Kim, Young C.

Japanese journalists
and their world

DATE			

Japanese
Journalists
and Their World

Japanese
Journalists
and Their World

YOUNG C. KIM

UNIVERSITY PRESS OF VIRGINIA
CHARLOTTESVILLE

This volume is a publication of the
American University Public Policy Symposium.

THE UNIVERSITY PRESS OF VIRGINIA
Copyright © 1981 by the Rector and Visitors
of the University of Virginia

First published 1981

Library of Congress Cataloging in Publication Data
Kim, Young C
    Japanese journalists and their world.
    Includes index.
    1. Journalism—Japan. I. Title.
PN5404.K55   079'.52   80-25720
ISBN 0-8139-0877-9

Printed in the United States of America

Contents

Acknowledgments

It is with a deep sense of appreciation that I acknowledge my indebtedness to all those who contributed to the preparation of this book. I want to express my profound gratitude to the many reporters of the *Asahi, Yomiuri, Mainichi,* and *Sankei* newspapers who consented to personal interviews, sharing so generously their thoughts and experiences. Similarly, my deep gratitude goes to the many officials of the Japanese government—members of the Diet and senior officials of the Ministries of Foreign Affairs and International Trade and Industry—for providing me with their perspectives and insights. Indeed, interviews with these reporters and government officials constitute the most important and valuable source of data for this volume. In compliance with the pledge given at the time of interviews, these contributors to the volume will remain anonymous. Without their generous cooperation, this book could not have been written.

Many friends rendered valuable assistance during the phase of field research in Tokyo. In particular, I want to express my sincere appreciation to Kimura Shuzo, Ichikawa Masaaki, Tsunoda Jun, and Honda Michiko. I am also thankful to the officers of the Japan Newspaper Association for the many courtesies and assistance they provided.

The funds for the conduct of research in Japan were provided by the Social Science Research Council, the Earhart Foundation, and the Institute for Sino-Soviet Studies of The George Washington University. I wish to take this opportunity to thank the officers of these institutions for making this study possible.

A special note of appreciation goes to my good friends and colleagues, Hugh LeBlanc, Bernard Reich, and Gaston Sigur of The George Washington University for their continued support and encouragement during the entire phase of my research and writing. Cho Sung Yoon of the Far East Law Library and the staff of the Japanese Section, Orientalia Division were particularly helpful during the initial phase of library research in Washington. I express my sincere appreciation to them.

Dan Nimmo and Kondo Ken gave a critical reading of portions of the manuscript for which I am very grateful. I want also to thank Corisa Bernard, Dorothy Wedge, and Sheila Murphy, who cheerfully undertook the task of transforming the original manuscript into a more intelligible and legible form.

Jeung Ai alone can assess the implications of a marriage to an academic who takes a commitment to research and writing a bit too seriously. She, along with Martha and Claire, can better attest than I to the magnitude of the impact that my systematic and protracted inattention has had on their lives.

I also wish to express my gratitude to Dr. Robert A. Bauer, Director of the American University Public Policy Symposium, under whose auspices this volume is published by the University Press of Virginia.

Japanese
Journalists
and Their World

Introduction

A terrifying homogeneity of opinion, a left-wing orientation, and an antigovernment stance are some of the familiar characteristics attributed to the Japanese press. Indeed, editorials on political questions are conspicuous for their ambiguity in their use of expressions and in the positions taken. A comparison of random issues of major Japanese dailies demonstrates extraordinary uniformity or similarity in the angles employed and the degree of emphasis allocated to particular news items. The expressions used in headlines and subheads as well as the items chosen for major treatments are remarkably similar.

There are other intriguing aspects of the Japanese press. Anyone browsing through the Japanese press coverage of the People's Republic of China (PRC) in the late 1960s and early 1970s—before the normalization of relations between the two countries in 1972—would be struck by the reports consistently glorifying the developments in China, with critical reporting virtually absent. The lack led numerous critics to condem the "biased" reporting on China and the "subservient" attitudes of the Japanese press toward the PRC. To their chagrin and dismay, the Americans recall the intensity and persistence with which the Japanese press condemned America's involvement in the Vietnam War. Sharp American reaction included a charge—lodged by high-ranking government officials in the form of congressional testimony—that the Japanese press had been infiltrated by Communists.

Americans generally fare better than Russians. In recent years the Japanese press has generally become more outspoken in expressing anti-Soviet feeling and a sense of distrust toward the Russians. One example is the sentiments expressed in the newspapers during the period of Japanese-Soviet negotiations leading to the conclusion of two fisheries agreements in 1977.

A reader of Japanese newspapers for a sustained period of time would obtain impressions that would not be at variance with those conveyed in the preceding paragraphs.

I have long been intrigued by such tendencies and particularly by the nature of the substantive contents of newspapers, the underlying frameworks of analysis, and the allocation of emphases. My initial fascination with Japanese newspapers arose from the query: "In what ways and to what extent does the press influence Japanese foreign policy making?" This question represents a broader focus than that which sustained my interest in the present research. This book has a more limited objective. It is intended to throw light on the question of why the nature of substantive contents of newspapers is what it is. The primary focus of the present research is on the reporters: their background, career patterns, role orientations, news-gathering and news-processing activities, and their product.

Although no systematic inquiry has been conducted, the student of Japanese foreign policy has been sensitive to the question of the nature and the degree of impact the newspapers have on foriegn policy decisions. The relevance of this question is not confined to the student with theoretical interest. From the perspective of American policy makers, too, the question of the proper weight to be given to the manifest content of the Japanese press has long been a matter of substantial importance. Policy makers as well as analysts have often pondered the question of the extent to which opinions expressed in mass media reflect true rather than manufactured public opinion or the opinion of a significant segment of Japanese society. Both analysts and policy makers are in search of an accurate assessment of their attempt to foresee the impact media opinions will have on Japanese foreign policy making and the proper weight to be given to them in formulating United States policies toward Japan. It is hoped that this book will provide a useful perspective in this regard.

This inquiry into the process of news gathering and processing in Japan hopefully contributes to our generic knowledge of the process. The addition of findings on Japanese reporters' recruitment, orientations, and behavior should deepen our understanding of the comparable processes found in the United States and elsewhere.

The most critical element in the entire process of newspaper making is obviously the reporters themselves. They are the gatekeepers, playing a decisive role at various stages. An attempt was made in the present research to identify and assess the significance of the various factors shaping the activities of the gatekeepers at different points during the newspaper-making process.

What kind of background do Japanese reporters bring to the process? Why did they aspire to be journalists? After they enter the field, what career patterns do they follow? These questions are explored in chapter 3. What values, beliefs, and attitudes do they bring to bear on their work? Obviously, among other things, their conception of the proper role of newsmen and their conception of what constitutes news shape their news-gathering activities. Questions of this sort are explored in chapter 5. The assumption here is that the characteristics of the reporters—conceived both in terms of individual and collective attributes—do affect their work.

Japanese newspapers represent a professionalized and highly differentiated communication system. The reporters operate in a complex organization. Standard operational procedures and the extensive division of labor, as well as the nature and demands of the work itself, shape their operations and the product. Chapter 4 is concerned with such organizational factors.

The nature of the Japanese press is, of course, related to the characteristics of Japan's socioeconomic and political developments. These include a high rate of literacy, high technological development, a competitive market economy, a legacy of American occupation, the essentially libertarian, democratic character of the postwar political system, and the underlying dominant political values. In this vein, chapter 7 examines legal aspects of the operations of newspapers: the nature of legal constraints as well as the protection accorded the operations of newspapers. However, it is not merely the presence of legal norms that shape newsmen's activities. It must be kept in mind that the vitality of the Japanese mass media is shaped and sustained by the structure of political power and the dynamics of a political process manifested in the activities of the parties, the Diet, and interest groups.

Chapters 8, 9, 10, and 11 are devoted to an analysis of the selected product, i.e., the contents of newspaper articles. Four issues will receive special attention: (1) press coverage of the Vietnam War and American involvement in it; (2) reporting on China; (3) attempts to influence reporting by the government and by individual politicians; and (4) the impact of ideology and major norms such as objectivity and neutrality on reporting.

In order to understand the nature of the product, it is also necessary to examine the orientations and activities of government officials concerning the transmission of news. Officials are the target for news gathering and are the main source of news for political reporters. This is particularly so because of the reporters' club system in Japan. The conception that officials hold about their own role as well as about the reporter's role shapes their interactions with reporters and their performance as a source. For example, it would make a difference whether the official holds the normative conception of his role as that of a mere transmitter of information. Likewise, the official's conception of what constitutes the legitimate function of the press affects his behavior, which in turn has a bearing on the scope and effectiveness of the reporter's activity. Whether the official's role conception is congruent with that of the reporters has implications for the behavior of all parties concerned. These questions are dealt with in chapter 6.

Two sources of data were used in preparation of this volume: (1) interviews with a sample of reporters and government officials and (2) books, monographs, and periodicals. Field research in Japan, conducted for approximately six months during 1975-76, consisted of three phases. The first phase was concerned with data gathering from secondary scources at the Diet Library and the Library of the Japan Newspaper Association. The second phase involved the preparation and pretesting of an interview schedule (see Appendix). The third phase concerned the conduct of interviews with a sample of reporters from the four major dailies, the *Asahi*, *Yomiuri*, *Mainichi*, and *Sankei*, and a sample of officials from the Ministries of Foreign Affairs and International Trade and Industry and from members of the National Diet. The details of theoretical assumptions and methodology are given in the pertinent chapters that follow.

CHAPTER I

Japanese Newspapers: Major Characteristics

Before the four major dailies selected for study are examined in detail, a brief note on the variety of newspapers in Japan is in order. By convention, the country's daily newspapers are classified into three broad categories: general, sports, and specialized. General papers in turn are divided into national papers (*zenkokuski*) and local papers (*chihoshi*). The national papers refer specifically to the following five papers: the *Asahi*, *Mainichi*, *Yomiuri*, *Sankei*, and *Nihon Keizai*. These national papers, with editorial offices and printing plants maintained in two to five different cities, enjoy nationwide circulation. The local papers encompass prefectural papers published in the capitals of prefectures, with their circulation limited to a single prefecture, and the so-called bloc papers such as *Hokkaido*, *Chunichi*, and *Nishi Nippon*, with their circulations extending to several prefectures. Some of the bloc papers are published in more than one city.[1]

Throughout the 1960s there was a small increase in the share enjoyed by national and bloc papers in the total circulation figure. Beginning in 1972, the relative share of national papers has been on the decline slightly. Another computation shows that in the 1960s national papers in general grew faster than local papers. This is particularly true of the *Asahi*, *Yomiuri*, and *Nihon Keizai*. National papers together with bloc papers have penetrated significantly into the share of other local papers.

1. *Gendai Janarizumu* 2 (Tokyo: Jiji Tsushinsha, 1973): 78; Susumu Ejiri, *Characteristics of the Japanese Press* (Tokyo: Nihon Shimbun Kyokai, 1972), pp. 2-4. Japanese names in this book are transcribed in the normal Japanese order, with family name first, except when Japanese authors are cited for their English-language works.

The share of local papers still remains substantial, but even if the growth of sports and specialized papers is taken into account, the ascendancy of national papers is conspicuous.[2]

As of the latter half of 1974, the three national papers, the *Asahi, Yomiuri,* and *Mainichi,* accounted for 43.5 percent of total newspaper circulation in Japan. The *Sankei* and *Nihon Keizai* accounted for 8.5 percent and the three bloc papers for 10.3 percent. When the above-mentioned eight papers are combined, they jointly accounted for 65 percent of the total circulation. Since 1960, the relative shares of the three or the eight papers have remained relatively stable. If one keeps in mind the fact that circulation figures of specialized and sports papers are included in the total figures computed by the Japan Newspaper Association, one may say that there has been a gradual increase of shares by either the three or the eight papers.

A major characteristic of Japanese newspapers is their extraordinarily large circulation. Normally, morning and evening editions are published under the same name and sold as a set. The stories are so edited as to provide continuity. For computing circulation figures, a set of morning and evening papers is counted as one copy. A combined edition, compiled from the morning and evening editions, is available for distant areas where delivery of evening papers is impossible.[3] As of October 10, 1974, the total circulation of the 112 dailies—constituting the membership of the Japan Newspaper Association—was 40,006,000, in which "set newspapers" are counted as one. Set

2. *Gendai Janarizumu* 2:79-80. A review of the history of newspapers attests to an intense expansionist policy of five major dailies into other areas of Japan. In 1950 the *Asahi* and *Mainichi* began publishing in Nagoya, and by 1952 the *Sankei, Nihon Keizai,* and *Yomiuri* began their publications in Sapporo. The *Sankei* began its publication in Tokyo and the *Nihon Keizai* in Osaka. By 1959 the *Mainichi, Yomiuri,* and *Asahi* began publishing in Hokkaido by the introduction of facsimile, or the Kanji-teletype system. In the early 1960s, the *Yomiuri* expanded its operations into Takaoka and Kita Kyushu while the *Nihon Keizai* moved into Fukuoka. *Nihon Keizai* moved into Sapporo in 1970 and via "delegated printing" into Hirosaki in 1975. Through the use of *Mutsu Shimpo* facilities, the *Asahi* began publishing in Hirosaki in 1975 and in the same year the *Mainichi* and *Yomiuri* began publishing in Aomori. Such a series of expansion by national papers has come to pose a threat to local papers.
3. Ejiri, p. 7.

newspapers accounted for 44.5 percent of the total circulation. Combined edition papers and morning-only papers accounted for 49.7 percent. The circulation of evening-only papers and the evening edition of the set papers sold on the street accounted for the remaining 5.8 percent. If the morning and evening editions of the set newspapers were counted separately, the total circulation figure would have been 57,820, 419.[4]

As for the rate of dissemination for the entire country, the figure was 1.23 copies per household, or one copy for every 2.74 persons. In terms of total circulation figures, Japan ranks third, following the USSR and the United States. Japan ranks second in terms of dissemination rate.

The annual increase of circulation during the period 1964-74 was about 3.6 percent, though the figure for 1974 showed an increase of only 0.4 percent, due to a sharp rise in subscription rates in 1973.[5] The total circulation grew about 1.5 times during the period 1960-70, and the number of persons per copy was reduced from 3.89 to 2.89. However, the growth in terms of copies per household remained small, 1.24 over 1.18. This may suggest that the increase in circulation is owed primarily to the increase in the number of households due to the dispersion and movement of families into the cities.[6]

The high rate of newspaper dissemination in Japan is usually ascribed to several factors. Density of population, availability of transportation facilities, a high rate of literacy, and introduction of advanced technology come readily to mind. In addition, and perhaps of more importance, intense competition among national dailies and the system of home delivery must be cited.[7] Over 90 percent of the total circulation is on a subscription basis with the papers delivered to individual homes. (Newspapers are published twice daily except on newspaper holidays, and no evening editions are published on Sundays.) According to the 1975 data, 91.2 percent of the total circulation is home delivered, 8.1 percent is sold by newsstands, and 0.7 percent is sold through the mail.[8]

4. *Japanese Press: 1975* (Tokyo: Nihon Shimbun Kyokai, 1975), p. 56.

5. Ibid.

6. *Gendai Janarizumu* 2: 75-78.

7. Ibid.

8. *Japanese Press: 1975*, pp. 56-57.

The practice of home delivery is deeply rooted in Japanese custom. As of February 1974 there were 20,908 newspaper distribution stores or agencies in Japan. Of these, roughly 70 percent are exclusive sales stores that are bound by contract to handle the distribution of a particular newspaper.[9] These stores promote sales of the newspaper and insert flyers and other advertisement materials in the newspapers they deliver. They collect monthly dues and sell weekly and monthly magazines and books published by the newspapers they serve. Some stores handle multiple numbers of newspapers. Income for these stores comes from sales commissions and some subsidies from the newspaper firms.

In February 1974 the number of persons employed by these stores was 347,940, over half of which were newsboys from among junior and senior high school students. Their age ranged from twelve to eighteen. The number of those over eighteen decreased since 1958, and in recent years the number of women employees increased; in 1974 women constituted approximately one fifth.[10]

The employees promote the sale of their newspapers by canvassing each household in a given area. Pressure for increased circulation is intense, and some distribution stores occasionally offer giveaways and presents to obtain new subscribers and to retain the old. Such a practice is forbidden by law, and some newspaper companies have been warned and served injunctions by the Fair Trade Commission to desist from such unfair sales practices.[11]

A truly astonishing feature of the Japanese press is the large-scale operations of the national papers. The national papers under study are published in several cities scattered throughout Japan. The *Asahi*, the *Mainichi*, and the *Yomiuri* each maintain five separate offices throughout Japan.[12]

9. Ibid.

10. Ibid., and *Gendai Janarizumu* 2: 103-9. Due to economic growth, overall shortage of labor, and poor working conditions, the newspaper distribution stores have found it difficult to recruit employees in recent years.

11. *Japanese Press: 1975*, pp. 57-59.

12. The *Asahi* has four main offices and one branch office; the *Mainichi* has four separate main offices and one "printing" office; the *Yomiuri* has three main offices and two branch offices; and the *Sankei* has two main offices.

As of April 1977, the number of employees of the *Asahi* was 9,721. The *Mainichi* and *Yomiuri* each has about 8,000 employees. Each paper maintains extensive domestic and foreign networks. For example, the *Asahi* maintains 10 domestic branch news bureaus, 275 correspondencies, and 23 overseas bureaus (3 general bureaus, 20 branch bureaus, and 3 correspondents).[13] This newspaper has a network larger than the national news agency, collecting local news for different local editions. It issues at least one edition for each prefecture and sometimes two to seven editions to cover separate parts of a prefecture so as to attract readers on a nationwide basis.

National dailies publish pages that are common to a number of their local editions. But even of these common pages, the papers publish numerous morning and evening editions. Daily production reflects a continuous process of up-to-date changes in the pages of each edition. In terms of the number of editions published daily, Japan's national papers surpass all other papers in the world.[14] In the face of this competition posed by national papers, the local papers themselves publish a multiple number of editions, each of which is further divided into sublocal issues.

The variety of related and "extracurricular" activities carried on by the Japanese national dailies is truly astounding. Each of the four dailies is involved, though in varying degrees, in extensive publication programs. Included are weekly newspapers, weekly and monthly magazines, and annual publications. The following is a partial list of the *Asahi*'s publication list:

Daily papers: *Asahi Shimbun*; *Asahi Evening News*

Weekly papers: *Asahi Towns*, *Asahi Family*

Weekly magazines: *Shukan Asahi*, *Asahi Journal*, *Asahi Graph*

Monthly magazines: *Kagaku Asahi*, *Asahi Camera*, *Modern Medicine*, *Home Doctor*

Quarterly magazines: *Japan Quarterly*, *Asahi-Asia Review*

Annuals: *Asahi Yearbook*, *Asahi Junior Year Book*, *Wings of the World*, *Cars of the World*, *Ships of the World*, *Railways of the World*, *Asahi Shimbun News Photography*, *Japan Market Analysis by Prefectures*, and *Lexicon of Newspaper Vocabulary*.

13. These figures for 1977 were provided by the Personnel Department of the *Asahi*.

14. Ejiri, p. 5.

The newspapers and magazines published by the *Mainichi* include: *Mainichi Daily News*; *Mainichi Weekly*; *Mainichi Daily Newspapers* for primary and secondary school students; weeklies such as *Sunday Mainichi, Economist, Mainichi Graph*; monthly magazines such as *Camera Mainichi, Mainichi Life*, and *Monthly Economist*. In addition, the *Mainichi* publishes annuals, bimonthlies, quarterlies, and a series of books on Japanese arts and culture, literary works, history, and so forth.[15]

The contact with their readers is not limited to newspaper pages and other printed matters. The papers go directly to the people, participating in numerous cultural activities.

Each of the four papers under study sponsor numerous cultural activities such as art exhibitions and concerts. The Leningrad Symphony Orchestra and the London Symphony Orchestra visited Tokyo in 1958 and 1963 under the auspices of the *Asahi*. The programs sponsored by the *Mainichi* are just as varied. They include recitals, art exhibitions, go-chess games, student championship games in judo and kendo, karate and sumo. The purpose of these cultural activities is to enhance the prestige of the newspapers, thus helping to increase circulation and advertisement revenues, though no direct, immediate results are expected.[16]

Programs sponsored by the *Yomiuri* have included art exhibitions of the works of Rembrandt and Renoir and an art exhibit from the New York Metropolitan Museum and performances by the Bolshoi Theatre Ballet Troupe, by the Paris National Theatre of Opera, and by Arthur Rubinstein. The *Yomiuri* has established a nonprofit welfare foundation, the Yomiuri Light and Love Association. The association has conducted free medical examinations for children in schools for the blind and has extended financial aid to cover the expenses of those individuals who need treatment and operations to regain their eyesight. The association provides cash gifts and other aids to needy homes with physically handicapped children. The Yomiuri Nippon Symphony Orchestra, with 100 players, gives an average of 130 performances a year. It provides international cultural exchanges and frequently makes foreign tours.

15. *Minasanno Mainichi Shimbun*, pamphlet (Tokyo: Mainichi Shinbunsha, and n.d.).

16. Ejiri, p. 12.

The *Yomiuri* owns and operates junior colleges of science and engineering in Tokyo and Kita Kyushu. In 1975 a total of 1,878 students were enrolled in Tokyo and 753 in Kita Kyushu. All of these students are taking advantage of the *Yomiuri* scholarship program, which offers a long-term scholarship designed to benefit students who deliver *Yomiuri* newspapers. The *Yomiuri* clinic provides medical consultation and treatment on a non-profit basis to the readers of the *Yomiuri* and citizens at large. The clinic is housed on the third floor of the Tokyo Yomiuri Building. It has nine divisions, staffed by fifteen doctors, four pharmacists, one dental and two 'radiological technicians, and sixteen nurses.

Moreover, the *Yomiuri* is involved in multiple enterprises. The *Yomiuri* personnel have been sent to twenty-three companies in which the *Yomiuri* holds more than 50 percent of the stock. Nippon Television Network Corporation, Yomiuri Telecasting Corporation, the Hochi Shimbun, the Fukushima Minyu Shimbun, Yomiuri Travel Service, Yomiuriland, and Yomiuri Kogyo Company are prime examples. This last-named company owns and operates the Tokyo Yomiuri Giants of professional baseball's Central League and produces television programs and telecommunications equipment. The Yomiuri Travel Service in Ginza maintains three regional offices and thirty-five local branch offices throughout the country. Yomiuriland operates a huge recreational complex and two eighteen-hole golf courses in Tokyo. The kinds of extracurricular activities of national newspapers sketched above give some idea of the versatility and a complexity of the operations of the Japanese national dailies.[17]

As of January 1, 1975, the number of regular employees of all newspapers in Japan was 68,480.[18] (The total number of personnel employed by 121 newspaper companies affiliated with the Japan Newspaper Association was 71,216.) In 1976, 26.4 percent of the employees were in the Editorial Department's, 28.1 percent in printing, 8.3 percent in administration,

17. Each of the major dailies is housed in an impressively modern, mammoth building. For example, the *Mainichi* building, located near the Imperial Mall, measures 211.2 meters east-west and 50 meters north-south. It is nine stories above ground and has six floors underground.

18. *Shimbun Keiei*, no. 52 (July 1975), p. 86.

17.1 percent in business operations including mailing, 13.6 percent constituted an external work force assigned to local bureaus and Communication Departments, 2.9 percent were in publications, and 3.5 percent had other duties. Two characteristics of newspaper employees may be noted. First, the number of female employees is small. According to the data of the Office of Prime Minister, the ratio of male and female for non-agriculture-forestry employees of Japan for 1973 was 100 male vs. 49.3 female. The corresponding figure for newspaper employees for the same year was 100 vs. 7. The second characteristic is the relatively high level of educational attainment and advanced age of the newspaper employees. The average age of employees of all industries was 32.1 for 1974, whereas that of the newspaper industry was 36.7. While 13.7 percent of the employees of all industries were college graduates, 48.4 percent of the newspaper employees were college graduates.[19] Both of these characteristics make newspaper labor relatively more expensive.

Of the fifty-one companies whose data are available for the period 1971-75, the following characteristics are discernible:

1. The number of personnel has been increasing at the rate of 1 to 2 percent.

2. Female employees account for around 6 percent of the total employees.

3. In terms of age composition, the proportion in the 20-40 bracket is decreasing, while the 40-55 category is increasing. The average age was 35.7 in 1975 as compared with 35.1 in 1971. This is higher than the average age for all employees of all industries, which is 32.1.

4. The proportion of those with employment of less than ten years is decreasing, whereas those with twenty to thirty years of experience is increasing.

5. Overall, the annual rate of termination has been around 4 percent. As for reasons for termination, retirement accounts for about one-fourth (24.1 to 28.2 percent), voluntary resignation a little over half (56.4 to 60.8 percent), and other reasons such as death account for the rest. Over the years, the trend shows a decrease in the proportion of those who voluntarily resign.[20]

19. *Shimbun Kenkyu*, March 1975, p. 73.
20. *Shimbun Keiei*, no. 52 (July 1975), pp. 86-89.

Perhaps one of the most peculiar characteristics of the Japanese newspapers is the incredibly small size of their own capital. This is particularly surprising in view of the mammoth scale of operations discussed above. Most newspapers rely for their capital on money invested in the company by the management and the employees. Of the seventy-six joint-stock newspaper companies that are members of the Japan Newspaper Association, those having more than half of their shares owned by people within the company constitute 60 percent and those with less than half, 40 percent. The larger the newspaper, the bigger the ratio of shares held by people within the company.

According to the Commercial Code of Japan, joint-stock companies must make their shares available to the general public. However, a special law enacted in 1951 exempts newspapers from this stipulation. The law was enacted after the newspapers argued that such a law was necessary to enable them to perform their mission as a public organ. The rationale was that such a measure would make it possible to guard against possible loss of independence through economic domination by outsiders. At the same time, however, the legal stipulation has led to the inability of newspapers to increase their capitalization and their presumed susceptibility to banking interests.[21]

Some statistics on the financial status of newspapers are presented below. Of ninety-seven stock companies affiliated with the Japan Newspaper Association, sixty-six companies disclosed the composition of their stockholding. Of the sixty-six, fifteen rely 100 percent for capital on internal sources, twenty-two rely over 50 percent on internal sources, and twenty-nine companies rely less than 50 percent on internal sources. The amount of their own capital is remarkably small. In 1974 the companies whose capital exceeded 500 million yen numbered five: *Sankei* (2 billion yen), *Mainichi* (1.8 billion yen), *Nihon Kogyo* (1 billion), *Nihon Keizai* (800 million), and *Kyoto* (600 million). The twelve companies whose capital fell within the 200-500 million yen range included the *Asahi* (Osaka) and the *Yomiuri* (Scibu). Twenty-four companies, including the *Yomiuri* (Tokyo) fall within the 100-200 million

21. Ejiri, p. 2.

Table 1. The status of capitalization of four dailies, 1975

	Capital (1,000 yen)	Stocks issued	Number of stockholders	% of internal ownership
Asahi	280,000	2,800,000	1,286	100%
Mainichi	1,800,000	18,000,000	7,556	100%
Yomiuri	153,300	1,533,000	696	100%
Sankei	2,000,000	4,000,000	undisclosed	undisclosed

Source: *Shimbun Kenkyu*, July 1975, p. 68.

yen range. Fifty-six companies, 57.7 percent of the total, had less than 100 million yen of their own capital.[22]

The *Asahi, Mainichi,* and *Yomiuri* depend entirely for capitalization on their own internal sources, the management, and the staff (see table 1). Comparable data on the *Sankei* are unavailable.

The *Yomiuri,* which recently constructed a new building worth 40 billion yen, has its own capital of 0.1 billion. Intense competition among the major national dailies prompted massive investment in equipment and the introduction of new technologies in the sixties, aggravating the financial dependence of newspapers. This financial vulnerability allegedly makes the newspapers susceptible to intervention and control by the government and financial circles.[23]

Total sales of the newspaper industry for 1971 reached 490 billion yen, about four times the 1959 figure and over twelve times that of 1951. This means about a 10 percent increase per annum. In terms of the composition of earnings, advertising revenues exceed those of sales. In 1960 sales revenues accounted for 52.17 percent and advertising revenues of 43.0 percent, with revenue from all other sources accounting for the remainder. The relative weight of sales and advertising was reversed in 1962, and by 1970 advertising revenues accounted for 52.9 percent, whereas sales accounted for 36.8 percent, with other sources adding 10.3 percent.[24]

22. *Shimbun Keiei,* no. 52 (July 1975) pp. 66-67.
23. *Gendai Janarizumu* 2: 88-90.
24. Ibid., pp. 111, 121. Total newspaper circulation apparently reached a saturation point, as indicated in the rate of dissemination—1.24 copies to one household. On the other hand, newspaper advertising expenditures increased 3.2 percent in the 1962-71 period. The high growth rate of the Japanese economy was reflected in the growing demand for advertising space, and advertising revenues have become a principal source of income for Japanese newspapers.

Table 2. Composition of revenues

		Sales	Advertising	Other business income	Others
A	1972	39.9%	47.5%	9.2%	3.4%
	1973	36.6	51.7	8.2	3.6
	1974	36.3	51.2	8.9	3.6
B	1972	39.0	49.9	7.2	3.9
	1973	36.1	53.1	7.4	3.4
	1974	41.4	46.9	7.5	4.2

Source: *Shimbun Keiei*, no. 50 (1975), pp. 74-76, no. 52 (1975), pp. 70-71.

Of the data presented in table 2, those in section A were derived from a survey conducted by the Japanese Newspaper Association in 1974 of thirty-one (out of sixty relevant) companies that customarily conduct accounting during the first half of the year. Data in section B pertains to thirty-eight (out of fifty-four) companies that conducted accounting in the latter half of 1974. As compared with a comparable period of the previous year, the total income was increased by 20.1 percent for A group and 22.8 percent for B group.[25] This was due to the increase in sales and the rise in subscription rates effected in the summer of 1973. There was a slowdown in advertising revenues due to the recession and the shortage of newsprint after the October oil crisis.

Table 2 shows that advertising revenues comprised half of the newspapers' total revenues, and they have consistently carried greater weight than sales. Newspapers have consistently outranked other media as a channel for advertising. For the 1972-74 period, newspapers accounted for 34.1 to 35.1 percent of the total advertising expenditures as compared with 32.3 to 33.5 percent for television advertising. Incidentally, the proportion of advertising, the ratio of the amount of advertising to the entire space available in the papers during the recent years, has been within the range of 39.7 to 43.3 percent. It is useful to keep in mind that postal regulations concerning the mailing of printed matter serve to restrain this proportion of advertising per space in a newspaper. Table 3 shows the composition of expenditures. The table shows that personnel costs account for

25. *Shimbun Keiei*, no. 50 (1975), p. 73, and no. 52 (July 1975), p. 70ff.

Table 3. Composition of expenditures

		Newsprint	Materials	Personnel	Business expenses	Others
A	1972	18.5%	2.2%	39.3%	34.1%	5.9%
	1973	16.4	2.2	40.6	33.8	7.0
	1974	17.8	2.2	42.5	32.0	5.5
B	1972	18.5	2.3	38.6	35.2	5.4
	1973	17.8	2.2	38.2	35.1	6.7
	1974	16.3	2.5	41.5	33.0	6.7

Source: *Shimbun Keiei*, no. 50 (1975), p. 83, no. 52 (1975), p. 77.

about 40 percent of the total expenditures.[26]

The quality of their contents is another noteworthy feature of Japanese newspapers. It is difficult to discern clear-cut differences between national and local papers in this regard, unlike the case in some Western countries. With the exception of some small community papers, both national and local papers generally feature national and international political news on their front pages. If a newspaper enjoys a large circulation, this is generally regarded by the Japanese as indicative of the high quality of that paper's contents.

A study of the pages of ten newspapers—three national dailies, one bloc paper, and six local newspapers of various types—found the relative weights given to various subject matters. Space allocated for news of different types was:[27]

Political news	32.7%
Economic	14.8%
City	14.8%
Cultural	21.0%
Home	7.7%
Sports	9.0%

Implications

Japanese newspaper organizations must operate in a society where the rate of newspaper dissemination is one of the highest

26. *Japanese Press: 1975*, pp. 62-72. Japan's advertisement expenditures in 1974 totaled 1,169,500 million yen, an increase of 8.6 percent over the previous year. This means minus growth when the rise in prices of more than 20 percent is taken into account. Moreover, the 8.6 percent increase was due to an increase in advertisement rates.

27. Ejiri, pp. 12-13.

in the world. This high rate is correlated with a high level of literacy, a high standard of living, and an advanced technology and is reinforced by fierce competition and promotional campaigns among the major dailies.

The high degree of newspaper concentration, as reflected in the dominance of the national dailies, tends to sustain the high quality of the Japanese newspapers in general. The significance of this high concentration is great, particularly when the close linkage between the major dailies and television and radio stations is kept in mind. The newspaper thus constitutes, potentially at least, a formidable instrument of influence in the Japanese society..

The national dailies under study are characterized by a stupendously large scale of operations and circulation and are locked in intense competition for the maintenance and expansion of their respective shares of the readership. These characteristics are related to the tendency of the papers to avoid alienating any significant segment of the public. Thus, injection of overtly partisan attitudes must be avoided. Each paper exerts a constant effort to enhance its visibility and prestige, and the involvement of the papers in a series of extracurricular activities is in part related to this consideration. Each paper must try to appeal to the broadest spectrum of the population and must cover a wide range of interests, needs, tastes, and preferences of the present and potential readership.

The peculiarly small size of internal capital of a typical major daily—all the more surprising in view of the mammoth scale of its operations—makes the daily at least potentially and theoretically vulnerable to the exercise of influence of financial and business interests. The substantial share of advertising revenues relative to sales revenues reinforces its potential susceptibility.

CHAPTER II

The Readers:
Major Characteristics

This chapter is intended to portray major characteristics of Japanese newspaper readers. More specifically, it examines the degree of the reader's access to the newspapers, the useful information he feels he derives from newspaper reading, the opinions he has of the newspapers, and the social composition of the readership of the four national dailies. The theoretical rationale for such an examination is twofold. First, the readership constitutes the environment in which newspapermen operate, for the attributes of the readership as understood by newsmen may have some relevance to their behavior. Second, the characteristics of the readership constitute an "objective" factor, shaping the degree of the influence newspapers have on the readers.

In the present chapter, to the extent available, the data regarding other media, television and radio, will be presented. Such data will serve as a norm for comparison as we examine the data on newspapers, and our understanding of the role and weight of newspapers will be facilitated. We will begin with the reader's access to mass media. According to the Nippon Hoso Kyokai (NHK)'s nationwide survey of 1969 (N=3,600), about 74 percent of the sample said that they read newspapers everyday. About 92 percent read newspapers with varying degrees of frequency.[1]

In another sample survey conducted in Tokyo in April 1974 (N=534) the following question was asked: "On the average, how much time do you spend reading both morning and evening papers a day?" The model category was thirty minutes, accounting for about 29 percent of the sample. Seventeen percent of the sample spent about twenty minutes, and 16

1. NHK Hoso Seron Chosasho, ed., *Seikatsu no naka no Hoso* (Tokyo: Nihon Hoso Shuppan Kyokai, 1971), pp. 34-35.

Table 4. Types of news and frequency of reading (Tokyo, 1974)

Types of news	Frequency of reading		
	Read always	Read occasionally	Don't read at all
Stocks/Trade	12.5	33.5	54.0
Economy	28.7	57.7	13.7
Science	6.9	62.1	31.0
Editorials	25.6	58.5	16.0
Politics	46.0	46.3	7.7
Foreign News	22.3	69.2	8.5
Music/Theatre Arts	25.6	62.7	11.7
Literature/Book Reviews	15.4	66.0	18.7
Sports	44.2	42.3	13.5
Letter to the Editor	18.1	67.7	14.2
Society	51.3	45.2	3.5
Local News	31.3	62.5	6.2
Radio/TV Programs	54.2	42.3	3.5
Home/Women	34.0	41.3	24.6
Health	22.9	66.0	11.2
Travel/Leisure	20.0	68.5	11.5

Note: N=520 (excludes 14 who do not read newspapers).

percent about one hour. On the average, Tokyo residents spent forty-one minutes. The time spent in reading papers increased with age and with education. This Tokyo survey also found that 25 percent of the sample watched television two hours and 28 percent for three hours. The average viewing time was two hours and 58 minutes.[2]

The Tokyo survey also attempted to ascertain the types of newspaper articles read by the readers. As indicated in table 4, the most frequently read items were radio-television programs, social affairs (including crime), politics, and sports. The fact that a large percentage was in the area of politics may have been due to the timing of the survey; it occurred immediately before the House of Councillors election. However, the percentages for editorials, foreign news, and economy were also substantial.[3]

As for the characteristics of television viewing, the most widely watched programs are news, drama-movies, documentaries, sports, and music (popular songs).[4]

2. Nihon Shimbun Kyokai, ed., *Masukomi to Seikatsu* (Tokyo: Nihon Shimbun Kyokai, 1975), pp. 23-24.
3. Ibid., pp. 36-37.
4. Ibid., p. 37.

A detailed analysis of the Tokyo survey data shows that the occupational categories of the respondents do not meaningfully correlate with the readers of different categories of news articles. Society pages are read by all occupational categories in roughly the same proportion. So are political/economic pages, though the proportion of manual workers reading the political/ economic pages is the smallest of the four categories—white-collar office workers, managerial, professional, and trade-commerce.[5]

Why do the people read newspapers? What is the reader's own assessment of the utility of newspaper reading? A nation-wide survey (N=2,539) conducted by Chuo Chosa Sha for the Office of Prime Minister in December 1968 throws much light on these questions. Of all media, newspapers are relied upon most for the purpose of "knowing current developments in politics and the events in the society." Newspapers are also read to obtain knowledge useful to daily living. Television, radio, and weeklies are sought after for consolation, amusement, and enjoyment.[6]

Another Tokyo survey in April 1975 yielded similar findings. As indicated in table 5, the readers approach newspapers primarily for educational and utilitarian purposes: to learn of developments at home and abroad and trends of public opinion, to form a basis for judgment and opinion, to enhance the level of their culture, and to be useful in their work and daily living. In these respects, newspapers outweigh other media significantly. As compared with the little value given to newspapers as a medium of entertainment, notice the utility of television seen in terms of amusement. This was followed by the perceived usefulness to the reader's hobby and the contribution to topics of conversation.[7]

A detailed analysis of the Tokyo survey data of 1975 shows that the degree and type of the respondent's education are associated with his reliance on the newspaper and television media. For example, with regard to the first five categories of

5. Ibid., pp. 42-43.
6. "Waga Kuni ni okeru Masukomi Hodo no Shomondai," *Chosa Geppo*, Aug. 1972, pp. 48-50.
7. *Masukomi to Seikatsu*, pp. 53-56.

Table 5. Objectives for media access (Tokyo, 1975)

Objectives	Types of Media				
	Newspapers	TV	Weeklies	Radio	Unclear
To learn of developments at home and abroad	53.9%	39.7%	1.1%	4.3%	0.9%
To learn of trends in public opinion	60.1	30.7	4.5	3.4	1.3
To use as a basis for judgments and opinions	60.5	28.7	5.2	4.3	1.3
To enhance the level of one's culture	61.4	22.8	4.7	5.2	5.8
To make it useful for work and daily living	46.3	35.6	6.6	8.2	3.4
To make it useful for one's hobby	19.9	49.4	18.7	6.6	5.4
To enrich conversational topics	23.8	46.1	19.5	8.1	2.6
For amusement	2.6	80.3	9.7	5.4	1.9

Note: Percentage figures exceed 100 due to multiple response.

objectives listed in table 5, the more educated tend to utilize newspapers rather than television. Likewise, roughly speaking, with minor exceptions, office workers and readers in professional and managerial occupations depend on newspapers for these objectives more than do readers in other occupational categories.

However, the nationwide survey conducted by NHK in 1969 yielded findings contradictory to those of the Office of Prime Minister. The respondents were asked to identify which medium they used frequently to learn information concerning the following three kinds of problems: (1) problems related to living conditions or events of the area in which they resided, (2) political and economic problems of Japan, and (3) trends in political, economic, and social conditions of the world. The media listed were newspapers, weeklies, monthlies, NHK radio, NHK TV, and personal conversations with others.

What is noteworthy about the NHK survey findings is that a greater proportion of respondents apparently utilized television rather than newspapers for information concerning the first two types of problems. This is the opposite of the findings of the Office of Prime Minister. Even if the response to the first type of problem cannot definitely be said to be contrary, because of different phraseologies or possible changes in the substance of the meaning, the response to the second type of problem appears inconsistent with the Office of Prime Minister survey. It is possible that the awareness of the respondents of the survey's sponsorship by NHK may have contributed to the exaggerated weight given the television medium.

The degree of confidence the reader has in the mass media is indicated in the *Mainichi* surveys of October 1969 and September 1970. In 1969, 57 percent of the respondents declared newspapers to be the most dependable or trustworthy source of information. Television was so named by 35 percent and radio by 3 percent. A year later, the figures for newspapers, television, and radio were 46 percent, 42 percent, and 3 percent respectively. This may indicate an upward trend in the degree of confidence the people have in television relative to newspapers.[8]

A *Yomiuri* survey of October 1970 found the majority of readers had a positive image of their newspapers. Table 6 indicates that a small fraction (about 3-6 percent) of the respondents thought the newspapers "are bad or very bad" with regard to accuracy, speed, fairness, specificity (details), and interest. About a third (28-39 percent) gave high ratings, with about one-half of the respondents indicating average rating in these regards.[9]

Table 7 presents the occupational categories of subscribers to the four dailies that are household heads. Data on *Asahi*, *Mainichi*, and *Sankei* subscribers were collected at the same

8. Nihon Shimbun Kyokai, *Shimbun e no Shinrai o takameru tameni* (Tokyo: Nihon Shimbun Kyokai), p. 11.

9. Ibid., p. 14.

Table 6. Popular images of newspapers

Attributes	Rating					
	Very good	Good	Average	Bad	Very bad	Don't know
Accuracy	6.3%	32.2%	49.0%	2.4%	0.3%	10.0%
Speed	7.1	28.9	48.8	5.2	0.8	9.3
Details	7.4	29.7	47.7	4.6	0.4	10.2
Interesting	7.4	21.0	55.0	7.9	0.8	10.0
Fairness	5.2	22.4	53.3	4.0	0.6	14.7

Table 7. Occupational categories of subscribing household heads

Categories	Asahi*	Mainichi*	Sankei*	Yomiuri[†]
Office	43.3%	33.1%	28.0%	26.7%
Labor	18.0	25.7	26.7	21.8
Trade-Industry-Service	17.5	19.6	29.2	38.8[‡]
Free-Managerial	11.5	7.9	6.8	12.1
Agriculture-Forestry-Fishery	6.4	10.3	6.7	— — —
Others	3.3	3.4	2.7	0.6[§]

* As of March 1975.
† As of October 1974.
‡ Includes the following two categories: retail and service stores, 17.8%; trade-industry, 21.0%.
§ Others and unemployed.

time by the Mass Media Research in March 1975 and hence are comparable. The data on the *Yomiuri* were collected by the *Yomiuri* company in October 1974, and since slightly different categories are employed, a comparison is somewhat difficult. The *Asahi* is conspicuous in its larger proportion of white-collar office workers among its readers as compared with other papers (43 percent vs. 33 percent of the *Yomiuri* and 28 percent of the *Sankei*). Obversely, the proportion of manual workers among the *Asahi* readership was smaller than that of other papers. The *Sankei* readership contained a larger proportion of those with commerce-industry-related occupations than other papers. However, what is most significant about the table is that the readership composition of each paper was remarkably similar. The readership of each paper was distributed widely among the different occupational groupings.[10]

Data on the level of annual income of households subscribing to each of the four dailies are given in Table 8. One may note a somewhat larger proportion of subscribers in a relatively high income bracket—with income over 2.2 million yen—among the *Asahi* readership (55 percent vs. 47 percent of *Mainichi* and 44 percent of *Sankei*). The *Yomiuri* data are hard to compare, but the pattern of overall distribution closely resembles that for the other papers. It is evident that all four dailies were subscribed to by families with substantially the same level of annual income as well as with similar kinds of occupations.

10. Nihon Shimbun Kyokai, *Zenkoku Shimbun Gaido* (Tokyo: Nihon Shimbun Kyokai, 1976).

Table 8. Annual income of subscriber households (as of March 1975)

Unit 10,000 yen	Asahi	Mainichi	Sankei	Yomiuri
Less than 100	3.6%	4.4%	5.0%	1.4%
100-119	3.5	4.3	5.5	{ 5.9% 100-149
120-139	5.0	5.9	5.1	
140-159	5.7	7.1	7.9	{ 13.0% 150-199
160-179	5.1	6.2	4.8	
180-199	6.9	8.4	9.0	
200-219	11.1	11.8	11.4	
220-239	5.3			61.4% Over 200
240-259	7.8	{ 47.2% Over 220	{ 43.8% Over 220	
Over 260	42.0			
Unknown	4.0	4.8%	7.5%	18.3%

The 1975 data on the educational background of the heads of households subscribing to the various dailies indicate that the subscribers to the *Asahi* were more or less equally divided among three categories: graduates of junior high schools, senior high schools, and colleges and universities.

In the case of the other three dailies, *Mainichi*, *Yomiuri* and *Sankei*, the proportion of junior high school graduate subscribers ranged from 38 to 46 percent, with senior high school graduate subscribers accounting for 38 to 43 percent. The proportion of college-educated subscribers ranged from 5 to 21 percent for the three papers.[11]

Implications

The data presented in this chapter indicate that Japanese newspapermen operate in a generally friendly environment so far as the mass public is concerned. An overwhelming majority of the readers feel that the newspapers should not be partial to a particular political party and believe that their newspapers are politically neutral or impartial. A substantial proportion of the people express confidence in, and give positive ratings for, accuracy, fairness, specificity, and appeal of the papers they are reading. Regarding these attributes, only a very small

11. Asahi Shimbunsha, *Asahi no Dokusha, 1976* (Tokyo: Asahi Shimbunsha, 1976), pp. 8-38.

fraction of the public indicates a negative rating. About a third feel that the papers should be critical of the government, whereas about one-fifth feel that papers should be cooperative. How the elite sector of society evaluates the newspapers will be discussed later.

About 90 percent of the Japanese read the newspapers with varying degrees of care and frequency, with 74 percent reading a paper every day. The newspapers thus constiute an extensive channel of communications and are in a position to exert significant influence in shaping the attitudes and opinions of the Japanese. Although it is the social affairs pages that command the most extensive readership, the political-economic news and editorals, too, are read by a substantial proportion of the public.

We have seen that the two dominant objectives sought by the reader are: (1) to keep abreast of current developments and (2) to obtain information and knowledge useful to daily living. To the extent that newspapermen are conscious of the readers' needs and orientations, some measure of impact on the newspapermen's behavior may be assumed. This question will be explored in a later chapter.

Survey data on the types of news articles possessing wide appeal to the readership and the reasons for media access have been assumed to affect the contents of the papers. The editors must be concerned with the variety, as well as with the educational content and quality, of stories provided. Even a cursory look at the Japanese major dailies would impress one with the rich variety, the comprehensiveness, and the high quality of articles, as well as with the large numbers of special features.

That there are little differences in social composition among the readers of the four dailies means that these dailies must compete for essentially the same public socioeconomic groups. The resultant competition tends to sustain a continuous search for innovations, comprehensiveness of coverage, and enrichment of the contents. At the same time, it contributes to the standardization of the paper, as indicated in the similarities in format, angles adopted, and substantive contents.

CHAPTER III

Reporters: Recruitment and Career Patterns

This chapter is concerned with the process of initially recruiting the reporters and their placement and promotions after their entry into newspaper organizations. One must begin with a fact of fundamental importance, namely, that the Japanese reporters are recruited through a formal, systematized means of selection. Aspirants must pass highly competitive written and oral examinations. As a general rule, major dailies conduct the examinations at about the same time annually, usually during the summer or fall, with the date of employment effective the following spring. Of the four dailies under study, the *Asahi, Mainichi,* and *Yomiuri* usually conduct their written examinations on the same day, while the *Sankei* gives its examination a day before or after the examination date of the other dailies. Thus, the aspirants are denied the opportunity for multiple applications at the major dailies. To a certain extent, this results in self-screening on the part of the applicants, thereby reducing the number of applicants a particular newspaper firm must cope with.

The number of applicants each newspaper firm processes varies somewhat from year to year and between newspaper firms, but generally falls between 1,000 and 3,000 annually. A keen, intense competition is the rule as each firm recruits only a very small number, somewhere between 10 and 20. For example, in 1972, from a total of 2,539 applicants for editorial work, the *Asahi* selected 24 persons. The *Asahi* also employed 13 out of 590 applicants for business-related work.[1]

In the same year, the *Yomiuri* hired 16 reporters out of 1,570 applicants. Out of 1,308 applicants, the *Sankei* took 25, 10, and 1 respectively for editorial, business, and technical

1. Chuo Daigaku Masukomi Zeminaru, ed., *Masukomi e no Michi* (Tokyo: Hitotsubashi Shoten, 1973), p. 483.

work. The competition ratio for the *Asahi* the following year was 58 to 1; 27 applicants out of 1,567 were accepted for work in editorial-related fields. The ratio for the 1974 exam was 88 to 1[2]; the *Asahi* took 22 out of 1,940 applicants. The competition ratio for work in noneditorial fields was lower, with the figures being 13 to 1 and 41 to 1 for 1973 and 1974 respectively. The ratio for the 1976 exam was 70 to 1 as the *Asahi* took 49 out of 3,412 applicants. The 1976 exam covered both categories of employees. The *Yomiuri* took about 20 out of 1,000 applicants in 1976, whereas in 1975 the *Mainichi* hired about 20 out of 3,000 applicants.

Exams and Criteria Applied

The written exams given by all of the four newspaper firms encompass a subject called "common sense," writing a composition, and a foreign language test (usually translation of English into Japanese). In addition, the *Yomiuri*'s list of exam topics includes a Japanese language test, a sample piece of news article writing, and translation of Japanese into a foreign language.

The written exam lasts approximately four hours. The section on common sense lasts about two hours, while the foreign language test and the written composition each last about an hour. The *Yomiuri* exam lasts somewhat longer as about one hour is devoted to article writing, even though Japanese is combined with common sense. The subject common sense takes the form of multiple-choice questions covering a wide range of topics including history, economics, politics, law, physics, chemistry, music and arts, current international affairs, literature, geography, and sociology. Whereas the subject of common sense and the foreign language exam test the level of acquired knowledge, the composition requirement serves several purposes. First, in the words of a *Yomiuri* reporter, a piece of composition provides much insight into the writer's way of thinking, cultural background, political tendencies, character, and personality. Second, a piece of composition demonstrates one's writing ability and potential as a writer. The topics for

2. The exam was given in 1973 for work to begin in 1974.

composition in 1972 included "Reflections on My Student Life" (the *Asahi*); "Dialogue" (the *Mainichi*); "Professional Ethics" (the *Yomiuri*); and "The Year 2000" (the *Sankei*).[3]

A review of exam questions used for the past several years indicates the truly amazing breadth of knowledge and very high quality of thinking that are expected of the applicant. In fact, in the words of directors of the Department of Personnel of a few newspaper companies, the written exam is designed "to flunk as many applicants as possible." The function of the written exam is seen as a practical means of reducing the number of applicants to a manageable proportion for the purpose of conducting subsequent oral examinations. The task of interviewing over 1,000 applicants would be too staggering to contemplate. As a rule of thumb, the number of applicants allowed to pass the written exam, i.e., the number retained for the oral exam, is approximately several times the final number of candidates to be hired. No ranking is made among those who survived the written exam phase; they are treated equally before a panel conducting the oral examination. The oral exam lasts from fifteen to thirty minutes per person.

Of the two kinds of exams, written and oral, the oral exam is given greater weight in making a final selection. Some firms conduct interviews twice. For example, in 1975 the *Yomiuri* eliminated approximately 930 applicants through the written exam. Then the remainder of 70 were interviewed for approximately fifteen minutes each by a panel of examiners, and about 35 applicants were interviewed for the second time by another panel for about thirty minutes each. The first panel of examiners consisted of about ten members drawn mostly from department heads. The second panel was smaller, consisting of members of the Governing Board such as the vice-president (who served as editor-in-chief), the director of the Editorial Bureau (the managing editor) , the head of the Personnel Department, and an editorial writer.

A *Yomiuri* official declared that a reporter's potential and suitability can be assessed through interviews. In an interview many things about an applicant are observed: his comportment when entering a room, the first impression he makes, as well as his hair style, attire, speech, and sitting posture. Examiners

3. *Masukomi e no Michi*, pp. 37-38.

are interested in the applicant's bearing, personality, family upbringing, circle of friends, hobbies, outlook on life, political tendencies, capacity for making judgments, and zeal for the work of a reporter.[4]

The *Asahi* employs a two-step process of interviews. Those who successfully passed the written exam are divided into small groups for the purpose of group discussion. Each group is composed of seven or eight persons, and each person is assigned a topic and allowed about five minutes to organize his thoughts. Each is given the opportunity to express his views for several minutes, and this is followed by a free discussion. Each person's participation is observed by a panel of examiners, mostly senior staff with the rank of department head. The group discussion lasts approximately fifty minutes. The results of the evaluations are taken into account at the time of the second interviews, which are conducted individually. The individual interview is conducted by a panel of about six officials, including the executive vice-president in charge of editorial matters, editor-in-chief, director of the Editorial Bureau, and head of the Office of Research. The interview is designed, in the words of an *Asahi* official, to "determine whether the applicant is fit to be a reporter." The *Asahi* deems the following qualities as desirable; strong convictions, cooperativeness, quality of and capacity for judgment, creativity, integrity, action potential, and so forth. Overall, in addition to integrity of character, the *Asahi* is particularly interested in a person with a sense of mission, which is interpreted to mean enthusiasm for and devotion to work, and with a full appreciation of social and cultural significance of the role of newspapers.[5]

According to the director of the Personnel Department of the *Sankei*, the most important attributes a reporter should have may be summarized by three powers: "will power, physical power, and knowledge power." He went on to enumerate other attributes, such as "the ability to collect information, facility in oral and written expressions, capacity to make judgments on the relative weight of the issues." Then he said, "Of course, another important quality is one's countenance [*kaotsuki*], though one need not be handsome."

4. Ibid., pp. 43-48.
5. *Asahi Shimbunsha Annai*, May 1974 and Sept. 1975.

Profile of the Chosen Few

Successful candidates are invariably college graduates within the 24- to 26-year-old age bracket and mostly fresh out of college. Eligibility for the entrance exam stipulates that the applicant must either be a college graduate or expecting to graduate in March of the following year. This is true of all four newspapers. As for the age requirement, the *Sankei*, *Yomiuri*, and *Mainichi* require the applicant to be under the age of twenty-six as of April 1 of the following year, the date they would report to work. The *Asahi*, which until recently had twenty-seven as the upper age limit, has relaxed it to include all those under the age of thirty as of April 1 of the following year.

Perusal of the roster of the new entrants to the *Asahi* in 1975 indicates the following characteristics. Of twenty-two recruits for editorial work, ten were fresh college graduates, i.e., those who had graduated in March 1975; seven had graduated in 1974; three in 1973, and one each in 1972 and 1971. Of eleven recruits for business-related work at the *Asahi* (accounting, sales, advertising, computer, etc.) in 1975, nine had just completed college and the other two had graduated the previous year. Regarding the educational background of these new entrants, one is struck with the consistency with which several universities provide a larger proportion of successful candidates. Universities such as Waseda, Tokyo, Keio, and Kyoto are striking examples. Of twenty-two *Asahi* recruits for editorial work in 1975, six were graduates of Waseda University, four of Tokyo University and three of Kyoto University. Other universities contributing one recruit each included Keio, Jochi, and Hitotsubashi. Of eleven recruits for the business field, four were graduates of Waseda. In 1976 the *Asahi* recruited thirty-two people for editorial work; ten were graduates of Tokyo University, seven of Kyoto, six of Waseda, and three of Osaka. The following universities provided one successful candidate each: Hitotsubashi, Kobe, Chuo, Tokyo-Gaigokugo, Tokyo-Toritsu, and International Christian University. Of seventeen recruits for the business field, four came from Waseda.

Corresponding data on other national dailies for 1975 are unavailable. However, comparable data for 1973 are available

Table 9. Educational background of recruits, 1973

	Newspapers			
	Asahi*	Yomiuri†	Sankei‡	Nihon Keizai§
Waseda	10	8	8	22
Tokyo	8	2	3	6
Kyoto	4	0	1	4
Keio	3	0	2	10
Hitotsubashi	3	1	0	2

* Nine other universities contributed one recruit each.
† Five other universities contributed one recruit each.
‡ Handai, Chuo, and Hosei contributed two each, with fourteen other universities contributing one each.
§ Togai, Jochi, Rikkyo, Dukukyo, Yokohama Shiritsu, and Doshisha contributed two each, and eleven other universities contributed one each.

on the *Asahi, Yomiuri, Sankei,* and *Nihon Keizai* (see table 9). Since the data on all applicants are unavailable, no inferences are warranted, but it is conspicuous that for the four dailies, Waseda, Tokyo, Kyoto, and Keio universities provided a disproportionately larger number of entrants than did the other universities. Waseda supplied ten out of thirty-seven entrants for the *Asahi,* eight out of sixteen for the *Yomiuri,* eight out of thirty-eight for the *Sankei,* and twenty-two out of sixty-seven for the *Nihon Keizai.*

As for the sex of the recruits, the number of successful female candidates is almost infinitesimal. In 1973 *Sankei* hired one female out of 165 female applicants. She was the only one among *Sankei*'s 47 successful candidates. Out of 1,567 editorial applicants, the *Asahi* hired 27 persons in 1974; only 3 were female.

In terms of the major field of their formal education, Japanese reporters represent diverse backgrounds. Of the new *Asahi* recruits for 1975, five majored in law, four in political science, three in economics, five in literature, and three in foreign languages. Humanities, i.e., languages and literature, are predominant.

Why Aspire?

What are the motivations underlying the pursuit of a career in journalism? A survey conducted by the Editorial Department of

Table 10. Motivations for becoming reporters

Job is/provides	Ranks 1st	Ranks 2d	Ranks 3d
1. Free/unfettered	19.4%	14.9%	13.9%
2. Leader/guide of society	9.9	6.9	7.5
3. Masculine/manly	3.4	5.3	6.5
4. Bright future	1.8	1.3	1.8
5. A star of the times	2.5	1.7	3.6
6. Can demonstrate one's individuality and ability	28.7	24.7	11.6
7. Can experience things others normally can't	11.8	20.9	16.8
8. Can associate with anyone on equal terms	4.7	8.3	12.6
9. Enjoy writing	10.2	10.4	14.2
10. Just thought I might as well become a reporter	6.2	1.5	6.3

Source: *Shimbun Kenkyu*, Oct. 1973, p. 72.

the *Shimbun Kenkyu* (*Studies on Newspapers*) in June 1973 provides useful insights.[6] A questionnaire was sent to a random sample of 1,900, chosen from a population of 13,451 reporters. Of the 1,169 reporters (61.5 percent of the total sample) who returned a usable response, 652 (60.9 percent) were employed by the so-called central dailies: the *Asahi, Mainichi, Yomiuri, Nihon Keizai,* and *Sankei.* The rest of the respondents worked for "bloc papers," "local papers," and press agencies. A question asked was: "What motivated you to become a reporter? Please select three from among the following items with ranking indicated." The results of tabulation are shown in table 10.

As table 10 indicates, over half of the respondents cited the following three reasons for their career choice: (1) the job of reporter provides the opportunity for demonstrating one's individuality and ability; (2) the job is free and unfettered; and (3) the job enables a reporter to have experiences that others normally cannot enjoy. About one-third of the respondents said they wanted to become a reporter because they enjoy writing. Only one-quarter of the respondents said that they chose the job because the reporter is the leader or guide of the

6. *Shimbun Kenkyu*, Oct. 1973, p. 8.

society. This is surprising in view of a traditional conception the Japanese have about the job of a reporter, namely, that reporters are supposed to be embued with a sense of mission and that they are guides (*bokutaku*) of society.

About 15 percent of the respondents said they were attracted to the job because of its manly nature. Incidentally, young reporters within the age bracket of 25-29 comprised 18.8 percent of the total sample. Many of the older reporters occupying management posts whom I interviewed hold the view that young men these days are attracted to the job because "it looks nice [*kakko yoi*] or it is masculine [*otoko rashī*]." They added that many old-timers were driven by what they took to be the mission of newspapers, i.e., the guide of society. As will be shown later, their own motivations, as they responded to my questions, were complex, with only a small percentage of respondents mentioning the conception of the guide.

The survey of the *Shimbun Kenkyu* in fact demonstrates that the proportion of the respondents citing the concept of guide increases with age. This is, of course, related to whether or not they received most of their formal education in a prewar educational system.[7]

With regard to the reasons for seeking a career in journalism, several findings emerged from an analysis of the interviews that I conducted with forty reporters. The unstructured, open-ended question put to each reporter was: "How did you become interested in the job of a reporter?" The response was, to borrow a Japanese expression, *Junin toiro*; that is, "So many men, so many minds." The question evoked a variety of responses, with only a few categories overlapping with those used by the *Shimbun Kenkyu* survey. Some respondents gave more than one reason for their initial interest in journalism. What follows is a classification of spontaneous responses in terms of dominant reason given by the respondents themselves. Of the forty respondents, seven said that they thought their personality and character were suited for the job. "I am not suited for office work." "Well, I majored in literature. Of the only two things I am trained to do, be a teacher or a reporter, I thought my personality was suited more for a reporter." Five

7. Ibid., pp. 40-43.

respondents said they sought the job because they enjoyed writing. Five recalled the difficulty of finding employment in the years following the end of the war and said that a newspaper company was one of the few places where one could hope to enter on the basis of ability. They tried the exam with success.

The largest number of respondents pointed to the nature of the work itself as the thing which attracted them. The job was described variously as "free," "unfettered," "manly," "full of variety," "colorful," "dynamic," "active," "socially significant," "an enlightenment movement." Two respondents said they were influenced by acquaintances—one by a friend who was a war correspondent during the Korea War, the other by a local politician. One respondent said that he had somehow come to adore a reporter's job from childhood and recalled that he was actively involved in the making of a student newspaper.

There were five responses that reflected more positive attitudes toward the work of a reporter. Two reporters said "I wanted to witness with my own eyes the mechanism or scheme of politics [*seiji no karakuri*]"; another said he wanted to assert his views; another said, "I wanted to exercise influence in the society"; and the fifth reporter said, "I wanted to 'touch' or observe at the front line the tides and changes of the times."

Six respondents referred to what may be called "the sense of mission," "duty," or "service to the nation." One remarked, "I had been interested in politics and wanted to realize my political ideals." However, he could not elaborate on why he chose a career in journalism over a more direct entry into politics. Another recalled the period of confusion following the end of World War II and remarked, "Reflecting what the future of Japan will be and should be and how I can contribute, I thought the work of a reporter would be very important." Another respondent recalled his two years spent in the Imperial Army, saying: "Upon my return, I thought a good deal about where Japan was headed, what course Japan should pursue and how I could be useful to the society. Finally, I came to realize the importance of the work of the newspaper." In the words of a reporter with twenty-one years of service, "With the end of the war, I saw a collapse of Japanese militarism and the beginning of the construction of such a new society by joining the democratic force of the newspapers."

A pattern in the distribution of the respondents is evident when the factor of age is considered. Relatively older respondents, who held high positions in the organizational hierarchy tended to respond in terms of a sense of mission, duty, and service. They tended not to respond in terms of the nature of the work or the suitability of their personality for the work. The single conspicuous exception was the case of a newspaperman with twenty-three years of service who held a high managerial post. His response was rather disarming. He said, "I majored in foreign languages and wanted the opportunity to go abroad. I was interested in doing some work related to foreign countries."

Patterns of Work Assignment and Promotion

New entrants undergo a brief orientation program for a period ranging from a week to a month. Training at the Tokyo Head Office lasts for a week for *Asahi* entrants, a week to ten days for *Sankei* entrants, and a month for their counterparts at the *Yomiuri* and *Mainichi*. The *Asahi* operates on the assumption that new entrants should be exposed to and confronted with real, practical problems at the earliest possible date. After a short indoctrination program concerning what the *Asahi* man is, recruits are sent off to various local bureaus throughout Japan. The *Sankei* recruits are given the opportunity to observe directly and familiarize themselves with various aspects of the news production process. In addition, they are given twenty-four hours to go out and sell thirty subscriptions. The *Mainichi* recruits are expected to observe the operations of various departments and then are asked to deliver newspapers to homes. Experiences in sales, as in the case of *Sankei* recruits, or delivering papers, as in the case of *Mainichi* recruits, are designed to sensitize and compel them to recognize various problems related to the newspaper enterprise.

In the case of all four dailies with which we are concerned, the first assignment following the orientation program is invariably to a local bureau of their respective news organizations. A tour at a local bureau usually lasts two to three years and a reporter may be called to the home office at that point, but more likely he is sent to another local bureau for two or three years before he returns to Tokyo. In most cases, a reporter serves at a local bureau for three to six years.

While assigned to a local bureau, a reporter goes through practical on-the-job training. He is expected to prove to be and function as a full-fledged reporter, covering all kinds of news such as crime, politics, and the economy. Upon completion of his local tour, he is assigned to a department at the Tokyo Head Office.

Home office department heads are generally acquainted with the work of a particular reporter directly or indirectly. They themselves notice and read articles appearing in the local editions of their newspapers that are written by a reporter assigned to a local bureau. Also, they hear about a reporter through the channels: the chief of his local bureau and the head of the Department of Local Communication who makes annual inspection tours of each local bureau. While on his inspection tour, the department head gets to know and collect information about the ability of reporters.

The chief of a local bureau under whose supervision a reporter works gets to know the reporter very well—his strengths and weaknesses. He and the head of the Department of Communication (or the Department of Locality in the case of the *Asahi*) play important roles in the further placement of the reporters. The chief of the local bureau often transmits to the Home Office assignment preferences of the reporters under his supervision. Of course, personnel needs of each department and availability of slots determine assignments. Personnel needs are met by taking into account such factors as demonstrated competence and fitness for a particular subject area—as indicated in informal evaluations mentioned earlier—and preferences of individual reporters.

Decisions about whom to assign to which department at the home office are made for all practical purposes by the head of the receiving department, be it a department of politics, economy, or social affairs. Formal approval is given by the director of the Editorial Bureau.

Once returned to Tokyo to become a member of a particular department, the reporters are assigned to cover a specific government agency or a significant social group. The reporters who belong to the Political Affairs Department are assigned to such places as the official residence of the prime minister, each

of the five political parties, and the Diet, as well as each government agency. Members of the Economic Affairs Department are
assigned to Kabutocho (the Japanese stock market), the Bank
of Japan, private economic organizations such as Keidanren,
or the Federation of Economic Organizations, as well as such
government agencies as the Ministry of Finance and the Ministry of International Trade and Industry. Members of the Social
Affairs Department are assigned to cover various law enforce-
ment agencies.

Ranking of a sort exists among the various beats, but there is
no established pattern of work assignment. For example, the
official residence of the prime minister is considered the most
important beat among political reporters. For economic reporters, the Ministry of Finance and the Bank of Japan are
important assignments. Veteran reporters cover these important
areas by serving as captain of a team. Usually, several reporters
from the same newspaper are assigned to cover a major government agency. A political affairs reporter often begins with the
official residence of the prime minister under the direction of a
veteran "cap," then moves on to a party and a government
agency, but there is no regular sequence of work assignments.
There are many variations with a single news organization and
between news organizations.

Decisions on assignment to a particular beat are made by the
head of the department in consultation with the deputy head
of the department. A reporter usually leads the life of a cub
reporter for about five to seven years, each assignment lasting
about two or three years. Upon completion of beat assignments, the reporter is elevated to office work, seldom returning
to cover news at the front line. A position of responsibility
available at this point of one's career is "desk'," i.e., deputy
head of a department. The number of these positions available
is limited. For example, the Political Affairs Department and
Economic Affairs Department each have about four or five
deputy heads. The Social Affairs Department has a somewhat
larger number of deputy head positions available. At the time
of the field research conducted for this volume, deputy heads
of the four major dailies had been with their organizations for
about fifteen to eighteen years. Selection of deputy heads is
made by head of the department with formal approval of the
director of the Editorial Bureau.

Those who are not given the post of a deputy head of their respective departments may be sent to head a local bureau or to supervise a group of reporters of a major beat. Some may be assigned as a department head to other departments of lesser standing, such as research and liaison, radio, or television. Some of them become editorial staff members, editorial specialists, or editorial writers. These positions may or may not carry the rank of "deputy head treatment." Some may become a plain member of a particular department without any specific assignment. Decisions at this level are made by department heads and chief and deputy chief of the Editorial Bureau. Editorial writers are selected by the chief of editorial writers (*ronsetsu Iinchō*) in consultation with the director of the Editorial Bureau or by the editor-in-chief (*Shukan*) in consultation with the executive officer in charge of editorial matters.

A deputy head serves approximately four to six years before he can be elevated to the post of department head. Not all deputy heads make it to the post of department head. Selection is made usually by the director of the Editorial Bureau in consultation with deputy chief of the Editorial Bureau and/or with the executive officer in charge of editorial matters.

Those who do not make it to the post of department head will usually become editorial staff members, editorial specialists, directors of a major local bureau, or editorial writers with treatment equivalent to department heads.

The deputy director of the Editorial Bureau is usually selected from among department heads with four to six years of experience in that post. Selection is made by the director of the Editorial Bureau with the consent of the editor-in-chief (at the *Mainichi*) or with the Executive Board (at the *Asahi*).[8]

Selection of director of the Editorial Bureau is made by the editor-in-chief with the consent of the Executive Board (at the *Mainichi*). In the case of the *Asahi*, the executive officer in charge of editorial matters makes the selection with the consent of the Executive Board. No minimum length of service as deputy director is considered essential.

On the whole, the so-called managerial posts are filled largely on the basis of merit and achievements, where the positions of

---

8. The *Yomiuri* has a position called *somu*, which is between a director and deputy director of the Editorial Bureau.

the editorial staff tend to depend on seniority. Personnel decisions beyond the level of department head are essentially
political.

Mandatory retirement age for all four dailies is set at fifty-
five. It is extremely rare for a company to retain those who
retire. As of February 1976, the *Asahi* had only two employees
who were over fifty-five. The figure was the same as of July
1977. However, there is a system whereby those who retire
may be rehired as consultants. As of July 1977, the number of
consultants of this type was 574.

The system of lateral entry is practically nonexistent. Heads
of Personnel Departments could recall only a few cases which
happened many years ago where reporters of other newspapers
joined their organizations. The number of resignations is extremely small. The reasons for resignation include the desire
to become a university professor, to inherit the family business,
to become a private secretary to a politician, and to run for an
elective office.

Implications

Of fundamental importance is the existence in Japan of a formal channel for the recruitment of reporters. A career in journalism is open to a wide stratum of the population on the basis
of achievement. The system of a highly competitive, rigorous
examination geared to college graduates appears conducive to
the development of professionalism.

Regarding the educational background of the reporters, it
is relevant to note the absence of a preponderance of Tokyo
University graduates. This contrasts sharply with the central
government bureaucracy. Newspaper organizations are staffed
with graduates of diverse universities, though certain universities contribute a disproportionate share to the world of
journalism. Another feature of interest is that a preponderant
number of reporters have a background in humanistic studies.
How educational background is related to the orientations and
behavior of reporters—especially as they interact with government bureaucrats—will be explored in a later chapter. A sense
of identification and bond stemming from a common alma mater

does not seem to affect personnel decisions significantly. It is common socialization experiences—exposure to the same university tradition—rather than the fact of common alma mater which may be of significance.

It will be recalled that lateral entry into news organizations is virtually nonexistent; i.e., there is no mobility between newspaper organizations. The rate of resignation is astonishingly low, and each reporter works for the same firm until his retirement. The sense of job security and the weight of seniority consideration contribute to the intense loyalty and sense of identification with "my own company." This factor appears to be related to some characteristic patterns of behavior of Japanese reporters.

The fact that reporters enter the profession in their early twenties is also significant in that they are exposed to the same subculture and tradition of a particular news company. The work socialization experience they share may be significantly related to their orientations and behavior.

It is also relevant to note that in Japan a sense of hierarchical relationships pervades those who are involved in production and processing of news. They are hierarchically organized effectively and meaningfully—in terms of age and the year of entry. The reporters who are actually interacting with government officials for the purpose of news gathering are normally in their twenties and thirties. Older reporters are elevated to managerial posts progressively removed from news gathering, writing, and even processing. Under these circumstances a columnist of the great stature of the American press cannot be expected to emerge. Clear generational gaps exist betwen the young reporters and their sources of news (government bureaucrats, politicians, and leaders of other social groups) and between managerial personnel and front-line reporters. What conflicts exist in their role conceptions, and how this is related to their behavior, will be explored in a later chapter.

CHAPTER IV

News Gathering
and Processing

Before we examine the procedures of news gathering and processing in some detail, a brief discussion of the organization of a newspaper firm is in order. Since the four national dailies under study resemble each other very closely in organization, an examination of the organization of one newspaper company will be sufficient. As of November 1, 1975, in addition to four offices and six committees placed under direct supervision of the president, the *Yomiuri* had the following bureaus:

General Affairs Bureau (3 departments and 3 sections)
Accounting Bureau (4 departments and a clinic)
Editorial Bureau (21 departments, 1 office, and 1 section)
Advertising Bureau (7 departments)
Circulation (sales) Bureau (9 departments, 2 sections)
Production (printing and engineering) Bureau (6 departments, Aomori Printing Plant)
Cultural Promotion Headquarters (2 departments, 1 section)
Publication Bureau (3 departments, 3 sections)

The primary focus of this study is on the Editorial Bureau; hence a brief sketch of the bureau is useful. The following departments are subsumed under the *Yomiuri* Editorial Bureau:

Makeup Department 1
Makeup Department 2
Political Affairs Department
Economic Affairs Department
Societal Affairs (city news) Department
Foreign News Department
Cultural Affairs Department
Science Department
Women's News Department
Sports Department
Photograph Department

Local News Department
Intranational News Department
Commentary Department
Proofreading Department
Communications and Aviation Department
Liaison Department
Materials/Data/Reference Department
English Papers (the Daily *Yomiuri*) Department
Sunday Pages Editorial Section
General Affairs Department
Public Opinion Survey Office
Protocol/Liaison Section

The organization of other dailies is quite similar though there are some variations in nomenclature. As of July 1, 1977, the Editorial Bureau of the *Asahi Shimbun* (the Tokyo Main Office) had the following departments: (1) Independent Senior Writers, (2) Makeup, (3) Political Affairs (political news), (4) Economic Affairs (economic news), (5) Societal Affairs (city news), (6) Cultural News, (7) Scientific News, (8) Sports News, (9) Foreign News, (10) Photography, (11) Liaison (communication), (12) Reference, (13) Provincial News, (14) Aviation, (15) Public Opinion Survey, (16) Proofreading, (17) Evaluation, (18) TV and Radio, and (19) Sunday Supplement Section.

In the *Yomiuri*'s Tokyo office alone, more than 1,000 reporters are assigned to diverse news sources and to cover news on a round-the-clock basis. News collected and manuscripts prepared by these reporters are sent to the home office via telephone or messenger. All incoming manuscripts are scrutinized by the desk, the deputy head of a subject matter department, say, political affairs. The desk makes judgments on the news value of a story, sometimes correcting misspelling, rewriting to enhance readability, or adding related stories and commentaries.

The revised manuscript is sent to the Makeup Department where judgments are made on the value of a news item; decisions are made about how big a treatment to give it; and appropriate heads and subheads are prepared. From there the manuscript goes to the Liaison Department.[1] (In some cases,

1. If the manuscript is recorded in duplicate, one copy is sent to the Liaison Department.

each department submits a manuscript directly to the Liaison Department, which, after using the Kanji-teletype monitor, submits it to the Makeup Department.) After punching with the use of Kanji-teletype monitor, the "manuscript" is forwarded to the Printing Production Department where it goes through typesetting (an automatic Monotype setting machine), composition for printing, and then on to packaging and delivery.[2]

As mentioned earlier, the Editorial Bureau is divided into many departments. Each substantive department is responsible for collecting news in a particular subject area. There is a sense of rivalry and tension among various departments. There is little respect between the reporters who deal with the so-called hard news items, such as politics and economics, and their colleagues in a "soft news" department, such as societal affairs. The former view the latter's alleged excitement over murder and suicide with some disdain, while the latter reciprocate the feeling for the former's preoccupation with high national politics and the illusion that they are big shots because they deal with celebrities in political and financial circles.

Tension is due, in part, to the sense of rivalry and to personality characteristics, but it is also due to the peculiar way in which the makeup of different pages is done. Take a morning edition of any national daily. Page one is allocated to the so-called general/comprehensive edition covering major news items of the day. This is followed by pages on domestic politics, foreign news, economy, stock news, editorials and commentaries, special feature stories, sports, home and women, radio-television programs, and city and local news. Responsibility for each section is assigned to a particular department. In general, a page devoted to home-women's affairs is exclusively comprised of news submitted by that department. Those reporters assigned to a particular department are more or less exclusively concerned with the affairs under their jurisdiction, often ignoring even major news that could be put on the front page if it is not in their specialty. The Department of Social Affairs, for example, is supposed to cover city news and is allotted two pages. Of course, it wants to give space to the stories developed by its own reporters; however, occasionally, it must reluctantly give

2. Shimbun Shuzai Kenkyukai, ed., *Shimbun no Shuzai* (Tokyo: Nihon Shimbun Kyokai, 1968), 1: 26-31.

space to social news emanating from other departments. Rigidity in organizational spheres of activities is such that, for example, classical music is covered by a reporter of one department, while popular music and jazz are covered by his colleagues in another department. This sometimes results in a hiatus in covering news and in a failure to cover newsworthy events.[3]

In order to understand the process of news gathering, it is essential to examine the vital role played by what the Japanese call reporters' clubs. A reporters' club is to be found at each governmental agency and at major social, political, and economic organizations. About 50 to 100 reporters, representing various departments (political, economic, social, and local) of various news organizations, frequent a club. They commute to their respective clubs daily directly from home. The number of reporters assigned to each club varies with the agencies. As of 1966, the Keishicho club had 140 reporters and the Foreign Ministry club had 180. About 120 reporters are assigned respectively to the clubs of the Ministry of Agriculture and Forestry, Ministry of Industry and International Trade (MITI) and Ministry of Finance. The Supreme Court club had 71 reporters, the Liberal Democratic party 150, the Japan Socialist party 133, the Tokyo Stock Exchange 120, the Bank of Japan 72, the Ministry of Labor 94, and the Ministry of Education 75. The National Diet club had representatives from 131 news organizations, and the registered membership was around 5,000. The Cabinet Reporters club had about 300 reporters representing about 70 news organizations.[4]

Generally speaking, these clubs are located either on the second or third floor of each government agency building, near a minister's office. Some agencies have more than one club. With the exception of Keishicho club, which provides separate, partioned rooms for each company, the government agencies allocate one large room for use by the club membership. A typical set of equipment available for a news company consists of one or two large desks, a set of sofa and chairs, a locker, a blackboard, telephones, a television set, a set of go and chess games, and a mah-jongg table. A room is usually messy, hardly a prime example of orderliness or neatness.[5]

3. Ibid., pp. 38-41, 44-45.
4. *Gendai Janarizumu* 2: 29.
5. *Shimbun no Shuzai* 1: 84.

At any one time around fifteen or twenty news organizations are represented at the reporters' club of a government agency. Some companies, including the four dailies with which we are concerned, assign a multiple number of reporters to a club. These reporters go to work around 10:30 to 11:00 a.m. On Tuesdays and Fridays when a cabinet meeting is held, they go to work a little earlier. The morning is spent covering press conferences given by a minister after the cabinet meetings or reading newspaper clippings and newspapers. At noon they watch NHK news and have lunch, staying at the club until around 1:00 p.m. when the deadline for the evening edition is passed, waiting for possible unexpected developments. For them, the hours between 1:00 to 3:00 p.m. are relatively free and relaxed. During this period some zealous reporters make the rounds of senior officials' offices in search of news.[6] At some government agencies such news-gathering activity is banned during the business hours. In any case it is difficult to catch these officials during the daytime, as they are frequently in meetings or attending Diet sessions, and so forth. Even if caught, they remain evasive, seldom coming forth with news-worthy items. Their reticence and caution may be overcome by personal ties or by friendship developed through a long association, but the short duration of a reporter's duty at a club, about two years, impedes the development of close relationships. In view of the difficulties of news gathering, and their often futile efforts, some reporters spend time playing mah-jongg, go, or chess or taking naps.

The time of government pronouncements is 3 p.m. Every day, between three and six in the afternoon, a government agency issues a series of announcements, bombarding the reporters with written materials, commentaries, lectures, and briefings. Since this large group of reporters, representing different news organizations, is exposed to the identical source of information and written materials, it is not surprising that the stories appearing in the papers are substantially similar. The reporters are not happy about this situation and do complain about their very limited access to officials. They try, to the extent possible, to gather news independently, but they cannot afford to neglect the government pronouncements, such as press

6. *Gendai Janarizumu* 2: 30.

releases. Besides, there are some constraints on news-gathering activities independent of the club.

According to the principles governing the operations of the clubs originally envisaged and adopted in October 1949, the clubs are designed to promote friendship and goodwill among the reporters assigned to a particular club. The club is not supposed to be involved in the matter of news gathering.[7] Contrary to this principle, the club is intimately and directly involved in news-gathering activity and has become a primary conduit and instrument of news gathering. The reporters whose organizations are not members of a club are not allowed to cover press conferences on the ostensible grounds that the conferences are sponsored by the clubs, not by the public organ. It is difficult to classify press conferences either as government-sponsored events or as sponsored by the club. If they are serious about the claims of club sponsorship, it would contravene the clause of the 1949 understanding that the club should not be involved in news-gathering activity. As a matter of fact, however, nonmembers are barred from using the reporters' room. This directly contravenes the principle that any reporter should have access to the facilities of the press room. Moreover, some reporters' clubs, for example the two attached to the MITI, have bylaws that stipulate openly that the clubs are to "expidite the process of news gathering."[8]

At any rate, as the number of government announcements and handouts has increased, it has become more difficult for a particular news organization to achieve a scoop. The increasing volume of government handouts has tended to dampen enthusiasm for independent efforts at news gathering. This is related to the often-heard charge that all newspapers are alike in content, and that the club members often withhold news by mutual agreement. In fact, a violation of informal agreement among club members concerning the off-the-record nature of a briefing, protection of news sources, and embargo could, and at times have, resulted in a ban on the access of a news organization to a particular club.[9]

7. *Shimbun no Shuzai* 1: 82-83.
8. Ibid., 1: 86-87.
9. Ibid., 1: 99-104.

Political affairs reporters at times have been criticized for being timid about news concerning a series of "black mist scandals" involving politicians. It has been asserted that the reporters' sensitivities have been numbed because of their daily contacts with the apex of the power structure or because of the sheer prevalence of corrupt practices. At any rate, they are said not to be vigorous enough in exposing dishonesty and corruption among politicians.[10] They are described as being afflicted with an "adult mentality" and are known for excessive introspection and circumspection. They are seen as tending to compromise with the power holders and are without much zeal in the quest for social justice. A popular belief is that the prolonged exposure to corruption and decay within the power structure dulls a reporter's critical sense and contributes to his adult mentality.

A few comments have been offered in defense of these reporters. Inasmuch as politics involves interest and ideology in a most intense way, and any hasty judgment by the reporters would have serious consequences, the reporters find it necessary to collect data exhaustively, to explore the matter in depth, and to weigh the evidence cautiously.

Political affairs reporters are expected to apply a criterion different from that of social affairs reporters. For the latter, immediately observable phenomenan, such as murder and traffic accidents, constitute news. On the other hand, political affairs reporters are expected to discern the forces behind a surface phenomenon and judge its significance. This calls for in-depth analysis, contributing to adult mentality.[11]

Another argument made by sympathizers is that political affairs reporters feel that there should be a limit to their moralizing strictures toward politics and politicians. If criticisms about defects of the corrupt political practices are carried to the extreme, they might negate the parliamentary democratic system itself. If strict provisions governing elections are carried to the letter, 99 percent of the elected would have to resign. If criticisms of corrupt practices attending elections are pursued to their logical conclusion, the efficacy of the electoral system itself might have to be questioned.

10. Ibid., 1: 76.
11. Ibid., 1: 181-82.

Another argument is that political affairs reporters are constrained by the principle of objective, nonpartisan reporting, the motto of the Japanese press. Adherence to this principle in a world of politics characterized by intense conflict requires circumspection.[12]

A few characteristics of political reporting in Japan are worth noting. Inordinate importance is attached to coverage of the prime minister's residence and the ruling party relative to other government agencies and opposition parties. News emanating from these sources commands great attention. In a sense, this is natural and rational inasmuch as it reflects the reality of power distribution. However, such an emphasis stems partly from a tradition that stresses personnel changes in the cabinet and in major posts of the ruling party. Personnel changes in these posts have long been thought to constitute politics and have traditionally been the major target of news gathering by political reporters.

The general decline of "faction reporters" has given rise to a few problems. First, it has become difficult to gather news about the moves of various factions. Second, factional leaders now give press conferences at their residence that are open to other reporters, and hence the opportunity for individual contacts leading to a scoop is diminished. This, in turn, has decreased the reporters' zeal for news gathering.

Each central newspaper organization has about forty political affairs reporters. These reporters are expected to do what reporters at press agencies in other countries would do, i.e., collect all the news themselves. In addition to their regular assignments, they are often expected to contribute special feature stories. Unlike the Social Affairs Department, the Political Affairs Department does not have "roving reporters" (yūgun), and when the need arises, reporters attached to other clubs are mobilized.

The fact that a political affairs reporter is assigned to a particular club impedes adequate coverage of political news in a broader sense. The reporters tend to concentrate on and chase news regarding a government agency from the perspective of that agency. Assigning veteran reporters to achieve a broader coverage has been tried but without much success. Aside from a

12. Ibid., 1: 180-83.

shortage of reporters, the inability to discharge responsibility adequately is apparently due to the prevalent attitude among political affairs reporters that the job of a reporter is to collect information at a reporters' club.

The reporters on assignment to specific clubs are given a special "functional" assignment to aid in developing a specialty as well as in acquiring a broader perspective, but this, too, has not met with much success.

Intense competition among the reporters for a scoop about a cabinet reshuffle is indeed remarkable. They are consumed and obsessed with news of this kind. This is done at the expense of proper attention to the underlying socioeconomic ideological forces shaping the political process.[13]

In discussing political affairs reporters, reference should also be made to the problem of *habatsu-kisha*, or faction reporters. The relative weight in Japanese politics of factional politics within the ruling party has been on the decline in recent years. In the days of such towering Liberal Democratic party factional leaders as Kono Ichiro and Ono Bamboku, the corrupt practices or evils of faction reporters were abundant. The reporters developed intimate personal ties with particular factional leaders, often serving as confidants and agents of political bosses. Kono was known to ban any unfamiliar reporters, i.e., those who were not attached to Kono, from his residence. News gathering in political affairs requires contacts with politicians, trust, and good personal ties between the politicians and the reporters. These are of critical importance. If politicians erect walls around themselves, shutting out any unknown and un-proven reporters, it is necessary for the reporters to win recognition and to gain admission inside the wall. To obtain trust, some reporters have acted in a manner unfitting for a reporter, serving as hirelings of the factional political leader whom they are supposed to cover.[14]

Economic affairs reporters are sometimes called an elite group of reporters. Other reporters are conscious of their own inadequacies in comprehending the questions of economy and yet fully acknowledge the relevance and importance of economy in understanding the trends in politics and society. Economic

13. Ibid., 1: 186-95.
14. Ibid., 1: 190-201.

affairs reporters are thought to belong to a special group responsible for a technical field and are held in high esteem. Economics stories are not widely or carefully read or even discussed
at the daily critique session of newspapers, however. Most
reporters have humanities backgrounds and are weak on figures.
The technical terms used are not easy to understand, and technical economic questions do not arouse much interest.[15]

Economic affairs reporters are dissatisfied that their stories
are not properly appreciated, but their dissatisfaction is tempered by the knowledge that they are thought of as specialists
responsible for covering a most important area. The sense of
fulfillment they experience appears greater than that of crime
reporters.

The image of economic affairs reporters is one of gentle,
cautious, well-groomed, and meticulous gentlemen. Their
attitude toward the government agencies they cover and toward
the voluminous materials issued by the agencies is different
from that of political affairs reporters. Economic affairs reporters can demonstrate their own specialization and depth of
knowledge even if the same materials issued by the governmental agencies are used. The quality of an article on economic
affairs depends relatively more on the reporter's ability and
accumulated experience than does one on political affairs.
Moreover, the economic stories require accurate figures, and
hence an economic affairs reporter is not so critical or skeptical
as a political affairs reporter toward government materials.[16]

"Night Attack"

Night attack refers to the practice where a reporter visits a
news source at his home late at night to elicit information. The
reporters in the Social Affairs and Political Affairs Departments
go on night attack duty frequently. Suppose a murder has taken
place. A social affairs reporter assigned to Section 1 of the
Metropolitan Police does news gathering at the place of the
crime and at night visits the homes of the detectives and high-
ranking police officials.

15. Ibid., 1: 206.
16. Ibid., 1: 215-18.

The targets of night attacks by political affairs reporters are most frequently the cabinet secretary, cabinet ministers, major leaders of the ruling and opposition parties, and ranking officials of government ministries. Reporters from various newspapers flock to the private residence of the target at night, especially when major developments are taking place, around 10:00 to 11:00 p.m. Since the officials cannot possibly meet with reporters individually, they often hold press conferences. About twenty reporters regularly participate in a night press conference given by the cabinet secretary or secretary general of the ruling party. Some politicians hold regularly scheduled press conferences a few times a week. Some reporters manage to obtain individual interviews. The desire for private, intimate talks with the target that might lead to a scoop or to a more accurate and fully developed story sustains long vigils and perseverance by the reporters. They often wait outside until other reporters have left the target.[17]

Night press conferences are far less formal than daytime conferences. Politicians' remarks then may be susceptible to different interpretations, depending on the perceptions of the reporters. The possibility of obtaining a scoop even in such joint conference settings cannot be ruled out.

The practice of night attack is usually justified on the following grounds.[18] (1) It is difficult to have individual access to news sources during the day. At some government agencies, news gathering is forbidden during the day. Since political leaders, cabinet ministers, and other high-ranking officials are busy, it is difficult for reporters to gain access to them, especially for private talks. (2) In the daytime, one cannot expect more than a formal response at the press conferences. This is in part due to the fact that reporters from several media, including television and radio, are present. In such a setting, it is difficult to carry on frank and in-depth conversations. (3) Television and radio may excel in speedy news reporting, but newspapers are superior in being able to provide high-quality news. In this connection, the kind of news likely to be collected through the night attack circuit is not so readily transferable to film as are fires or traffic accidents. (4) Night attack is necessary

17. *Shimbun no Shuzai* 2: 22.
18. Ibid., 2: 42-44, 26-27.

to obtain scoops. Scoops are necessary to overcome skepticism and the misconception that newspapers are not much different from one another—a misconception caused by the public relations activities of government agencies.

In 1959 Ryu Shintaro urged that the practice of night attack be discontinued. He suggested that the practice deprives politicians of the time needed for private study, and that it leads to unwholesome ties between the reporters and politicians.[19] Those who favor the abolition of the practice point to additional advantages: reduction in the long working hours, reduction in the expenses involved in news gathering,[20] and protection of the private lives of the reporters. Incidentally, the interviews I conducted with a sample of Japanese reporters clearly demonstrate that they consider the long and irregular hours required and the sacrifice of family life that this entails as the most negative and painful aspect of their job.

It appears that the practice of night attack in some measure has contributed to a corrupt relationship between reporters and officials. Some reporters have placed the goal of winning the confidence of the news source above the need for objective and impartial reporting. Politicians have leaked information beneficial to themselves, consciously utilizing reporters for their own interests. On the other hand, reporters have knowingly allowed themselves to be utilized so as to win the confidence of the news source.

At a meeting of political affairs department heads of Japanese newspapers in March 1959, there was general acceptance of the following points.[21]

1. In principle, it is desirable not to make a call on politicians in the middle of the night. However, since major political developments occur at night, it is impossible to do away completely with the practice of night attack.

2. Since major decisions, such as personnel reshuffling of cabinet and party posts, are announced in the middle of the night, night press conferences with the cabinet secretary are a

19. Ibid., 2: 22.
20. Expenses include transportation, often the use of chauffeur-driven cars, food, and drinks. The reporters consume food, beer, and sake while waiting for the commencement of a night attack.
21. Ibid., 2: 28.

necessary evil. However, no complimentary sake should be served to the reporters.

3. The reporters should not and will not press politicians for interviews at night if the politicians take a stand that they will not be available at home at night for interviews.

4. The reporters are invited to politicians' homes and treated as if they were private soldiers.

Department heads then agreed that excessive employment of the practice should be curtailed and that self-restraint was in order. The problem surfaced again in 1965, and the same conclusions were reached. It is practically impossible to abolish the practice, and there is no alternative but to exercise self-restraint. However, a pledge was made to attempt to find a more rational way of gathering news.[22]

Another problem is that night attack causes the families of the politicians and officials great inconvenience. The custom of entertaining reporters with food and sake is no longer widely followed, but late-night visitors cause inconvenience. This problem is more acute in the case of crime reporters because detectives and prosecutors, the targets of their night attacks, often do not have living accommodations suitable for receiving guests.[23] The practice of night attack also has adverse impact on the family life of the reporters. Traditionally, the model reporters are thought to be those who are so completely preoccupied with news gathering that they are beyond concern for the family or monetary intersts. Many reporters have accepted such a life-style, although a younger generation of reporters might not be willing to sustain family sacrifice.

Subject Matter Editors

It will be recalled that the Editorial Bureau has four to six deputy chiefs (*bujichō* or *fukubuchō*) called the desk. They are the most vital link in the news organization, responsible for the making of the newspapers. They direct the reporters in news gathering; they make judgments about news value, revise and polish incoming manuscripts, and plan special feature

22. Ibid., 2: 32-33.
23. Ibid., 2: 38.

stories. The position is considered to be a managerial one and is a stepping stone to higher posts in the organization.[24] The magnitude of the burden with little time for rest literally consumes the bodies and minds of the incumbents.

They attend to their duty, covering news twenty-four hours a day by taking turns. A deputy chief reports to work in the mid-afternoon and assumes the responsibility for the morning paper from the early edition to the final edition. In a department with four deputy chiefs, for three months out of a year he stays up at night until early morning. After finishing work on the last edition of the morning paper around 3 a.m., he either takes a nap at the office until a desk in charge of the evening edition reports to work around 9 a.m. or goes home at dawn to catch some sleep. (Always short of sleep, he usually spends his holiday sleeping.) He reports back to work in the afternoon, assisting a desk who is responsible for the evening or morning editions. On the third day, he is technically off but usually assists in planning special feature stories. On the fourth day, he becomes a desk in charge of the evening paper. He reports to work around 9 a.m. and assumes the responsibility for the evening paper from the first to the last edition, until 5 to 7 p.m. On the following day, he returns to "night work," being responsible for the morning paper.

For all practical purposes, a desk has the entire responsibility for the pages in his subject area. Although nominally the head of the department is responsible for the area pages, the deputy director and director of the Editorial Bureau are responsible for the contents of the entire newspaper. They are consulted on matters of great sensitivity and importance.

It requires a good deal of concentration, skill, and expertise to read, revise, and polish stories prepared by others under tremendous pressures of time. A desk in charge of the evening paper operates under greater time constraints than a desk in charge of the morning edition. He seldom has the time to send a reporter back for additional news gathering or to order the manuscripts rewritten. A desk charged with the preparation of the morning paper has the opportunity to "create his own pages." He is likened to a chef with his cutting board and knife ready, waiting for good materials to arrive. He can decide on the

24. Ibid., 1: 58.

top stories with a more measured pace and can afford to ask for more information and in-depth analysis of items that have come to his attention.

In addition to editorial responsibility, deputy chiefs are expected to assist department heads in administrative and personnel matters. As we have seen in an earlier chapter, deputy chiefs are selected from among the able veteran reporters with more than ten years of experience and usually are in their late thirties or early forties. A very small proportion of deputy chiefs move upward to become department heads, but most of them are said to "wither away" both physically and mentally after a tour of several years.[25]

The "Ten Commandments" for a desk include the following two points that attest to the trials and tribulations of the work involved.

1. A desk must be in excellent health.

2. He must not be bound to a family. Fear of a wife is the primary reason for the failure of a desk. In order to devote full time to the preparation of papers, he must be prepared to abandon his family.[26]

Makeup Editors

After review by the subject matter editorial staff, manuscripts are forwarded to the Makeup Department (*seiribu*). There, makeup desks make judgments on news value and determine heads and subheads and the layout of each page. The department is important not just because of the work involved in transforming all the manuscripts into the form of a newspaper with a limited number of pages. It is here that each item or story is evaluated in terms of news value. Until it reaches the Makeup Department, each item, however important or interesting it may be, remains a separate and individual story. By the

25. Recall also that they are not sent back to the front line for news gathering. These veterans are condemned to be administrators. They are no longer expected to play an active role in news gathering, and if any of them are assigned to a reporters' club, it is likely to be considered a demotion.

26. Ibid., 1: 80-81.

time the item leaves the Makeup Department, it has been transformed into a story occupying a certain space with a head and subhead and arranged in a suitable layout, attractive to the readers.

The volume of incoming news always exceeds available space. The makeup desks feel that their work involves printing as much news and as soon as possible, selecting from among the most important and newsworthy items, transforming each item into a concise and readable form, and compressing all this into a day's space. The work of makeup, therefore, demands a capacity for value judgment and aesthetic expressions, a deep understanding of the problems of writing, a capacity for resolute judgment, and a special skill for bringing all these items into a newspaper. It is inescapable that judgment on news value in part varies with those who make the judgment. A makeup desk's judgment may not be consistent with that the readers would have made. Items that receive great play in one paper may be given small treatment in other papers. The judgment of the Makeup Department staff is in large measure shaped by the contents of materials submitted by the news-gathering departments. The work of makeup presupposes familiarity and knowledge about various subject areas such as politics, economics, laws, society, sports, and culture and the capacity for speedy and appropriate judgment on the value of news items. The very nature of news items demands the prompt attention of the makeup editors so that these items can be processed in time for deadlines. Makeup desks in charge of various substantive areas are constantly making decisions and racing against a series of deadlines for different editions. They must make decisions in a matter of minutes and sometimes within a few seconds. They are confronted simultaneously by several scores of events, each demanding appropriate judgment on news value. They must process the items within the shortest possible time. They operate with the conviction that the value of a news item depends very much on the speed of reporting. A report appearing the day after other papers have published it would have no news value.[27]

27. Miki Seikichi, *Shimbun no Henshu to Seiri* (Tokyo: Gen Janarizumu Shuppankai, 1966), pp. 9-29.

Even when the makeup staff is working on final composition and layout, news of a major event may come in, requiring their immediate decision about its relative weight and the treatment it is to be given. This time pressure facilitates the operation of other factors that influence the process of news gathering and processing: one's subjectivity, preconceptions, prejudices, honest errors, desire for sensational news, and desire for scoops.[28] Makeup editors feel that they must report as much news as possible, and this has meant that the amount of coverage per item has to be reduced as much as possible. They try to make news stories concise and accurate. At the same time, they feel that they must use appropriate sensational expressions. In short, they believe that headlines must meet the requirements of conciseness, appropriateness, accuracy, and sensory expressions.

A survey of Tokyo residents in 1962-65 revealed that the proportion of the newspaper readers who read beyond the heads on a "hard" news story about foreign affairs, politics, or economy is very small. The proportion of careful readers of political items was 33 percent, while those who regularly read these heads was 47 percent. By comparison, the proportion of careful readers of city news (social affairs pages) was close to 70 percent.

Makeup editors attempt therefore to make the readers read the contents by using sensory expressions, especially on items dealing with politics. This effort is not directed to heads alone. The size, location, and arrangement of heads and subheads are determined so as to give each page the maximum sensory effect, appeal, and attraction.[29]

Makeup editors are also expected to have, and they do have, deep appreciation of the problems of writing—composition as well as style of writing. They must often delete parts of stories due to space restrictions and other considerations, and that requires much understanding of the problem of composition.

Given the amount of printed material contained in a daily paper and the limited amount of time the readers usually

28. Ibid., pp. 26, 34-42. A few extreme cases of news manufacturing have occurred. For example, in September 1950 the *Asahi* carried an exclusive interview by its reporter with a Japanese Communist party official at his mountain hideout. The story proved to be total fabrication by the reporter.

29. Ibid., pp. 58-59.

allocate, the importance of headlines is evident. Heads serve as makeup editors' recommendations and their allocation of emphasis to which the readers' attention is called. Headlines serve as an index of a sort, and the readers decide which stories to read on the basis of heads. For this reason, heads must be concrete and specific. And yet, this requirement contradicts another requirement of conciseness.

The Japanese speak of the three C's that are desirable for newspaper writing: being correct, concise, and clear. These qualities are expected of heads as well. In the case of heads, two additional qualities are mentioned—choice and charm. To make a judgment on news value is an exercise in choices. After selection, they must express important points accurately, concretely, and clearly and must charm the readers into reading the contents.[30]

Director and Deputy Director

In the pages to follow, the daily activities of ranking officials of the Editorial Bureau will be sketched. The director of *Sankei* Editorial Bureau comes to the office around 10:30 a.m. At 11 a.m. he presides over a meeting of department heads where a critical review of the day's morning paper is undertaken and discussions take place about the ways to deal with important items for the evening paper, about special feature stories, and about various problems related to the morning paper of the following day. Until the deadline for the evening paper is passed, he attends to any important questions that may arise regarding that paper. Much of his time, however, is spent on administrative matters such as personnel and expenditures. He usually leaves the office around 8 p.m. to attend various functions and then goes home.

The actual work in the making of a newspaper is handled mostly by each department. The director of the Editorial Bureau is involved in newspaper making by participating in the planning of various features and by making decisions on major problems. During the interview, the director remarked. "The most important thing for a bureau director is to establish the principles and guidelines for the newspaper. My responsi-

30. Ibid., p. 192.

bility is to formulate and indicate clearly what my company's stand is on a given issue, especially on matters which have bearing on national interests."

Very seldom, if ever, does the director review or revise a manuscript or rewrite a news story. He has the final authority to decide on what items get into the paper, and it is he who will be held responsible for what appears. However, normally the head and deputy head of each department are entrusted with day-to-day operations. Occasionally, differences of views arise among the ranking officials of the Editorial Bureau, for example, between a head of a subject area and a department head of the Makeup Department. In the case of a conflict of views on major issues unresolved at the level of deputy director, the director makes the final decision.

Editorials are generally outside the supervision of the director of the Editorial Bureau, although he meets with the editorial writers once a week. Editorial writers are in effect removed in their daily activities from the director.

On the newspaper owner's role in news gathering and processing, the bureau director remarked that, after all, "editorial rights" are in the hands of the company, and the views of the bureau director must be compatible with those of the owners. He said he consults the owners about extremely important issues in establishing the direction and the position of the newspaper. On other matters, the director's own judgment suffices.

We shall now look at the daily activities of a deputy director, in this case, of the *Mainichi*. When he is responsible for the evening paper, the deputy director comes to work around 9 a.m. At 9:30 a.m. he presides over a meeting of desks where he comments critically on the morning paper of the day and listens to the plans for news gathering by each department for the day. His office work ends at about 5:30 p.m. (When he is in charge of the morning edition, he comes to work in the afternoon and works until late at night.) He sees the major responsibilities to be in the area of management and newspaper making. His time is divided equally between these two tasks. He sees his participation in newspaper making to be more in terms of overall planning and laments the time he spends attending numerous meetings.

Formally speaking, he said, the ultimate and highest authority in editorial matters lies in the hands of the editor-in-chief (*henshu shukan*). However, the highest authority in day-to-day operations lies with the director of the Editorial Bureau. In actuality, the deputy director of the Editorial Bureau exercises that authority. Of course, matters of lesser importance are resolved in accordance with the judgments of desks and department heads. Decisions involving what items should be given top treatment on the front page and what should be given top play on the social affairs page are made in consultation with the deputy director. To reiterate, most cases are handled by desks, and only the issues of the political significance of, for example, cabinet reshuffling and major policy changes would invite the involvement of department heads. The deputy director of the *Mainichi* said, "My central concern is whether a right angle or standpoint is employed in developing a story and whether heads are appropriate."

According to the deputy director of the *Asahi*, he sometimes revises the contents of news stories, although his concern is more with the angle or perspective taken by a reporter and with the question of whether the story reflects a balanced perspective. Sometimes he is attentive even to minor details of a story if the nature of subject is delicate. Usually, a desk or department head consults the deputy director in advance on what are likely to be controversial and sensitive issues, but there have been times when he intervened after the composition of a paper was finished just before printing. It is clear that the bureau chief is only marginally involved in the daily making of newspapers. A deputy director of the Editorial Bureau is more deeply involved in the process. All the deputy directors interviewed say that approximately 50 percent of their time is devoted to newspaper making, the rest being spent attending to various management problems.

Heads of the Political Affairs Department

A department head at the *Sankei* comes to work around 11 a.m. to attend a meeting of department heads which lasts about an hour. From 12:00 to 2:30 he is concerned with any problems related to the evening paper. Following that, he is generally concerned with the making of the morning paper. He goes over the items with the desk and the reporters on the beats. By 8 p.m., an outline of the morning paper emerges, and unless any major happening detains him, he leaves the office to attend other functions.

As for the role of a department head, he said, normally the desk attends to and handles matters related to the newspaper making. If a major event occurs, he as department head goes over it. "In principle, rather than trying to comment on the product, I try to advise and instruct the reporters on the beats in advance about the perspective from which to deal with a problem. When a major event happens, he stays in close touch with the reporters on the beat and decides how much news should be processed that day. "Of course, all of us desire a scoop," he said, "but we are also constrained by a desire for accuracy and therefore want to have news firmly confirmed before going to press."

The head of the Political Affairs Department of the *Asahi* comes to work sometimes between 11:30 and 12 noon. He attends a meeting of department heads at 2 p.m. which lasts one or two hours. He stays in the office until 6 p.m. and then goes out to attend various functions, often dinner with political and business figures. At 9 p.m., he returns to the office to look over the early edition of the morning paper. He goes home sometime between 10 p.m. and midnight.

Although as department head he is fully responsible for the product, a desk takes care of "ordinary news." The *Asahi* department head said: "The most important thing for a department head is to help the members of his department to develop their full potential and to provide them with the environment for meaningful work. One thing I ought not to do is to show partiality for any one reporter. . . . To my dissatisfaction, I spend too much time in management, especially personnel problems. Only half of my time is devoted to newspaper making. . . . I respond to the questions from desks, and I advise them. I have little time to utilize my experience as a writer in the making of a daily paper."

When no major events are happening, a department head of the *Mainichi* comes to work around 11 a.m. He is busy attending to administrative chores. He attends meetings, receives reports from reporters on beat assignments, and receives guests. "As for my participation in the making of the paper," he said, "I convey to the desk my views on the morning paper, and when the early edition of the evening paper is ready, I let my reaction be known to the desk and other reporters concerned. At 6 p.m. I am through receiving guests or taking care of administrative chores. As the preparation of the morning paper begins, some reporters on the beats begin to return. I listen to them, giving them instructions. Usually, I return home sometime between midnight and 1 a.m."

While the evening paper is prepared, he confers with the desk on and off. In most cases, decisions concerning stories are made by the desks. There are two qualifications, however. "In case of major news items, the desk consults me," he said. "In a really important case, I consult with the deputy director or director of the Editorial Bureau. Even if the early edition is already out, when I, department head, find fault wth a story, I order a revision, often requiring a full development of a story. This kind of instruction is hard to comply with because of the time constraint in the case of the evening paper."

Ranking officials of newspaper companies maintain contacts with high-ranking government officials and political leaders on a more or less regular basis. For example, once or twice a month, the Editorial Bureau directors of several major newspapers jointly invite political leaders and high-ranking officials to the Japan Reporters' Club to give talks. A request for meetings sometimes comes from the latter. Similar meetings with politicians and government officers at levels involving deputy directors, editorial writers, and department heads occur. In addition, each of these newspapermen has his own private individual contact with a specific member of the political, economic, and government circles with whom he has developed personal ties over the years since his days as a cub reporter. From the perspective of newspapermen, these individual contacts provide the opportunity for news gathering, confirmation of significant news obtained by their subordinates, deep background briefings, acquisition of insights and the proper perspective to be employed in treating a specific event, as well as authoritative sources of potential scoops.

Asked about the contacts he maintains with politicians, a department head said, "For a political reporter, it is too late if any event has occurred. The most important thing is for him to predict how a thing may develop. For this purpose he needs to stay in touch on a personal basis with politicians and high-ranking officials." In view of the personal relations he has developed, he can, when necessary, telephone them and elicit some information. To be more effective, a visit to their home in the evening is necessary.

Deputy Heads of the Political Affairs Department

An *Asahi* political affairs desk's day usually begins at 9:30 a.m. when he is in charge of the evening paper and at 3:30 p.m. when he is in charge of the morning paper.[31] He begins his day attending a meeting of desks of various departments which lasts about one-half to one hour. When in charge of the evening edition, his official working hours will be over around 7:00 p.m.; when in charge of the morning edition, he usually works until 2:00 a.m. The day following the late night duty is supposed to be his day off unless an emergency occurs or unless the Diet is in session. When the Diet is in session, he goes to the Diet to supervise news gathering and dispatching of news articles from there.

The desk said he occasionally issues instructions about which items are to be treated as newsworthy. He is in touch with and frequently consulted by the captains of various teams assigned to different beats. He said that the reporters call in occasionally to make strong requests that the news they have gathered be printed, and they ask for his judgment before they go on a night attack.

As for feature stories, the initiative comes from the department head or desk. In carrying out the functions of the desk in charge of morning and evening papers, he decides independently

31. At the time of this study, the *Asahi* Department of Political Affairs had forty members. Six of them had the rank of deputy head. Four worked as desk at the home office, while the other two served as captains of the *Asahi* reporters' team at the Cabinet reporters' club and the Liberal Democratic party reporters' club.

on how to compose the pages of that day, although he checks with and obtains the approval of the department head on major issues. He consults with the department head regarding scoops, sensitive expressions, and headlines. He saw no basic major differences between himself on the one hand and the reporters or the department head on the other. Sometimes he revises news stories and, if time permits, requests rewriting when the stories are inadequately developed.

He has limited opportunities for contacts with outside sources. He felt that he should see the sources himself. He said he tries to hear the reporters directly on the beat as much as possible when they stop by the office.

Protests regarding political affairs articles are usually directed to the department head. He as deputy head has listened to oral protests on behalf of the department head. The duty of a desk also involves personnel matters concerning which he renders advice when requested by the department head.

When asked whether there are major differences of views between the desk and beat reporters about his work, a *Sankei* desk replied that there are no major differences. However, he added: "The dilemma I face is whether everything should be reported as long as it is true and factual. What happens to national interest in diplomacy? The beat reporters usually operate with pure or naive sentiments and prepare articles that expose everything they know. However, the position of a desk is confronted with the 'wall of national interest.'"

The beat reporters decide what stories to write, often in consultation with the captain of the team. It is the desk that determines which news to print. Most of the stories submitted are printed, but when a large number of stories are available on a given day, some must be dropped. The decision to drop a story has little to do with ideological reasons. In addition to the amount of space available, low news value and poor writing are considerations. Other than expressions, no substantive revision is made unilaterally. When a point is unclear, he asks for rewriting and, if necessary, instructs a reporter to undertake further news gathering.

Although the *Sankei* desk did not know much about the relations between the owners and editors, he felt that the owners have at times intervened and that such intervention has had some impact on editorial guidelines. As for his relations with the department head, he is left with the responsibility for practically everything concerned with editing. On major questions involving the composition of pages, assignments, and headlines, he consults with the department head, and sometimes the department head issues instructions.

As a *Yomiuri* desk saw it, the most important duty of a desk is to review all the incoming news stories sent in by reporters and to make a judgment on the newsworthiness of these items.[32] His job also involves rectifying inadequacies and transforming the stories into "fair" articles. Asked who decides what to write and print, he replied that in principle and in general the reporters on the beats decide in consultation with a captain on what stories to write that day. Then he makes a judgment which is reviewed by a desk in the Makeup Department. He said that sometimes the instructions may emanate from him. The main concern at the level of a desk is to make sure a judgment on news value is proper and to check whether the information or the story is deliberately slanted or biased.

Important decisions are made by the department head, and the desk assists the head in special features and personnel matters. The desk is constantly in touch with captains and reporters on the beats. Each of the six desks in the *Yomiuri* Political Affairs Department has personal ties with politicians that they developed when they were beat reporters. From time to time the desks use their personal contacts to ascertain accuracy and to decide on the timing of news publication. When the Diet is in session, a desk himself is involved in news gathering. He can talk on the phone with his contacts, and more frequently it is the politicians who want to meet with the desk to make their views known.

"On a purely personal basis," a *Yomiuri* desk said, "I am agreeable to consultation with a politician-friend. However, the treatment we have him on our newspaper pages is tough and can be ruthlessly critical. To be on friendly terms with politicians is all right, but we should avoid deep entanglements."

Protests are usually conveyed to a department head or Editorial Bureau chief. As desk, he gets some, but mostly he

32. The *Yomiuri* has a forty-member Department of Political Affairs including six desks.

listens to complaints on behalf of the department head. He concedes that there have been some differences of opinion between desks and reporters on the manner in which news is gathered and processed. The differences, which occur once in a while, are most frequently over judgment on news value, what angle should be applied, and what kind of play should be given to a particular story.

Deputy Heads of the Makeup Department

For all practical purposes, it is the deputy heads (desks) of the Makeup Department that carry out the department's work. The department head usually does not see the incoming manuscripts. On major issues, a desk in charge consults with the department head, and on occasions, the views of the deputy director of the Editorial Bureau are solicited. When in charge of the evening paper, a *Sankei* desk comes to work by 9:00 a.m. and works until about 5:00 p.m.[33] When in charge of the morning paper, he reports to work at 2:30 p.m. and works until about 2:00 a.m. After reviewing the last edition of the morning paper, he frequently sleeps at the office, usually about ten times a month. He gets up at 9:00 a.m. to get ready for the evening paper unless it is his day off. So far as the Makeup Department is concerned, the deadline for processing the manuscripts for the evening paper is 1:30 p.m., and the deadline for the morning paper is 1:40 a.m. As a rule, the final edition contains some changes from earlier editions. It is not unusual to find that top stories in earlier editions have been replaced.

. A desk in the Makeup Department often revises and shortens stories submitted by substantive departments due to space limitations. Because of the lack of time, the desks cannot give each incoming story a careful reading. A desk in charge of the morning edition is better off in this regard. A desk can request rewriting by a substantive department, although this seldom happens. Unless it is a major news item, those items already treated in other papers will get restrained play. Sometimes the director of the Editorial Bureau himself makes suggestions concerning top stories or headlines.

33. The *Sankei* Makeup Department has twelve desks, most of whom have been in the position over ten years.

According to the *Sankei* desk, the most important job is to evaluate news value, deciding which stories to put on the first page. Most important news items are treated in the first three pages, called "Comprehensive News Pages." The first page is devoted to top news from all fields, whereas pages two and three are devoted to other important news concerning domestic politics, social affairs, and the economy. His criteria for selecting top stories are threefold: (1) international significance and importance in terms of probable impact on internal politics, (2) major domestic political developments such as cabinet reshuffle, and (3) developments intimately connected with, and those which would significantly affect, the livelihood of the people. When in doubt, he consults his department head, but very seldom major differences of opinion occur. In most cases, judgments on the news value of stories are identical. The Makeup Department in principle does not change the contents of the stories; the department can delete passages or shorten stories without consultation with substantive departments.

Next to the problem of news value, decisions on heads command the major attention of a desk. The *Sankei* desk said, "The heads must be vivacious and dynamic and such that at one glance the reader must be able to grasp the contents." An important consideration is that heads must make the contents easy to comprehend. Substantive departments suggest certain heads, but as the *Sankei* desk put it: "We are ready to listen, but the Makeup Department makes final decisions. The job calls for creativity and a quick mind, and substantive department staff are often unable to come up with suitable heads. Heads call for good sense and our experience." On the matter of layout, which is another important responsibility for a desk, the desk said, "Layout must be pretty and easy to read."

According to an *Asahi* desk in the Makeup Department, the manuscripts from the substantive departments start arriving around 10:00 a.m.[34] As he looks over them, he visualizes the newspaper pages, thinking about the top stories to be used. The stories are scrutinized first by the desks in charge of the comprehensive pages for possible use on pages one through three, and then they are distributed among the desks in charge of

34. The *Asahi* has four desks responsible for comprehensive pages, four desks for hard news, and four for soft news.

"hard" and "soft" news. Desks either make decisions themselves or sometimes consult with substantive department desks. The Makeup Department desks take into account the opinions of the substantive departments, and according to the *Asahi* desk, about 80 percent of these suggestions are accepted. He is quite emphatic that the judgment is the privilege of the Makeup Department. The comprehensive page desks consult with a desk in charge of each page and decide on the top stories.

As in other newspapers, the *Asahi* Makeup Department desks cannot add anything in the process of rewriting but can delete or shorten stories without consultation. When the time permits, he makes suggestions to substantive departments concerning the desirability of strengthening a given story or adding related commentaries.

In making judgments on news value, criteria applied are: (1) international significance and its degree of impact on Japan, (2) novelty, and (3) whether an item is interesting. In making up the pages, the primary goal is to make the paper readable. "The paper must be readable, which is our primary goal," said the *Asahi* desk. "Yet, the paper must also be aesthetically beautiful. As for heads, the most important objectice is to convey accurately the essence of news. Accuracy is much more important than shock value."

The deadline for the final evening edition is 5:10 p.m. The deadline for the morning paper is 11:40 p.m. in principle, but when necessary it can be as late as 2:00 a.m. The paper is delivered to the residents of the Tokyo metropolis (the thirteenth edition) can reflect the latest changes entered up to 2:00 a.m. The eleventh edition is delivered to the northern Kanto area and Chiba prefecture, with the twelfth edition delivered to the suburban areas of the metropolis.

According to the *Asahi* desk, the most important things he must do are: (1) make judgments on news value, (2) select top stories, and (3) formulate heads and subheads.

Later editions contain more recent news and more well-developed stories. Poor judgments made in the earlier editions can be corrected. The major dailies make a practice of exchanging the earlier editions of their respective papers. Thus, both the substantive and Makeup Departments have the time to review the so-called combined edition and the first of the so-called set editions of other rival papers, comparing the judgments on news value made by other papers. When a newspaper company has a scoop, it refuses an exchange, preventing an exodus of an earlier edition from the premises. Scoops appear generally in the eleventh edition, the first set edition. If the newspaper company is really confident that no other papers have a scoop it has, it withholds the item's publication until the last edition (the thirteenth edition) to beat other papers.

Editorial Writers

In the remainder of this chapter, the procedures involved in the preparation of editorials and the nature of work of editorial writers will be noted. All fifteen members of the *Sankei* Editorial Office meet at 11:30 to decide on the topics for the day's editorials. Following discussion, the chief editorial writer selects topics, decides on which direction editorials should take, and assigns editorial writers. A *Sankei* editorial writer said that there are no specific criteria for selecting topics, except that topics are chosen from among the most important news of the day. The guiding principle of a *Sankei* editorial is to highlight the merits of the issues concerned.

When an assigned writer completes a draft, it is reviewed by the chief editorial writer. If the draft is contradictory to the company's guidelines, he is asked to rewrite it. The most important quality required of an editorial writer is the ability to make judgments on news values. It will be recalled that editorial writers are usually recruited from among those who served as department heads or deputy department heads and that each editorial writer has a field of specialization.

Editorial writers have the opportunity to talk with politicians and government officials on a more or less regular basis. Three major types of personal interactions were identified by the respondent from the *Sankei*. First, editorial writers are invited to government offices for an exchange of views. There, in addition to written handouts, briefings are given. This occurs about once a month. Second, several times a year, editorial writers are invited to a restaurant by political and government leaders, including those in the Asakasaka district of Tokyo, for an informal exchange of views. Third, about once a month politicians and high-ranking officials are invited to a luncheon by editorial writers of several companies to discuss current issues. Another mode of interaction between the two sides is the use of the telephone. Editorial writers can, without difficulty, call up high-ranking officials such as vice-ministers and bureau chiefs.

Complaints come to the chief editorial writer. They involve alleged errors in figures and facts. Practically no complaints have been made about the direction or angle taken by an editorial. To the knowledge of the respondent, the *Sankei* has received no protests from government officials. He knew of no instance of complaints from the legislators of the Liberal Democratic party or the Democratic Socialist party, but he recalled protests from other opposition parties.

A *Yomiuri* editorial writer said that he comes to the office around 11:00 a.m. and at 11:30 attends a meeting of fifteen editorial writers which lasts between thirty and forty minutes. Being himself the deputy chief of editorial writers, from 11:00 to 11:30 he discusses with the chief suitable topics from among the major news stories that appeared in the evening paper of the previous day and the morning paper. When asked to specify criteria for selection, he replied that items for editorials need not necessarily be from the top stories, but they must be from among "important and big news" stories about which the views of the *Yomiuri* should be expressed. The *Yomiuri* editorial writers have the following fields of specialization: three members are in charge of politics (domestic and foreign policies of Japan and international relations of foreign countries); four are in charge of economic affairs; five of social affairs; and three of foreign affairs, meaning domestic affairs of foreign countries.

Once topics are chosen, the assignment of writers follows more or less in accordance with the subject matter to be dealt with. The chief and deputy chief assign specific editorial writers to prepare editorials for the day.

The meeting leads to agreement on the direction and logic to be followed in preparing an editorial. The chosen writers then prepare the drafts by 3:00 or 3:30. The drafts are then reviewed by the chief and deputy chief, who make minimum modifications, such as smoothing out expressions. Very seldom is the substance touched. If the contents of a draft are at variance with the sense of the meeting, the writer would be asked to rewrite. The galleys are ready at 4:30 and again at 5:30, at which time minimum revisions may be permissible. Even at this time, attention is paid to the appropriateness of wording, nuances of meaning, and suitability of heads.

On the average an editorial writer prepares an editorial a week. When not on a writing assignment, he spends time reading in his field of specialization. As for contacts with government officials, he attends meetings sponsored by a group of editorial writers of different newspaper organizations. The meetings are held once a week or every other week and political leaders and bureau chiefs are invited. Meetings of this type frequently take place at a restaurant on the second floor of the Diet building with each company paying a fee of 5,000 yen. Sometimes a group invites the prime minister to talk before the Japan Reporters' Club at the Imperial Hotel. On the question of interaction with government officials, the *Yomiuri* interviewee said: "I have many friends in the government. I have known many of them from my days as a beat reporter. Besides, when you work as an editorial writer for ten years, you get to know a good many politicians and government bureaucrats. I can do news gathering by phone. I can call up ministers and bureau chiefs, even if I don't know them personally. They call me, too. I get phone calls from Prime Minister Miki occasionally. In the case of good personal friends, I can get a lot out of them, but in many cases the information obtained is not useful. When you know the real background of an event well, it is sometimes difficult to write an editorial."

He said that he personally received no complaints about the editorials; protests are lodged with the chief. His impression is that on foriegn policy matters, confident and powerful countries seldom protest. Weak countries tend to show greater sensitivities to editorials. This is true of the groups at home. He rejected outright a suggestion that the newspaper owners intervene occasionally in the substance of editorials. Rather, on major controversial issues, the chief consults with the president of the company. Editorials often run counter to the views that the labor unions exert undue influence on the contents of the editorials.

At the *Mainichi*, the editorial writers' meeting begins at 11:30 a.m. and lasts for about an hour. The criterion for selecting a topic is "the importance of the matter to the people." The chief editorial writer makes selections at the conclusion of the meeting. However, in actuality, with the clearance of the chief, the deputy chief has already discussed possible topics with individual writers. Each individual writer can be called upon to prepare a piece on short notice because of his specialization. When not assigned to an editorial, the writers continue their study in their respective fields and meet with news sources.

By 3:30 editorial writers submit the drafts to the chief and deputy chief. Nearly all of the editorials are printed in the original form as they are prepared, with minor retouching in expressions. At 4:00 the galley is available and is submitted to the Makeup Department. While an editorial is in galley form, the writer can add final touches. The writer and desk determine a head for the editorial.

A *Mainichi* editorial writer interviewed said that he meets with high-ranking officials of the government and politicians two or three times a week on the average. Sometimes he meets with them alone, sometimes in a group with editorial writers of other companies. There are three groups to which he belongs. In the case of two groups, a meeting takes place once or twice a month. The other group meets irregularly. Contacts take a few different forms, but in his case a meeting is most frequently arranged with individual politicians at the offices of the latter. The editorial writer of *Mainichi* said that editorials do not always correspond with the news stories as they should. Most pages reflect the strong views of ranking members of the Editorial Bureau. The views of the younger reporters are well reflected too. The editorial writers' office and the Editorial Bureau do not keep in as close touch with each other as they should. Once a week there is a coordinating meeting of the director and deputy director of the Editorial Bureau with the chief editorial writer chaired by an executive officer in charge of editorial matters.

As for relations with the owners, the respondent said that the chief editorial writer is a member of the Board of Directors and hence coordination is achieved. In actual practice, however, the editorial work is directed by the chief editorial writer. One major exception to this rule was a case of intercession by the board, when it agreed, at the request of the People's Republic of China, not to use the official title of the Republic of China when referring to Taiwan. The editorial writers' office was not fully consulted.

At the *Asahi*, a meeting of all twenty-four editorial writers is held around noon every day to discuss the topics for the day's editorials. An editorial writer said that, in principle, the selection of topics is made from the "hot and latest news." The topics usually come from the important items of the morning paper and the evening paper of the previous day. Chief and deputy chief editorial writers make selections and bring them up at the meeting. Discussions lead to a clarification of the nature of the issues and the development of the structure of logic to be employed in preparing an editorial. The view of a writer specializing in that particular area is given deference, but useful suggestions may be made by other writers. The meeting lasts about two hours, and an editorial writer then has about two and a half hours to prepare an editorial, since a draft must be ready by 4:30. The length of an average editorial is about four and a half manuscript pages, each containing 400 cells for Japanese letters.

When given a writing assignment, the editorial writer interviewed said that he would talk with the reporter who has been covering that particular topic and telephone his own sources in the government. Depending on the topic, the sources include the cabinet secretary, secretary to the prime minister, leaders of the political parties, and ranking officials of ministries. The chief editorial writer goes over a draft of an editorial, making revisions rarely, if ever.

The following is a portion of the diary of an *Asahi* editorial writer which he graciously reviewed for me. It indicates a schedule of appointments and activities he pursued for twelve days immediately preceding the date of the interview:

Sunday
   Speaker Nakamura's gaffe; talked to the Speaker on the phone; prepared an editorial on the subject.

Monday

Attended meeting on the small electoral district system.

Tuesday

Talked with secretary general of the Komei party at a tea-room of the Diet Building at the latter's request; talked about the case of Director Masuhara's remarks about the emperor; prepared an editorial on the case.

Wednesday

Attended a party given in celebration of a publication on international labor movement; talked with labor leaders.

Thursday

Attended luncheon given by the Study Group on International Politics and Economy to hear Soviet Ambassador Troyanovsky's speech; attended a function sponsored by the *Asahi* to hear a speech by Professor M on the United States and the Third World.

Friday

Drank *sake*.

Saturday

Attended a meeting on the problem of irrigation.

Sunday

Rest.

Monday

Heard Foreign Minister Ohira's briefing on current foreign policy issues at Kasumigaseki Building. The meeting was initiated by a group of editorial writers of several papers.

Talked with Korean ambassador at the "Korean night" sponsored by the Japan Reporters' Club.

Tuesday

Blank.

Wednesday

Requested a foreign ministry official to come to my office to brief me on Japan's foreign policy toward China.

Thursday

At my initiative I met and talked with Secretary General Yano of the Komei party about a wide variety of matters while enjoying Korean-style barbecued beef; wrote an editorial on emperor and politics.

Implications

Each of the major dailies under study is sensitive to the contents of other rival papers, kinds of items selected as news, and values assigned. In addition to the institutionalized practice of a formal review comparing the pages of the major papers, the rival papers as well as their own are carefully read by the newspapermen at various levels of the organizational hierarchy. The sensitivity to the pages of rival papers, sustained by intense competition for a larger share of readership, reinforces the desire to be the first with a news item and the tendency to resort to sensationalism. It also leads to mutual emulation. In a sense, these papers collectively direct national attention to the events they treat as being newsworthy and important. The function of these papers is then one of agenda setting and creation of reality by influencing the salience of issues and shaping the cognitive world of the readers.

Specialization in news sources and exclusive concern with them contribute to a rigidity in the organizational sphere of action. This is compounded by interdepartmental rivalries, sometimes resulting in a hiatus in news coverage.

An overview of the entire process involved in the preparation of a newspaper indicates the immense time pressure under which the newspapermen operate. The requirement of speed pervades the entire process of news gathering and processing, making adherence to the norm of accuracy and preparation of well-rounded or in-depth analysis of news items difficult. These major papers under study, it will be recalled, are called a "set paper," published both morning and evening papers, each with multiple editions. The pressure of time is conducive to the operation of the preconceptions and prejudices of individual newsmen throughout the entire process of gathering and editing news.

The system of reporters' clubs provides an effective and useful channel of news gathering, but it also imposes constraints on news gathering. Individual initiatives and activities outside the framework of the system tend to be neglected or discouraged. The virtual absence of by-line articles in Japanese newspapers contributes to diffusion of responsibility and stultification of individual initiative. An assignment of multiple reporters under the supervision of a captain fosters team play, necessary for effective news gathering, but at the same time it tends to diminish incentives for outstanding individual performance. In a sense, the club system serves as a common defense against maverick reporters who might otherwise exhibit individualized behavior. It also provides a justification for self-censorship by way of agreement among the members not to report certain news items. So long as the club system is the main channel of news gathering and the clubs are intimately related to government agencies, susceptibility to government manipulation is present. What is more, the club system predisposes the reporters to view and assess matters from the perspective of the agency to which they are assigned. The opportunity for specialization in news sources is made somewhat difficult due to the relatively short period of time a reporter is assigned to a government agency.

The practice of night attack in part attests to extraordinary zeal and dedication that Japanese reporters bring to their work. But at the same time it occasionally gives rise to "factional reporters" with all the attendant corrupt practices and to difficulty in a more rational use of manpower.

News gathering and processing are also affected by the distribution of power or responsibility within the newspaper organization and the relations among the beat reporters, desks, and higher officials of newspaper organizations. We have seen that the desks hold the most important responsibility for the composition of pages. The beat reporters may be said to be front-line gatekeepers for they are the first to screen the multitude of facts coming their way. The desks participate in this process of first-stage screening to the extent that the reporters are sensitive to the preferences of desks and to the extent that desks provide guidance and instructions to the beat reporters. Desks then add their value judgment on the stories provided by the beat reporters, thus constituting the second-stage gatekeepers. Inasmuch as the desks consult and are sensitive to the desires of superiors (department head, director, and deputy director of the Editorial Bureau), the latter are part of this second tier of gatekeepers. These high-ranking officials at the same time constitute the third line of gatekeepers, at least to the extent that they maintain their own contacts with news sources, make judgments on news values, and communicate their views to their subordinates. The question of the extent to which a consensus on role orientations exists among them will be explored in the following chapter.

On the whole, the desk of each substantive department is the linchpin of newspaper making, and on his shoulders rests the heaviest responsibility for page composition. The responsibility of makeup desks is equally heavy, given the impact of heads and subheads—which, in turn, reflect value judgments—on the reader. The desks of substantive and makeup departments serve as the bulwark of conscience and the ethos of the newspaper company. Their political orientations have profound influence on the newspaper pages. True, their views are influenced and can be contradicted by their superiors, but the process of news gathering and processing is such that their role is crucial. Moreover, to the extent that the desks' views coincide with those of the beat reporters and are supported by them, they exert tremendous and decisive impact on newspaper making.

CHAPTER V

The Reporter's
Orientations

What is the normative conception reporters themselves hold of their jobs? What orientations do they hold about the various aspects of their jobs? What orientations do they bring to bear upon interactions with government officials? These are some of the questions examined in this chapter. This chapter is intended primarily to delineate the reporter's orientations and, as data permit, to identify correlates of these orientations. The major assumption underlying this facet of my research is that the reporters' overt behavior is significantly shaped by their orientations. In the chapter to follow, the orientations held by govern-officials will be presented.

Three specific theoretical assumptions guided the construction of that portion of the interview schedule used to gather and analyze data for this chapter:

1. The nature of the work of a government agency is significantly related to variations in the reporter's orientations. Thus, orientations held by the reporters covering the Foreign Ministry (FM) will differ from those held by the reporters who cover the Ministry of International Trade and Industry (MITI).

2. The nature of the responsibility of an individual or a class of reporters is significantly related to orientations. Thus, orientations held by the beat reporters, assigned to a ministry, would differ from those held by "the managerial group" of reporters at home (desk, i.e., deputy head, head of the Department of Political Affairs, deputy director, and director of Editorial Bureau, and editorial writers).

3. The four newspapers studied differ in the set of orientations held by their respective reporters; i.e., reporters from the *Asahi* would subscribe to orientations different from those of the *Sankei*.

Data were analyzed in terms of these assumptions, and unless specifically noted, no additional patterns of response were observable.

Data used in this chapter come largely from interviews that were conducted with a sample of forty Japanese reporters. Ten reporters were selected from each of the four newspaper organizations (the *Asahi, Mainichi, Yomiuri,* and *Sankei*). The following categories of the respondents were interviewed:

Home Office Reporters
Editorial writer	4
Director or deputy director of Editorial Bureau	4
Department head	8
Deputy department head (desk)	8

Beat Reporters
Reporters assigned to FM and MITI	16
Total	40

The Japanese sample may be considered as stratified, albeit crude, and the subsample of beat reporters at each ministry was random. Interviews with personnel department heads centered on their work and did not cover the whole range of questions used in other interviews. Consequently, the size of N (the number of interviewees) used for most categories presented in this chapter is thirty-six. Interviews were conducted in Japanese and, in most cases, lasted from two to three hours.

In addition to the Japanese data, comparable data on American and German reporters will be introduced when pertinent. One source is William Chittick's data on a sample of forty American reporters covering the Department of State.[1] Another source is data collected by John Starrels in the summer of 1973 in West Germany specifically for this research. Ten interviews with German reporters were completed.[2] They cover the Ministries of External Affairs, Finance, and Economics. A third source is the data David Nickels gathered in 1972 from ten American correspondents covering the Department of State. In view of the small size of samples involved, the data presented

1. Unless otherwise noted, the American data presented in chapters 5 and 6 are from William Chittick, *State Department, Press, and Pressure Groups* (New York: Wiley-Interscience, 1970).

2. They represent the following three newspapers: *Suddeutsche Zeitung, Die Welt,* and *Frankfurter Allgemeine.*

here must be interpreted with caution. The data collected by Starrels and Nickels will be used only for making a crude comparison. Their data will be cited when a predominant pattern emerges, especially in a direction opposite to that found in Japan. The analysis of Japanese data offered here should also be regarded as only suggestive.

Two questions were used to identify the reporters' normative conceptions about their job.[3] Responses varied, but the single modal response, constituting about a half of the sample, concerned the way a reporter should transmit information: "accurately," "fairly," "impartially," or "objectively." The remainder focused on the goal of a reporter's activity; about 15 percent mentioned "search for truth"; about 10 percent named "pursuit of social justice." The following categories for goals shared more or less equally the remainder: the enlightenment of the public, guidance of the public, reflection of public opinion in government policy, service as a "pipeline" or conduit between the government and the public, and service as an opinion leader.

All German reporters interviewed answered in unison, "to make reportage and to provide commentaries." One reporter used the adjective "informed," another "clear," during their responses. Otherwise, the absence of modifying words such as "accurate," "fair," or "objective" is striking. This may be indicative of the degree of internalization (and of acceptance by interaction partners) of the value of accurate and objective reporting in Germany. In any event, the German respondents did not appear to be acutely conscious of the problem and did not verbalize the kind of sensitivity their Japanese counterparts portrayed.

Ignoring, for the moment, the kinds and amount of news released by government agencies, the decision to write a given story lies largely with individual reporters assigned to the ministries. When questioned about "who determines what stories to write," most reporters interviewed declared instantly, "myself—sometimes in consultation with the captain and/or the desk." Generally speaking, the degree of autonomy of reporters increases with experience but inversely with the im-

3. "How would you describe the job of being a reporter? What are the most important things you should do?"

portance of issues. A captain, who heads the group of reporters from the same newspaper at a ministry, is consulted by his junior colleagues, and in turn, he consults, or is in touch, with the desk. On important matters, the head of the Political Affairs Department and, in some cases, the deputy director or even the director of the Editorial Bureau are consulted. A captain said: "Routine matters are taken care of by the reporters themselves. About 80 percent of the work is handled by us. On important matters we consult the desk." Another reporter stated that he alone decides on the overwhelming majority of cases. Sometimes, he added, he gets advice regarding angles from the desk. "Seventy percent of the work is by myself and the rest in consultation with the desk," was another response. Another said, "We decide through discussion among our reporters at the ministry."

In some cases, the instructions to prepare a given story originate from the Editorial Office, especially in connection with special feature stories that are planned for future use. It should be remembered that the reporters who cover the ministires usually return to their home office in the evening and have an opportunity to discuss ideas informally with the desk and department head.

The respondents were asked to identify the criteria they use in determining or selecting stories to write and publish on a certain day.[4] I was impressed with the general difficulty, or inability, of the Japanese respondents to articulate these criteria. A long pause preceded most of the responses, and the question elicited a wide variety of responses. For some respondents the importance of a particular piece of information is easily determined by their training and experience. A few swiftly identified as criteria those items of information judged to have major impact on politics or upon the life of the people. A few mentioned topicality as a consideration in major issues, and this is determined by the trends of the time. A few mentioned the prominence of news sources; i.e., other things being equal, preference would be given to more prominent personalities as newsmakers. Some mentioned newness, novelty, or unexpectedness of news items as of primary importance and, second,

4. "How do you determine what stories to write and print? What criteria are used?"

"follow up items," to maintain continuity in the news. A similar thought was conveyed when one respondent said "turning point in the development of an issue."

The decision to print is further influenced by practical considerations. The amount of available space is a determinant. Therefore, a news item may be buried if more newsworthy developments occur on the same day. For example, the news of President Nixon's proposed trip to China outweighed less important news items of the day. Another factor is the desire to provide more accurate information by delaying a day. This competes with the desire to achieve a scoop at the risk of some inaccuracy of details. Another factor may be a serious question about "angle" or the contents of a story, especially on a matter of acute political sensitivity. For example, a reporter pointed out editorial decisions not to "play up" certain news issues or their aspects, i.e., a decision not to give extensive coverage to pro-Taiwan activities.

Our respondents were asked if a majority of the news items they write are printed. The responses were an emphatic "yes," and their estimates of the proportion printed ranged from "80 percent," "90 percent," to "all items." No respondent was able to specify any particular kinds of stories that are difficult to get printed. Reasons generally cited for a story's not being printed were space limitations, poor writing, poor timing, and incomplete contents.

With a single exception, all respondents conceded that at times their stories are revised at the editorial office. Most respondents denied, however, that content is altered. A few conceded that sometimes rewriting is necessary on a topic of great importance. For example, a reporter's original assessment of the prospect of yen revaluation was revised in consultation with the editor's office (including the director). Another respondent recalled a case of an unbalanced article and the use of the improper angle which resulted in revision. Before revision, the writers are consulted. Every respondent insisted, however, that wording, expression, punctuation, or style occasion revision in most cases.

On what sources of information do they rely most heavily for their news stories? Choices given to our respondents were: press conference, background conference, news release, interviews with line officials, interviews with information officials, and talk with fellow newsmen. Every reporter singled out interviews with policy officials and politicians as being the most important source. In a typical account, background briefings given by the minister or vice-minister provide the reporter wth some hints, and he then tires to develop a story by interviewing policy officials (chiefs of bureaus and/or sections). The reporters preferred private interviews, and in this connection, they occasionally practice "morning run and night attack," whereby the individual reporter tries to conduct interviews with officials early in the morning at the official's home or en route to his office and late at night at the official's house. News releases and press conferences outweigh other sources for the reporters, but for the development of their own stories they rely most heavily on private conversations with policy officials.

In response to the question as to what they consider to be the characteristics of a good news story, the single, most frequently mentioned feature was "accuracy." A reporter said a good story is one in which the news source can be clearly identified. Other characteristics mentioned were "objectivity," "comprehensiveness of treatment," "the use of proper angle," and "the degree of usefulness to the reader." Several reporters referred to content, saying that the content must be "rich," "interesting," "unambiguous," "easy to understand," and "deep in background analysis."

There is no perceived difference between what the reporters like and what they think the desk prefers.[5] The reporters generally conceded difficulty in ascertaining what the public desires to read, pointing to the broad range of their readers.[6] A few commented that pages devoted to social affairs, shocking news, or human interest stories appeal most to the reader. Most news stories written by respondents are considered hard reading material, and they strive to make this material easier to comprehend. Other than this general concern, the public or readership does not appear to loom large in the minds of reporters.

It is significant that with a single exception, every respondent said that he sees his role as expressing and shaping public opin-

5. The question was: "What do the editors and ranking members of your department consider a good news story?"

6. The question was: "What kind of stories do you think your readers like to read about most?"

ion in addition to informing the public.[7] There was also near unanimity among the respondents that they do not see their roles as participants in government policy making.[8] Even the several reporters who responded affirmatively spoke in terms of the indirect effect that they believe their activities have on government policy making.

German respondents showed an opposite pattern to that of Japan. With the exception of two reporters, both from *Suddeutsche Zeitung*, the remaining eight reporters responded affirmatively; i.e., they see their role as participant. A reporter from *Frankfurter Allgemeine Zeitung* qualified his affirmative answer by saying: "This is not the most important role of a journalist. My first goal is to instruct the readers about an event. I do not pose as their guardian."

How do the Japanese reporters perceive the press-government relations? A remarkably skewed answer was obtained to the following question: "Do you feel the government press relations are basically conflicting or basically harmonious? How would you describe this relationship?"

Over 90 percent of Japanese respondents (thirty-four out of thirty-six) characterized government-press relations as basically conflicting. The remaining two saw them as basically harmonious. Two of the first group preferred the expression "tense relationship" to "conflicting relationship," and five qualified their responses variously by saying their posture should really be one of watchdog, offering constructive criticisms, or that it need not be conflicting. For most respondents the question brought a swift response: "conflicting; so it should be, and so it is." The employees of the *Sankei*, not the *Asahi*, showed a greater tendency toward a "conflicting" posture. Contrary to my initial expectation, not all economic affairs reporters assigned to MITI showed a moderate posture toward MITI officials; only one out of four did. No association exists between the perceived nature of relationship and individual characteristics of reporters such as age and amount of professional experience.

The pattern of response showed by the German reporters is

7. The question was: "Do you see a role for yourself in expressing and shaping public opinion as well as informing the public?"

8. The question was: "Do you see a role for yourself as a participant in government policy making?"

similar. Virtually every respondent described government-press relationships as "tension-filled" and "not harmonious." The American pattern is striking in its contrast. Of the forty American reporters, about 38 percent described their relations with department policy officers as either "usually cooperative" or "more cooperative"; 35 percent perceived the relations to be either "usually antagonistic" or "more antagonistic." Approximately 23 percent of the sample characterized relations as "both cooperative and antagonistic."

I attempted to get at the reporters' perceptions of the way and to what extent the press influences government policy.[9] The elicited responses varied considerably, but they can be grouped into three categories. The first category of response emphasizes government use of the press. One response was that the government uses the press for "trial balloon" purposes to gauge public reactions; another was that the government needs the support of the press to implement policies. In the second category, the press was said to change the direction or modify the content of government policy or to promote the adoption of a particular policy. The press was also said to politicize an issue which otherwise might not become political. As one reporter put it, the press keeps a "watchful eye" on the activities of the government. First and second categories of responses are similar in one fundamental aspect; that is, the influence of the press is presumed to operate through the press's capacity to shape "public opinion." The third category of the responses concerned the press as a source of information for government bureaucrats. For example, MITI officials often learn about the views of the Foreign Ministry through the press. The press also provides information through the reporters' participation in numerous government commissions.

Every reporter interviewed characterized the degree of press influence on government policy making as "considerable" or "very much." The responses revealed no meaningful variations among reporters except that the first group of responses came from the reporters assigned to the MITI. This is indicative of relatively closer relations between the reporters and economy-

9. The question was: "In what ways do you think the press shapes or influences government policy? And to what extent? Could you give some examples?"

related government agencies. Several respondents qualified their assessment by saying that the influence of the press is indirect, not direct. The press campaign for government legislation on campaign financing was cited as ineffective.

Chittick provides no comparable data, but the American correspondents interviewed by Nickels ascribed "medium" to "slightly high" influence to the press. The German reporters indicated a low rating. One person replied "a lot," but six reporters said variously, "measurably small," "in small degree," "strictly limited," "not very much," "very conditional," or "hardly any at all" (two did not answer). The German reporters perceived the path of influence as primarily indirect. Press generates publicity which, in turn, influences the government either to modify policy or to take into account their views.

The perceived high degree of press influence on government policy is related to the perception of the degree to which officials care about what reporters write and the officials' opinion of reporters. The reporters' unanimous view was that government officials care a great deal about reporting. The reporters were convinced that officials fear reporters and regard them as a nuisance. One reporter covering the Foreign Ministry put it, "Those fellows at the Foreign Ministry operate as though they are under the injunction *kisha o mitara dorobō to omoe*," literally translated as "When you see a reporter, regard him as a thief." Some respondents, however, added that the degree of personal friendship between a reporter and an official makes some difference. The perceived sense of distrust and "conflicting" relations was more intense and pervasive among reporters who covered the Foreign Ministry than their colleagues at the MITI.

Several questions were designed to elicit the reporters' views concerning the role of public opinion as a criterion for information transmission. The respondents were unanimous in accepting the view that public opinion should influence government policy. At the same time, there was near unanimity in rejecting a notion that government officials do in fact base their decisions on public opinion. All respondents shared the belief that government officials are obligated to inform the public of their activities to the maximum extent possible. The expressions used by the respondents included "everything," "to the greatest extent possible," "as much as possible," or "in principle, everything." About a third of the respondents qualified their remarks by adding, "with some exceptions in the area of foreign policy." Two gave an unqualified affirmative response, saying the public needs to be informed of "the whole thing." Nearly all the respondents were convinced that officials do not share this belief.

The reporters were asked to establish general criteria for releasing or withholding information: "To what extent do you feel that government officals should or should not do the following?"

1. Release information selectively because it may strengthen the government negotiating position.

2. Release information because it may promote domestic political support for official policies.

3. Release information because the public has a right to know.

4. Withhold information because it may endanger national security.

With regard to item 1, about one-third of the respondents said that the government should not; 20 percent thought the government should; and the remainder gave qualified approval by saying either, "it can't be helped," or "it is permissible." A greater proportion of American reporters approved such a practice. Three-fourths of the Chittick sample of forty thought the State Department officers should (1=may or may not; 2=should not; 2=may not). The German reporters' responses were similar to the Americans, with six responses affirmative, two negative (2=NA).

Concerning item 2, about half of the Japanese respondents thought this should not be done, whereas 15 percent thought the government should do so. About one-third of the sample thought it cannot be helped or is permissible. Almost three-fourths of the American sample approved the practice and one-third opposed it. The German responses were closer to those of the United States. Six gave affirmative answers while two were negative (2=NA). Again, a greater proportion of the Japanese reporters were opposed to the practice.

Item 3 brought a resounding "of course" or "definitely yes" from every Japanese reporter. This criterion found enthusiastic support both in the United States and Germany. Virtually every

American reporter accepted the proposition that the Department of State should release information because the public has a right to know: sixteen said absolutely must; nine said preferably should; thirteen said should unless the situation precludes it; one said may or may not; one gave no answer. All the German reporters (eight) who responded gave affirmative replies. Regarding item 4, about three-fourths of the Japanese sample accepted the proposition with varying degrees of reluctance. About the same proportion of American reporters agreed with the statement but with greater willingness. Of the eight German respondents, seven were affirmative, and one said that the practice is admissible. In comparison with both German and American counterparts, the Japanese reporters appeared least willing to approve this criterion as justifiable for withholding information. It should be kept in mind that the American data were collected before the recent controversy over the Pentagon Papers and the Watergate affair. American attitudes may have moved closer to the Japanese pattern in recent years.[10]

Returning to the Japanese reporters, the distribution of answers for items 1, 2, and 4 reveals no meaningful patterns. On item 2, however, nearly all *Asahi* reporters responded negatively, while a much smaller proportion of reporters of other newspapers expressed a negative attitude. This may be indicative of a relatively more critical attitude on the part of the *Asahi* toward the government.

The respondents were also asked, "To what extent should reporters do or not do the following?"

1. Report the facts without any interpretation.

2. Write without regard for the editorial guidelines of their news organization.

3. Attempt to influence government policies.

4. Act in the role of opposition or watchdog.

With regard to item 1, about three-fourths of the Japanese reporters said there was no question that an interpretation or a commentary should accompany news reports. The remainder said that there were some cases where an interpretation might

10. It is interesting to note that Nickel's data collected in the spring of 1972 show that four out of nine correspondents thought the officials should not, with the remainder indicating mild approval, saying either "preferably should" or "may do so."

not be necessary, but they too felt that news reports should be accompanied by an interpretation.[11] The German pattern is conspicuous, diverging from the Japanese response pattern. Of the nine German reporters who responded, eight said that the reporters absolutely must do so, i.e., reporters should report the facts without any interpretation, and one person said the reporter may not.

On item 2, practically every Japanese reporter thought that he should try to stay within the editorial policy guidelines of his news organization. However, several reporters added that they are not always conscious of the guidelines.

In probing their responses, it became clear that policy guidelines were perceived to be too broad to impose restrictions. When a supplementary question concerning editorials was asked, the responses varied somewhat. Several reporters, all of the *Mainichi*, felt that they should write without regard for the editorial views of thier papers, but they added that it would be desirable that their writings be consistent with those editorial views. The rest said that there should be compatibility between editorial views and their own articles. The *Asahi* reporters were more sensitive to and felt more obligated to follow editorial views than did the reporters of other papers. The *Mainichi* reporters, for instance, proudly recalled several incidents when such incompatibility occurred.

American responses offer a sharp contrast. Virtually every American reporter of the Chittick sample thought the reporter should write "without regard for the editorial views of their news organizations." The German data are closer to the American with five accepting and two rejecting the proposition (3=NA).

Item 3 revealed a near unanimity of the view among the Japanese reporters that the reporter should attempt to influence government policy. Of those who agreed with the proposition (thirty-three out of thirty-six), about 50 percent gave unequalified approval, with the remainder qualifying their approval by adding that it is permissible to do so "to certain extent," "sometimes," or "depending on circum-

11. Of the nine American reporters interviewed by Nickel, five disagreed with the statement. Three thought that the reporters might or might not do so, and one agreed with the statement.

stances." Only two respondents disagreed with the statement (1=no response). This response is interesting in view of their earlier statement that they do not see a role for themselves as participants in government policy making. Evidently, to the Japanese, an attempt to influence government policy does not constitute participation in policy making.

The overwhelming majority of the American reporters interviewed by Chittick (thirty out of forty) thought the reporters should not "attempt to influence policy officers," (6=should; 1=may or may not; 9=NA). In the case of the Japanese data, the wording was "to attempt to influence government policy." However, the Nickels data are based on the identical phrase as the Japanese version. Eight out of nine of these American reporters stated emphatically that the reporter should not. In the United States, the conscious desire to influence government policy does not appear to be pervasive. In this regard, the German data are closer to Japanese. Eight of ten reporters responded affirmatively (2=absolutely must; 1=should; 5=may do so).

With regard to item 4, nearly every Japanese reporter felt that he should act as an opposition element or watchdog vis-à-vis the government. Two thought they should not. Of the thirty-four reporters who gave affirmative replies, everyone gave a swift and unqualified response with the exception of two who said "only to a certain extent or depending on circumstances." As for the German sample, six reporters thought the reporter absolutely must do so, with another respondent saying the reporter may do so (3=NA). The Nickels study of American reporters indicates a tendency opposite to that in Japan and Germany. Six American reporters gave negative answers (1=absolutely must not; 1=preferably should not; 4=may not), whereas three were affirmative (1=absolutely must; 2=may).

To reject the proposition that the reporter should act in the opposition role is not to deny the presence of the norm of a critical attitude on the part of American reporters. Marvin Kalb has characterized the reporter's job as "to undress the administration" because the officials attempt to protect the administration. He speaks of the desirability of State Department correspondents developing a distant, detached, and

critical faculty by spending a few years in Moscow as a correspondent. I .F. Stone's injunction is unequivocal: "All governments are run by a liar. . . . This is a prima facie assumption."
No systematic data are available to substantiate the degree of
internalization this orientation has achieved among American
reporters, but the injunction may strike a responsive chord
among many reporters. However that may be, as compared with
their American counterparts, the Japanese reporters are more
likely to feel that they ought to influence government policy
and to act in the role of opposition or watchdog. Again, the
Pentagon Papers and the Watergate affair may have brought
about a change in this orientation.

Each respondent was asked whether he is satisfied with the
work of others with whom he interacts within his organization. Most reporters who cover the ministries in fact grouped
the desk and other superiors at the bureau as one group. Home
Office personnel, too, make such a distinction. Most of the
respondents at the Home Office (desks, department heads, etc.)
said they were satisfied with the way the reporters are doing
their work. On the other hand, most beat reporters (fourteen
out of sixteen) indicated their dissatisfaction with the way
editorial personnel at home offices are carrying out their
work. The source of dissatisfaction on the part of beat reporters
is that editorial personnel are preoccupied with administrative
work, devoting little time to the proper work of newspaper
making. These reporters-turned-bureaucrats are thought to be
deficient in news sense and out of touch with reality. They are
perceived as lacking the capacity to provide leadership in mold-
ing the opinion within the newspaper organization. This line of
criticism is directed primarily toward those who are above the
desk. The respondents were asked whether there is disagree-
ment or conflict between the desk and reporters regarding the
gathering and processing of news. About two-thirds of the
respondents said such conflict occurs occasionally, while the
rest denied it.

As a possible correlate of orientations, the party identification of the reporters was examined. The respondents were
asked which political party was near to their own thinking on
political matters. They were not asked to reveal party affilia-

tions but rather to identify a party whose policies generally came close to their political views. About 20 percent declared that there was no such party since it would depend on the nature of issues. The rest gave responses ranging from the Liberal Democratic party to the socialist party.

Most *Asahi* reporters characterized their political views as being close to the Socialist party. On the other hand, all of the *Sankei* reporters were located somewhere among the Liberal Democratic party and the Democratic Socialist Party. The *Mainichi* reporters ranged from the Liberal Democratic Party to the Socialist Party. The remarkable point is that this self-characterization by the reporters about their poltical views is identical to the popular and stereotyped images of the political stance ascribed to these newspapers.[12]

An attempt was made to identify the perceived social status of reporters relative to other occupations, especially government bureaucrats.[13] All respondents thought the social standing of the reporter has risen considerably since the prewar period. All of them ranked the professions of medical doctor and lawyer higher than their own. Relative to government bureaucrats (*seifu kanryo*), the ranking of the reporter was not unanimous. For about one-half of the respondents the reporter ranks lower than government bureaucrats. The remainder was divided: several gave the reporter a higher ranking, with the rest placing both professions on equal footing. On the whole, I was impressed with the degree of pride the respondents displayed in their profession. Those who saw the reporters' status to be higher than that of government bureaucrats held high-ranking positions within news organizations. The rest who spoke unequivocally of equal status tended to be younger members. An impression lingers that the younger the reporter the greater the pride and the stronger the belief that both professions are equal in status.

About 20 percent of the respondents said that they would not pursue that same career again, while another 20 percent were unsure but leaned toward "no." Of the rest, 40 percent

12. Corresponding data on *Yomiuri* reporters are unavailable.
13. The question was: "In terms of social prestige, where are the journalists placed in your country?"

declared unequivocally that they would choose the same profession willingly, whereas 20 percent would join the profession with some reservation or reluctance.[14]

All reporters were unanimous in identifying the long, irregular hours they must keep as a major complaint. The demand for physical endurance is enormous and a normal family life difficult to maintain. Yet many are still attracted to the profession because, as they said, the job is "interesting" or "it is suited to my personality." They apparently derive much satisfaction from the opportunities accorded them by being in the forefront of important events and mingling with prominent and influential persons. Their single greatest source of satisfaction is the sense of triumph when achieving a "scoop."

14. The question was: "If you were ever to begin again, would you choose the same career?"

CHAPTER VI

The Official's
Orientations

The present chapter approaches press-government interactions primarily from the perspective of the officials. What are the normative conceptions that the officials hold regarding the role of the reporter? Do they perceive any advantages in their interactions with the reporter? What orientations do they hold concerning various aspects of these interactions? These are some of the questions explored in this chapter. The underlying assumption here is that the activities of the officials, especially their news-transmitting activities vis-à-vis the reporter, are conditioned by these orientations. From the perspective of the reporter, the officials—with such orientations as they hold—constitute a target area or an environment in which he must operate. The reporter must cope with the officials' orientations, and his activity (including the nature, pattern, and degree of his access to the officials) is affected by them.

Data used here come primarily from interviews I conducted with a sample of twenty-six officials from the Foreign Ministry (FM), the Ministry of International Trade and Industry (MITI), and the members of the Diet. Nine officials, who held the rank of section chief and above, were selected from among the FM officials. They represented two geographic bureaus and a functional one (Bureau of Information and Cultural Affairs). Also interviewed were eight officials of the MITI, of comparable rank to the FM sample and representing two policy bureaus and the Information Section of the Minister's Secretariat.

Nine members of the Diet were chosen; two each from the Liberal Democratic party, the Komei party, the Japan Socialist party, and one each from the Japan Communist party and the Democratic Socialist party. In case of the first three parties, one member was from the House of Representatives, the other from the House of Councillors. One was a member of the Foreign

Affairs Committee; the other was of the Committee on Commerce and Industry. In the case of the remaining two parties, the members interviewed were in the Foreign Affairs Committee in the House of Representatives. Interviews, conducted in Japanese, lasted from one to two hours in most cases.

Several assumptions guided the structure of the questions and the analysis of the data. It was assumed that the orientations which the officials held:

1. Differ from those of the reporters.

2. Vary with the nature of the work of the ministry. Thus, the orientations held by the Foreign Ministry officials differ from those of MITI officials, and the orientations held by the legislators differ from the administrative officials.

3. Are influenced by the nature of the work of individual officials, i.e., the orientations of policy officials differ from those of information officials.

4. Vary with the ranks of officials, i.e., the higher the rank of the official, the more sensitive he is and the more favorably disposed toward the press and more likely to ascribe influence to it.

5. Vary with the perceived prestige of the newspapers that reporters represent. Officials have a more favorable attitude toward, show greater sensitivity to, and ascribe greater influence to prestigious newspapers.

A summary of interview data is presented here. The data obtained were examined from the perspectives underlying the above assumptions. Assumptions that appear to have received some support from the data are noted as such following a brief note on the distribution of responses for each category of orientations.

The normative conception the officials held of the role of reporters will be considered first. The question employed was "How would you describe the job of being a reporter? In other words, what do you think are the most important things a reporter should do?" The responses came swiftly and were unanimous: "reporting of facts," though a few respondents added phrases such as "to provide material for judgment," "to identify problems," and "to provide responsible commentaries." About half of the interviewees proceeded to specify what may be proper reporting by adding such adjectives as "accurate," "faithful," "fair," and "objective." It should be noted that this conception is quite congruent with the normative conception the reporter himself holds in respect to his job. Some excerpts from the officials' responses follow.

> The most important thing is to report facts accurately. If the reporters want to evaluate policies, they should give fair assessment. They should try to contribute to the shaping of public opinion from a fair standpoint. [MITI]

> The role of newspapers should be constructive. The reporters should view a problem from various angles and should realize that the responsibility of MITI includes more than just due sensitivity to consumer interests. The press tends to be sensational. It should try to help the public to make correct judgment on issues. [MITI]

> The most important thing is to write stories from a just and fair standpoint. The press voices opposition to various aspects of MITI administration, and it is good so far as it goes. I hope that the press gives an adequate evaluation of the policies in question instead of voicing only opposition. I wish they would write some nice things about us if they do so find. I wish they would reflect public opinion, not always manipulating it. [MITI]

> The most important thing is to report truth. It is necessary for the press to play the role of fair critic, but it should not oppose things just for opposition's sake. [MITI]

> The most important thing is to provide the public with accurate information so as to serve as a basis for judgment. The press is now involved too much in shaping public opinion. [MITI]

> The most important thing is the quest for and reporting of truth. I would say I am 50 percent satisfied and 50 percent dissatisifed. I think the press is too subservient to the taste of the masses. [MITI]

> My dissatisfaction is with speculative articles I find in the papers. Economic articles are generally free from ideological distortions, and the reporters are fairly neutral politically. [FM]

> Accurate reporting. At the same time, there should be more background information. Everything has a reason. No amount of hysteric writing about the rising prices would stop them. What is often lacking is a commentary explaining whys of rising prices. My dissatisfaction is that even if we explain the government's

positions on the matter written about in the paper, our explanation does not get printed. [FM]

Needless to say, accurate reporting of acts is most important. Commentaries could vary with the newspapers, but there should be a consistency in the position taken by a paper. Besides, often it is hard to tell facts from comments. My only wish is that the reporters should operate with a firm understanding of our national interests. [FM]

There is clearly anti-American bias on the part of most Japanese major papers. They seem particularly interested in printing stories which would embarrass the government. [FM]

The newspapers are not fair. Another complaint I have is that the reporters just walk into my office just about any time. I often find them standing right in front of me without warning. [FM]

The role of the press is to inform the public of the truth about politics. We are struggling within the framework of the parliamentary system to establish the parliamentarianism of the people. I am dissatisfied. The press places primary emphasis on the activities of the government, though I realize the editors must be concerned with business aspects of the newspaper organization. As for the press attitude toward the dissolution of the United States-Japan security treaty and neutrality question, the press lacks vigor. [Communist dietman]

The most important thing is to write fair articles. One's beliefs and values necessarily enter into a story, but a story should show high objectivity. [Komeito dietman]

To provide reportage with objective and accurate judgments. Generally speaking, I consider the editorials of major dailies to be valid. I do not find anything particularly contradictory to my position. They are close to my views. The editorials of *Sankei* are different. I think the editorials of *Asahi*, *Mainichi*, and *Yomiuri* are generally valid. The problem of the press is that it tends to emphasize current, immediate problems, particularly those of human interest, rather than dealing with long-range problems. [Socialist dietman]

I hope the newspapers report the truth. The papers are edited erroneously and with subjectivity. I am very much dissatisfied. There is too much subjectivity in reporting. The press suffers from commercialism. The reporters write stories that would sell. Often the stories reflect ideological tendencies. [Liberal Democratic dietman]

The primary responsibility of the press is to inform the public of the facts. It is all right for various interpretations and commentaries to appear, as long as the position of the writers is clarified. In Japanese papers you will find the authors of many articles remaining anonymous. [Socialist dietman]

The most important job for a reporter is to inform the public of the facts about everything accurately. I think the reporters are too much concerned with a big play their stories would get in the paper. [Democratic Socialist dietman]

I am not particularly dissatisfied. Although it depends on which paper you are talking about. Occasionally I feel articles have been written with much subjectivity. Regarding the press criticism of our party, Komeito, naturally these would not have been a problem if only press articles are based on the correct assessment of the party line and achievements of our party. [Komeito dietman]

What role do I expect of the press? The press should provide facts accurately and rapidly. The most important thing should be to speedily provide proper information—I mean free from ideological judgment. Press should be fair and be on the side of the weak. [Democratic Socialist dietman]

The most important thing is to report truth. The state of public opinion is reported erroneously. The reporters are too sensitive to the left-wing opinion and are sympathetic to the latter's views. The most conspicuous example is their belief in Marxism and Leninist theory. To them socialism equals peace and capitalism war. Japanese reports about China are often inaccurate. The Japanese reporters don't have moral courage to criticize China. They were responsible for the major disturbance over the Security Treaty. [Liberal Democratic dietman]

All the interviewees expressed some degree of dissatisfaction with the activities of the reporters. The sources of such dissatisfaction varied, although the following received frequent mention: (1) lack of objectivity, (2) dearth of factual reporting, (3) partial and unfair reporting, (4) tendency to concentrate on stories that embarrass the government, (5) abundance of speculative and inaccurate reporting, and (6) anti-American bias. The sense of dissatisfaction was especially strong among the FM officials. MITI interviewees generally articulated similar dissatisfaction, but with less intensity, and their dissatisfaction was directed largely toward reporters from the Social Affairs Department of newspapers, as distinct from those from the Economic Affairs Department. It will be recalled that economic affairs reporters on their part characterized their relationship with the officials in more satisfactory terms than do their colleagues from the Social Affairs Department.

The dissatisfaction felt by the officials toward the reportage is related to their perception of the criteria that the reporter applies in news selection. They were sharply critical of what they perceived to be dominant criteria. A question designed to identify these criteria yielded several responses. For some officials, "antigovernment stance" (usually combined with anti-Americanism) constitutes the major criterion. Some others mentioned "appeal to the mass public or human interest." Several pointed to the reporter's perception of a story likely to be accepted by the desk and, when pressed, named antigovernment posture to be the criterion. A few mentioned novelty of news and a major change in hitherto pursued policy. Still others thought the sensational character of a news item is a determinant. On the whole, the perceived criterion of antigovernment stance loomed large in the minds of the officials. It is noteworthy that only a few officials mentioned other criteria, such as novelty and major policy change, which the reporters themselves identified as being their criteria for news selection. There is then much dissatisfaction and resentment on the part of the executive officials and members of the ruling party towards the reporters.

Distrust toward the press is revealed in the response to what role the officials expect the press to play. About one-third of the respondents called on the press to eliminate antigovernment bias and to refrain from the "act of opposition for opposition's sake." About one-fifth repeated their call for accurate and/or fair reporting of facts. These two categories constituted about half of the respondents. Another third of the sample expressed a desire that the press more adequately reflect, rather than manufacture, public opinion. The remainder expressed a hope that newspapers would provide material reflecting diverse viewpoints so as to facilitate the reader's judgment. A few respondents deplored what was thought to be the practically identical manner in which the issues are treated in various major dailies.

Nearly every official stated that the views of the press are not equivalent to, nor do they constitute, the whole of public opinion. As one official put it, "the press certainly does not represent the view of the silent majority." Most respondents, however, conceded the difficulty of gauging "true public opinion."

In spite of the sense of distrust toward the press, the officials were not wholly negative toward interactions with the reporters. Not only were they resigned to the need for dealing with the reporter in a democratic polity, but they were also conscious of resulting advantages. Only one official declared flatly that he derives no advantage whatsoever. About half of the executive officials saw that the principal advantage lies in being able to gauge the mood of the public. While some of them appeared to be interested in public moods primarily from a manipulative standpoint, the remainder stated that such information is occasionally "instructive as it represents the viewpoint of the ruled." Other officials saw the chief utility as being able to learn of the attitudes and evolving policies of rival ministries on given issues. Others saw the press as a useful instrument in "educating and sensitizing the public" on a particular issue along the line their ministry is advocating. Several interviewees mentioned a "trial balloon" function. When asked specifically about this function, most of the respondents stated that a manipulation of the press for such purposes is difficult to manage.

During probes, officials said that they find it useful when they obtain through the press information on an overseas development before an official cable reaches them. When asked if they thought news commentaries are ever useful or enlightening, the response was generally negative. As most officials saw it, reportage or commentary is superficial, rarely going beyond a commonsense treatment. This assessment is related to the officials' evaluation of the attributes of the reporters. Except for a few reporters, both in the FM and MITI, thought to have a good command of the subject matter they are covering, most reporters are regarded by the officials as suffering from a deficiency in technical knowledge. We shall later return to the question of the officials' evaluation of the reporters with regard to other attributes. In general, the legislators had more positive attitudes than administrative officials toward contact with reporters. All the legislators stated that interactions with reporters provide them with valuable information on the activities of other parties, the government, factional politics, and the Diet. One legislator added that sometimes he obtains hints from reading newspapers about questions to be used at committee meetings.

The officials betray a high degree of sensitivity to press reportage. Most officials interviewed say they are sensitive to material written about their agency or themselves, while only a handful of officials professed to care little about it. This is consistent with the reporters' perception in this regard. About half of those officials who conceded their sensitivity recalled that they have communicated their reactions to reporters and/or editors. Occasions for such action arise under two circumstances—in the case of inaccurate information and the reporting of security leaks. Protest or complaint is generally communicated to the reporters assigned to the ministry, but in serious cases the department head and even the chief of the Editorial Bureau may be contacted. Matters involving interpretation are usually ignored as they presumably represent differences of judgment and protesting them would prove futile.

From the standpoint of government officials, the methods of communication most useful are press conferences and informal contacts with reporters. These two means are considered superior to other means such as press releases and formal briefings. It will be recalled that the reporters said they rely most heavily on interviews with policy officials. The same set of questions were used to elicit the officials' attitude about the transmission of information. Nearly every executive official interviewed agreed with a statement that information may be selectively released in order to strengthen the government's negotiation position vis-à-vis foreign countries. About half of those were unqualified responses, whereas the remainder added such qualifiers as "to a certain extent," "should be done cautiously," "not toward an ally such as the United States," or "only in relation to the Soviet Union." Of seven dietmen who responded, three were negative. Of the affirmative responses, one was unqualified while the rest were qualified. It will be recalled that about one-third of the reporters thought the government should not manipulate information in such a way. Of those officials who gave an affirmative response, a handful indicated that the government is involved in such a practice to a certain extent, and the rest declared that the government seldom practices it. A few respondents added that such a practice is usually ineffective. As for the American sample Chittick interviewed, nearly every official thought the Department of State should release information if it is thought to serve to strengthen the government's negotiation position.

Again with a few exceptions, all the administration interviewees agreed with the statement that the government official may release information so as to promote domestic political support for official policies. Four out of seven dietmen gave negative responses, with the remainder giving a qualified yes. Most of those administration officials who said that the government is actually doing so, with a few demurring that this occurrence is not frequent. It should be recalled that about half of the Japanese reporters thought this should not be done. Almost three-fourths of the American policy officers accepted the proposition that the State Department should release information because it might promote domestic political support for department policies.

It is noteworthy that most Japanese officials do not feel that they "ought to release information because the public has a right to know." Only one official replied affirmatively without qualification. A few agreed with the statement, with the provision that diplomatic secrets be excepted. For most officials it is not so much a matter of the public's right to know, but, rather, that it is beneficial to release information since it would enable them to gauge public reaction and to provide public understanding for government policy. The response of the legislators was strikingly different. Everyone agreed with the statement in question, although the position of two Liberal Democratic members was somewhat qualified. The responses of the officials contrasted sharply with those of the reporters, who unanimously endorsed the statement that the government ought to release information because the public has a right to know. As for the American counterparts, virtually every State Department respondent accepted the proposition that the department should release information because the public has a right to know. This feeling is, however, not intensely felt, since responses of about half of the sample were that the department may, rather than should, do so.

Regarding the question of whether government officials should withhold information "because it may endanger national security," Japanese responses were resoundingly affirmative— "of course." A few officials saw fit to enter a qualification that strict interpretation should be made concerning what constitutes a danger to national security. All legislators agreed with the statement, albeit with varying degrees of conviction. Some added a qualifying statement such as "in principle" or "to a certain extent." One legislator put his reservation more explicitly when he said: "In principle, I agree. The problem is how to stop its abuse. The trouble with our government is that it tends to hide anything inconvenient or embarrassing to the government under the cloak of national security." When asked this same question, it will be recalled, three-fourths of the Japanese reporters reponded affirmatively, with the remainder opposed. Almost without exception, American officials felt strongly that the State Department should withhold information which might endanger national security.

With the overall sense of distrust toward reporters described in the preceding chapter, it is remarkable that all the Japanese respondents claimed that their press relationship is "good."[1] A few of them said further that they "would not call their relationship cooperative, though it is not bad," but most went on to describe their relationships as either "usually cooperative" or "always cooperative." Various reasons were cited for the existing relationship. A few thought their candor in dealing with reporters explains it. Some declared it is "because I don't lie." Others ascribed it to the lack of prejudice, their openness to reporters, their willingness to spare time to hear the reporters out or of not deliberately misleading the reporters. The common theme underlying all these reasons is the candor and accessibility granted to the reporters.

---

1. The questions asked were: "How would you describe your relationship with newspapermen?" "What are the basic reasons, in your view, for the relationship being as it is?" "Would you describe your relationship with reporters as (1) always cooperative/conflictual, (2) usually cooperative/conflictual, (3) sometimes cooperative/conflictual, (4) seldom cooperative/conflictual, or (5) never cooperative/conflictual?"

In general, American State Department policy officials described their relationship with reporters in favorable terms. About 30 percent characterized the relationship as being both cooperative and at the same time antagonistic; about 43 percent of the sample described it as "more cooperative" or "usually cooperative" and about 15 percent said "more antagonistic" or "usually antagonistic." (The remainder gave no response.)

The American data also indicate that the reporter's perceptions of relations with State Department policy officials bear a remarkable resemblance to those of the policy officals themselves. The number of American policy officials perceiving antagonistic relations is indeed small. In Japan there is wide incongruity in the perceived interpersonal orientations so far as the cooperative-antagonistic dimensions are concerned. While every Japanese reporter perceived conflicting relations, nearly all Japanese officials characterized their relationship with reporters as cooperative.

There are some discernible differences between the MITI and the FM officials which are not clearly revealed in simple tabulation of responses presented above. What came through clearly is that on the whole the MITI officials revealed a strong awareness of an interdependent relationship with reporters and showed little antagonism toward the press. This is not to deny the presence of resentment they felt toward some reporters from the Social Affairs Department. The MITI officials explained their good relationship with the reporters much the same way their FM counterparts did. However, some of them offered an additional explanation: "the nature of the work of our ministry is such that we can afford to be open and candid." This, indeed is the crux of the matter.

Of course, the perceptions of the existing relationships are distinct from the normative conception. With the single exception, all FM interviewees declared that the relationship between officials and reporters should not be "basically conflicting" and deplored the perceived antagonistic, conflictual attitude of the reporters. This contrasts sharply with the reporters' orientation—their predominant view being that the relationship should be conflicting and that it is.

Our respondents held to a man a favorable evaluation of the basic intelligence and trustworthiness of reporters with whom they interact. The reporters' rating by administrative officials ranged from "poor" to "fairly high," with most responses falling within the category of fairly high. Some respondents used measures of their own. One official indicated the grade of B would be appropriate, another giving 70 points out of 100. Regarding the level of information deemed to be possessed by the reporter, the officials' rating was somewhat austere, ranging from "not much" to "fairly high," but with most responses still falling within the latter. There were no significant differences in the distribution of answers in terms of either the ministries or other factors. The only difference was that the ratings given by the legislators of the reporters' intelligence, trustworthiness, and level of information were uniformly higher than those given by administrative officials.[2]

The officials' perception of the social prestige of the reporters was somewhat more complex. Nearly all interviewees thought that the reporters' social standing was "good" or "fairly high" but was somewhat lower than that of other occupations such as medical doctors, lawyers, and bureaucrats. Only two executive officials deviated from the pattern; one indicated the reporters' social standing was comparable to that of the other occupations listed and another declared it to be higher than the latter. Of those who gave the lower occupational rating to reporters, several administrative officials observed that they would not give consent to their daughter's marriage to a reporter. One official went on to observe that the reporter is pampered and lacks decorum and a sense of propriety.

It should be noted here that the officials generally classified the reporters into two groups. One group consists of those whom they termed as representing first-rate or prestigious papers such as the *Asahi*, *Mainichi*, *Yomiuri*, and *Nihon Keizai*. The other consists of the reporters of lesser prestigious papers. With regard to the officials' ratings of the reporters, both in terms of specific attributes and social prestige mentioned

2. The pattern of distribution obtained in the United States by Chittick showed that about three-fourths of department policy officers rated reporters at "fairly high" on the qualities of "intelligent, informed, skilled, and helpful." The rating given by the information officers was somewhat higher, with three-fourth falling between the medium point to the highest.

earlier, about a third of the respondents felt it necessary to preface their remarks by saying that they were speaking of reporters of the first-rate newspapers. Their evaluation of the reporters of the second group, therefore, was lower. Another distinction the officials made about the newspapermen was between the beat reporters and those who serve as ranking members of the Editorial Bureau and editorial writers. The officials accorded the latter much respect and prestige. In sum, the officials treated the reporters (at least those of the first-rate newspapers) with some respect, but they rated themselves higher than the reporters in terms of occupational prestige and level of expertise.

There were several additional aspects of the reporters' activities about which the officials' orientations were elicited. The officials were not prepared to exclude interpretation or commentary, as distinct from reporting of fact, from press activity. Thus the administrative officials interviewed felt that it is "permissible" for an interpretation to accompany the reporting of facts. Their proviso was that the reporter's subjectivity be kept to a minimum. The legislators' attitude was more positive; they felt it is natural and desirable for an interpretation to accompany the presentation of facts. Some respondents added, however, that there are some things which may not require interpretation. This contrasts sharply with the American sample. Close to three-fourths of the American officials felt that reporters should be factual, avoiding any interpretation whatever. Regarding the question as to whether the reporter should write without regard for the editorial views of their newspapers, the predominant view among Japanese officials, both executive and legislative, was that there need not be consistency between the two. Most respondents thought such is the actual case. Several officials, all from the FM, thought that there should be consistency between the news stories and the editorials. Incidentally, the *Asahi* was singled out by them as being fairly consistent in this regard. They complained that editorials of Japanese papers are usually ambiguous, making it difficult to ascertain the position of a newspaper on a given issue. One of them suggested that editorials are deliberately made ambiguous as an escape hatch or a shield against possible criticism while the contents of stories in the paper clearly are allowed to denote an antigovernment bias which advocates a definite policy action.

A perfect example, according to one official, was the issue of the United States-Japan Security Treaty. The kind of headlines used and the contents of stories were clearly anti-Security Treaty, while the editorial views were ambiguous and demonstrated "good behavior" in the eyes of the government. He condemned such a practice as being improper. The overwhelming majority (just over three-fourths) of American State Department officials, both policy and information, felt strongly that the reporters' writings should disregard the editorial views of their news organizations. An overwhelming majority of the officials interviewed thought it all right or permissible to attempt consciously to influence the government's policy. Only four (10 percent) gave their negative response without qualification. Two gave wholly affirmative answers, but the rest qualified their affirmative responses by adding such phrases as "to a certain extent," "there should be a limit," or "it shouldn't be done excessively." One of the four officials who disagreed stated that this would be permissible if divergent viewpoints were expressed in the newspapers. He observed that the Japanese newspapers take practically identical postions on key issues, and hence the reporter should not. Another official, who avoided direct answer, said that "in any event, such is the result of the reporter's activity." The near consensus on the proposition may indicate a resignation to the de facto situation or a grudging acceptance of the principle rather than an accurate expression of internalized value. About half of the sample thought that the reporters are actually engaged in a conscious attempt to influence government policy. The other half declared that little of such an attempt is observable, because the reporters are driven by a search for a "scoop" and simply do not have the time to study policy questions thoroughly.

There appears to be no discrepancy between the reporters' orientations and those of the officials. It will be recalled that on their part most reporters felt in varying degrees that they should attempt to influence government policy. True, for the officials to say something is "permissible" is different from saying that it should be done, but the officials' responses are interesting. Comparable American data show that a majority of the policy officers and about three-fourth of the reporters accepted the preposition that reporters should attempt to influence policy officers.

With regard to the propriety of assuming the role of the opposition, nearly every official conceded that it is either "necessary to some extent" or "permissible" for the reporters to act as oppositionists. A few executive officials added a proviso that this should be done "fairly," "selectively," or "with due recognition that such is not a sole function of the press." Two executive respondents stated that the reporter should not act in the opposition role. For them it is wrong for a reporter to assume such a posture, for the report should evaluate government policies on the basis of merits of the issues.

As for the legislators, with a single unqualified rejection, all of them thought it necessary or permissible although qualified by such phrases as "depending on the case," "to a certain extent," "if there is an objective validity to the opposition." Some gave more elaborate responses: "Well, it depends on the nature of issues. . . . It is all right for a reporter to present logical, rational arguments so as to make the government proceed on the right course. However, he should not adopt anti-government postures on everything." Despite some reservations expressed about the role of opposition, no respondent objected to a reporter's assuming the role of watchdog.

Here again the MITI officials were more relaxed in attitude toward this than their FM counterparts. Several MITI officials remarked that very seldom had they experienced situations in which the press played the role of oppostion to the MITI. On the other hand, the FM officials' stand on this issue was ambivalent. It will be recalled that nearly every reporter felt that he should act as the opposition element or watchdog vis-à-vis the government. In abstract, nearly every official subscribed to a statement that the reporters may try to act in the role of opposition. However, the officials demonstrated considerable disapproval and resentment. Their verbal acceptance of the proposition appears merely to indicate a sense of resignation to a reality, unpalatable as it may be.

As for the perception that government officials have concerning the influence of the press, the responses of MITI interviewees were generally more positive than those of their FM counterparts. Several MITI officials went so far as to acknowledge considerable direct influence of the press on their ministry's policies, while every FM official denied the presence of direct influence, insisting that influence is at most indirect. Those MITI officials who perceived indirect influence were prepared to say that they take into account the view of the press. As for the FM officials, about half said that they pay attention to the views of the press while others said they do not take them into account but merely take note of them!

Direct influence is understood to occur when government officials, conscious of the views of the press, allow them to shape policy output. A MITI official recalled that when the press gave good coverage to the boycott against the high price of color television sets conducted by the League of Housewives, the MITI felt compelled to intervene. Likewise, newspaper reports about hoarding or dumping by a trade company led to MITI investigations.

CHAPTER VII

Legal

Constraints

There are no laws specifically regulating the mass media. Before 1945 there were general laws regulating the mass media, such as the newspaper law, publication law, and movies law, but they were repealed after the war. Under the present constitution, the only area placed under some legal regulation is broadcasting. However, there are parts of existing laws which provide the mass media with special benefits and privileges. For example, the Public Office Election Law contains stringent regulations on campaigns, particularly with regard to documents and drawings. Moreover, the law recognizes the mass media's freedom to report and comment on elections, provided that fair elections are not impaired by the abuse of freedom of expression such as false reporting.[1] As will be examined later in some detail, Article 230-2 of the Criminal Law stipulates that for the purpose of promoting public interest, an expression of opinion concerning matters of public interest will not be punished if evidence of the truth is available. In this connection, facts related to crime are considered a matter of public interest. With regard to political corruption charges, one needs only to prove truth. These provisions, together with a court ruling that in proving the truth one only needs to demonstrate that he had sufficient reason to believe it to be true, provide the mass media with special protection.

The newspapers enjoy a special status under the Commercial Law. This law contains an amendment allowing the newspapers to restrict the granting of stock to those who are connected with the newspaper enterprise. This was intended to protect the newspapers from being subjected to outside pressure. Under the Postal Law, the newspapers and magazines are given the special

1. *Jurisuto*, Oct. 1976, pp. 30-32.

privilege accorded to third-class mail. Since only a small fraction of the newspapers are sent by mail, this privilege may not be significant. However, when the proportion of advertisement exceeds 50 percent, the privilege is revoked. What is important is that the newspapers and magazines depend on the status of receiving the third-class permit for their freedom of reporting and commenting on elections; the revocation of this permit would mean the loss of that freedom. Potentially, the government has the power to control the amount of advertisement in the newspapers and magazines.[2]

Certain activities of the mass media are regulated by other existing laws. A typical example is the Youth Protection Rearing Ordinance enacted by various local public entities. In order to protect young people, restraints are imposed on the distribution of certain publications and the viewing of particular movies. Another example is the Juvenile Law, which provides a restriction on the reporting of the identity of a juvenile delinquent.[3] Article 44 of the Inquest of Prosecution Law requires a reporter to gain the court's permission to tape, record, broadcast, or take pictures of the trial proceedings.

There are many cases of indirect regulation of news gathering.[4] Several laws (Article 100 of the Public Employee Law, Article 34 of Local Public Employee Law, Article 59 of the Self-Defense Forces Law, Article 9 of the Postal Law) impose an obligation on public employees to safeguard official secrets. This makes it impossible for the reporter to gather information. The Public Employee Law (Article 111) makes an act of enticement a punishable offense. Indirect restraint is also operative since reporters can be compelled to disclose their news sources.

There are other laws, although not intended to be applicable, to the mass media, that tend to restrict the activities of the mass media. They include laws governing obscenity, defamation, intimidation, and invasion of privacy.

The present chapter is concerned with various legal aspects of the setting in which the reporters operate, i.e., the legal provisions that presumably govern the activities of the reporters. The following questions are examined: freedom of expression,

2. Ibid., p. 32.   4. Ibid., p. 34.
3. Ibid., p. 33.

defamation, right of privacy, freedom of reporting, and freedom of news gathering.

Freedom of Expression and Public Welfare

The leading principle established through a series of court decisions holds that basic human rights are constrained by the standard of the public welfare. Articles 12 and 13 of the Japanese Constitution are interpreted to mean that the freedom of expression cannot contravene public welfare. In principle, public welfare is held to take precedence over such fundamental individual rights as freedom of expression.

The decisions of the Japan Supreme Court, however, contain some passages implying variations in nuance. Some decisions seem to imply that public welfare does not necessarily take precedence over the freedom of expression and that both interests are of the same or equal value. Despite some contradictory passages, the Supreme Court nearly always upholds the priority of public welfare and its powerful constraining force. The logic underlying the decisions of the Supreme Court has consistently been:

1. The freedom of expression is a basic human right of extreme importance for a democratic society.

2. However, even such a freedom as that of expression is not absolute or limitless. Its abuse cannot be permitted and it cannot be allowed to run counter to public welfare.

3. If taking or not taking an action is in the interest of public welfare, then freedom of expression may be limited.[5]

It should be understood, however, that the Supreme Court is not condoning the limitation of freedom of expression simply through the application of the vague concept of public welfare without attempting to specify the substantive contents of the concept. Professor Shimizu has analyzed a sample of seventeen cases involving freedom of expression in order to delineate what the Supreme Court considers public welfare and to clarify

5. Uchikawa Yoshimi et al., *Koza: Gendai no Shakai to Kominikeshon*, vol. 3, *Genron no Jiyu* (Tokyo: Tokyo Daigaku Shuppankai, 1974), pp. 28ff. See also Arthur Taylor von Mehren, ed., *Law in Japan* (Cambridge, Mass.: Harvard University Press, 1963), pp. 205-38.

the legal position taken by the Supreme Court on the issue of freedom of expression.[6]

These cases are classified according to three categories: (1) those involving interests of state, (2) those involving interests of society, and (3) those involving interests of individuals. The first category includes the cases concerning the act of advocating nonperformance of citizen duties, the act of impeding a fair election or fair trial, and the act of urging dereliction of the duties of public officials. The smooth functioning of government agencies, free from external interference, is considered a most important interest. In these cases (the first category), the concept of public welfare appears to have replaced the notions of compliance with tax obligations, loyalty of public officials, and fair trials. It is sufficiently vague as to be usable as a means to limit freedom of expression for the convenience of a government agency. One such case involved the distribution of leaflets by the Japan Communist party during the Korean War which urged Japanese policemen to refuse to obey the orders of foreign imperialists and the traitorous Japanese government. The court decision states in part that even the freedom of expression guaranteed in the Constitution is not limitless. The wanton use of freedom of expression by individuals is not permissible and sometimes must be coordinated with public welfare. For example, inciting government employees to commit sabotage, an act which would lower governmental efficiency, would be to entice the dereliction of their important obligations to serve the interests of the people. Such an act would be contrary to the public welfare and would exceed the boundary of freedom of expression. In short, the maintenance of obligations by government and local public bodies takes precedence over freedom of expression.

In the second category, the cases include those dealing with public safety, the security of economic life, the preservation of sexual morality, and public health. The possibility of potential abuse by the government exists as in the case of the first category. This occurs when the concept of public safety is invoked in relation to demonstrations. In 1960 the Supreme Court ruled as constitutional a Tokyo prefectural ordinance concerning prior restraint of group (mass) acts or acts that might destroy

6. *Genron no Jiyu*, pp. 32-34.

peace and order. Through this decision, the system of general permits regulating group activity was declared constitutional. Some scholars considered the decision as one imposing prior restraint on freedom of expression, as being inconsistent with the principle of "clear and present danger," or the principle of definiteness. It would amount to placing the group activity outside the framework of Article 21 of the Constitution. According to the opinion of the Supreme Court, the expression of thought through mass action is different from a mere expression through speech or publication. Mass action is characteristically supported by a kind of potential physical force present in the strength of a group of people. Mass action is based on the law of mass psychology and also on real-life experiences that there exists a danger that a group could turn instantly into a mob and, by force, violate law and order. Public welfare is the protection of public peace. Therefore, such an act of mass demonstration containing danger can be subjected to prior restraints.

The Supreme Court defined a different substantive content for public welfare. A typical case involves the preservation of morality. The Supreme Court ruled in the famous case of D. H. Lawrence's *Lady Chatterley's Lover* and the marquis de Sade's *Juliette* that even though the material has some artistic value, if it is obscene, then to make such material the object of punishment in order to preserve order in sexual life and sound customs is consistent with the interest of the people.

Basically speaking, for the third category, the public welfare as envisaged in the Constitution is not contrary to, but rather consistent with the respect for individuals. However, to view the guarantee of individual rights as constituting public welfare would lead to some confusion about the concept of public welfare. In a case involving the distribution of a leaflet containing an expression of intimidation, the Supreme Court ruled that intimidation injures public welfare, exceeding the boundary of freedom of press and expression, and is antisocial behavior. Therefore, punishment of an individual for intimidation constitutes public welfare.[7]

As defined by the Supreme Court, the concept of public welfare is quite comprehensive in scope and is unclear. It is,

7. Ibid., p. 36.

therefore, not surpirsing that many criticisms have been voiced by the students of the Constitution and even within the Supreme Court. Among lower courts some criticisms have appeared concerning the concept of public welfare and its interpretation. A minority opinion on the Tokyo ordinance case states that freedom of expression should not be limited by such an abstract yardstick as the public welfare. It should be done by rational and clear criteria applied to each category of expression, including mass acts of group expression. Freedom of expression is particularly important under the Constitution and is different from other freedoms or rights. The point of controversy has been whether to use the concept of public welfare as a principle delimiting the freedom of expression. The Japanese scholars are divided on this legal interpretation. Although a majority of Japanese scholars seem to hold such a view, there still exists a controvery over the interpretation.[8]

Defamation and Invasion of Privacy

The question of freedom of expression arises also in relation to the protection of honor and privacy. By the latter half of the 1960s, attention was directed to the violation of honor and privacy by the mass media, occasionally giving rise to the advocacy of legislative regulation of the mass media. Both the freedom of expression and privacy/honor are protected by law and yet are in a sense mutually contradictory. This problem, however, had seldom been dealt with as an issue in Japanese constitutional law. In 1951 the Supreme Court of Fukuoka held that a newspaper article expressing contemptuous sentiments for others constitutes an abuse of the right of the freedom of press. The court held that it is the inherent mission of the newspapers to report facts about the happenings in society and that fair commentary should be allowed as part of freedom of reporting. However, freedom of reporting is not absolute. A newspaper would be abusing its right of press to carry an article expressing contemptuous sentiments for individuals and using insulting remarks in headlines and contents. This would exceed the proper conduct of newspapers. The Supreme Court took a

8. Ibid., pp. 37-41.

similar position in 1958, declaring that defamation is the abuse of the right of press. According to the decision, Article 21 of the Constitution does not guarantee freedom of press absolutely. If a newspaper carries an article defaming a person, it abuses the freedom of press. Moreover, such an action cannot be considered as falling within the framework of freedom of press guaranteed under the Constitution; defamations in the press are outside the framework of freedom of press.[9]

The Japanese traditionally have had a keen sense of honor, but it arises most often in relation to the groups to which they belong. Sensitivity to the insult of an individual has been relatively weak. This is reflected in the Japanese tendency to treat a matter of honor more as a matter of face. This is also reflected in the tendency of the Japanese to disregard the amount of damage and to emphasize the public printing of an apology for the restoration of honor, and in other cases to institute criminal proceedings for punishment rather than civil action.

As for the newspapers, they would rather pay damages than print an apology or retraction. In their reporting, they are, of course, aware of the potential problem of defamation and pay due attention to not injuring an individual's honor.

The newspapers seem especially concerned with the pursuit of truth, disregarding the legal considerations. This stems in part from the awareness that if the reported facts are true, they can evade responsibility both legally and morally. In the case of erroneous reporting, the newspaper assumes moral responsibility, even though it can manage to avoid legal responsibility. Therefore, they are concerned almost exclusively with the question of truth. This is the way the newspapers approach the question of defamation, and it represents a basic posture in the process of news.[10]

According to Article 230, paragraph 2 of the Criminal Law (the Penal Code), in a defamation case, if a published report concerns a matter of public interest, a defendant will not be punished as along as the report is true. The principle established through court decisions in Japan is that reporting

9. Ibid., pp. 194-95.
10. Shimbun Henshu Kankei Hosei Kenkyu Kai, ed., *Ho to Shimbun*, (Tokyo: Nihon Shimbun Kyokai, 1972), pp. 118-20.

which constitutes defamation is considered to lie outside the freedom of expression and of press, and hence is not worthy of constitutional protection. The principle embodied in Article 230 is that if a person's honor is injured, it meets a criterion of the offense of defamation, whether the allegation contained in the report is true or false. However, if the condition stipulated in paragraph 2 of Article 230 is met, the act of illegality is dismissed. Even if truth is being reported, one's honor is still impaired. Yet, one is exempted from criminality if his act is within Article 21 of the Constitution. In Japan, then, paragraph 2 of Article 230 gives substance to the spirit of Article 21.[11]

Privacy and Right of Portrait

The right of privacy refers to the "right to be let alone" or the right to keep private affairs from being made public. In a celebrated case, *After the Banquet*, the court defined privacy as the "legal guarantee or right to have private life not made public without permission." The right of portrait refers to one's right not to be photographed and made public without permission. Since the late 1960s the Japanese courts have begun to refer to the right of portrait without explicitly recognizing it as such. The Japanese position is, therefore, much closer to the continental European tradition in distinguishing the right of portrait from privacy. The Supreme Court in a 1969 case refers to the "freedom from unauthorized or indiscriminate photography of one's countenance and figures," adding a phrase "aside from the question of whether this is to be called the right of portrait."[12]

Incorrect or False Reporting

From the standpoint of a newspaperman, an incorrect report should be distinguished from false reporting. A false report is

11. Ibid., pp. 121-27. For an essay in English on this topic, see Lawrence Beer, "Defamation, Privacy, and Freedom of Expression in Japan," *Law in Japan* 5 (1972): 192-208.
12. *Ho to Shimbun*, pp. 128-31.

written with full awareness from the beginning that the story is a fictitious one. An incorrect report refers to a case in which the story was believed to be true at the time of writing but turned out to be incorrect later. The former reflects a deliberate act, while the latter is a mistake. For the object of news reporting, i.e., the reader, there is little distinction. To them it is simply a matter of varying degrees of error.

Legally speaking, aside from Article 230 of the Criminal Law, there is no distinction between the two since a wrongful act (tort, misfeasance) may result from either a deliberate or an erroneous action. So far as the courts' decisions are concerned, there has been no consistency. There are cases of incorrect reporting in which the courts upheld a defamation suit. Charges of incorrect reporting may be divided into two groups: (1) those involving errors in factual information reporting and (2) those involving errors in evaluation. A case in which a libel suit was upheld against a newspaper resulted from an article which gave the impression that a man was found guilty of all the charges, when in fact, he was found guilty of only a portion of the charges reported.[13] Another example involves a man who threw a bottle grenade at the Mitsubishi Bank Bill Center. Several newspapers reported it under the heading of "a case of bottle grenade robbery." The plaintiff sued the newspapers on the grounds that he did not intend a burglary but rather political act to awaken the center, which represented the stronghold of capitalism. Indeed, the police authorities treated the case as an interference by force in the execution of business. The newspapers lost the case as the Tokyo District Court ruled that the newspapers' evaluation of the events was erroneous. The court's reasoning was that in view of the fact that the plaintiff was found guilty and sentenced on the charge of trespassing and forceful interference in business execution, his act should not be called a burglary under criminal law. Moreover, since there was no information indicating the plaintiff's intention to commit the act of robbery, it was erroneous to judge his act to be robbery. Therefore the head of the article in question was not consistent with truth. In this case, the judgment expressed by the newspapers was in error.[14]

13. Ibid., pp. 111-12.
14. Ibid., pp. 138-40.

Newspaper reporters often use the expressions "it is said" or "according to investigations." However, they are merely techniques of expression in newspaper writing and have no bearing on the question of legal responsibility. So far as libel cases are concerned, what is important is not whether in fact there was such a rumor but whether the factual contents of the rumor printed in the paper are consistent with truth. A newspaper carried an article about the fund-raising activities of the Japan Communist party and used the expression "it is reported." The article reported dishonest fund raising accomplished through the use of the Medical Protection, Livelihood Protection, and Health Insurance systems. The newspapers also reported that the police authorities held the view that the party received financial assistance from abroad.

Even though the first section of the article implied that it was a rumor by employing the expression "it is reported," the printing of such a story was unlawful. The court's reasoning was: If a rumor is printed which would injure another's honor and has no regard for the truth of the substantive contents, even if the existence of the rumor is fact, the story would be ruled unlawful. Even if the story is in the form of "it is reported," a reader would acquire slanderous impressions about the contents reported.[15]

Newspapers themselves do not speak of news-gathering techniques. Direct news gathering by the reporter constitutes only a small portion of reporting. Examples are Diet proceedings, open trials, and traffic accidents. Much of the news comes from indirect news gathering, based on releases, material, and documents made available officially by all kinds of news sources such as government agencies, political parties, enterprises, groups, and individuals. In a broad sense, indirect news gathering is equivalent to gathering by hearsay. Hearsay news gathering is confined to indirect gathering from private sources, excluding public officials. In the case of such indirect gathering from a private source, the newspapers cannot be exempted from responsibility even if the source is clearly indicated. On the other hand, if the source is an official pronouncement from a public agency, the newspapers are exempted when the contents of the reports turn out to be incorrect.

15. Ibid., pp. 142-43.

Headlines plays a crucial role in determing the decision made in a libel case. A Chiba district court stated that determination of whether a particular newspaper article is contrary to fact and damaging to a person's honor shall be governed by the criterion appropriate to the general reader.

The court decisions have not been consistent as to what extent exaggeration or simplification is to be permitted. Some decisions concede the need for some exaggeration in the heads. A superior court in Hiroshima ruled that by their nature some exaggeration of expressions cannot be helped, since the heads and preambles are intended to arouse attention of the reader to get him to read the main text. However, if simplification and exaggeration are carried so far as to sacrifice accuracy, the newspaper is open to the charge of libel.[16]

Violation of honor and privacy is in part determined by the status and occupation of the victims. In the case of public figures, their rights of honor and privacy are considerably restricted. As mentioned above, paragraph 2 of Article 230 states that as long as the reported fact is truth, the newspapers are protected. As for privacy, the limitation on the privacy of public personages is recognized.[17]

In general, when a news report has been found to have impaired a person's right of honor, it must assume criminal and/or civil responsibility. Since the end of World War II, there has been no case resulting in criminal responsibility for a newspaper involving the members of the Japan Newspaper Association. However, in view of the prewar court decisions and postwar decisions involving magazines, if the case of responsibility should ever arise, the reporter and/or the desk would be held liable.

According to a theory of criminal law, libel is committed when a person, aware that he might impair honor, dares to publish an item. Individuals assisting in this publication will be held liable as well. In the case of criminal responsibility, only a natural person is punishable. In view of the legal theory and the function of a newspaper organization, the desk is expected to assume responsibility. Even though the primary responsibility is with the reporter who sent an erroneous report, the desk is the

16. Ibid., pp. 147-51.
17. Ibid., p. 163.

person who has the power to print or stop the publication of an item. Within news organizations, an unwritten rule is that everything printed is the desk's responsibility. As long as the desk is aware that an untrue story was printed, he will be held liable.

Under civil law, either a legal person or employers can be liable. Article 44 of the Civil Code specifies that when an organ of a legal person causes damage, it must assume the obligation of reparation. However, it is extremely rare for the organization of a newspaper, namely the board of trustees, to write an article and publish it. Article 715 specifies that when employees such as reporters commit libel, the employer (a newspaper) must pay damages. Even in this case, if an employer has paid due attention in selection and supervision of employees (reporters), the employer is deemed to be absolved of responsibility. However, in the case of libel by newspapers, there has not been a case in which the employers have been exempted from responsibility when the employees' faults have been established. Along with the newspaper, the employees such as reporters and desks have been sued. In certain cases, joint defendants included the newspaper, its managing director, its heads of political affairs and a reporter. The responsibility of the employer presupposes the responsibility of the employees, and legally speaking the responsibility of employees remains, even if a newspaper pays damages.[18]

When a newspaper loses a suit, it may feel that its employees deserve to be excused in certain cases. This might happen when the source of news could not be revealed or the reasoning of a court decision was not convincing. In cases of clear negligence, a reduction of pay, the issuance of a warning, and a transfer to another position might result. The relationship between a desk and reporter is one of trust, and therefore, if a reporter keeps filing erroneous reports, this trust would be destroyed. The reporter in question would no longer be given important assignments. To deny a reporter an assignment would be a fatal blow and would constitute a real punishment.

The newspaper may have to assume both criminal and civil responsibility. If civil responsibility is established in which a newspaper is found to be at fault, it may pay damages or print apologies and a retraction. According to criminal law, if crimi-

18. Ibid., pp. 209-17.

nal responsibility is established, libel is punishable by imprisonment for less than three years and a fine of less than 50,000
yen. Most often the fine is imposed rather than imprisonment.
However, in one libel case a magazine president and a magazine
editor were sentenced to imprisonment of one year and half and
one year respectively. There has been no case of criminal action
brought against a newspaper.[19]

Grounds for Exemption from Responsibility

In a case of libel action, as general principle, a person is exempted from both criminal and civil responsibility and no
punishment is imposed if (1) the act concerns the interests of
the public, (2) its objective has been to promote primarily
public interest, and (3) evidence for truth has been established.
This ground for exemption from responsibility applies to both
civil and criminal cases. The newspapers (as opinion leaders and
transmitters of news) can certainly be characterized as being
concerned with public interest. Therefore, as long as the newspapers are engaged in normal reporting activities, they would
be considered as being concerned with the public interest and
as aimed at promotion of public interest and, therefore, would
be exempted from both civil and criminal responsibility.

There have been some cases in which such a contention was
rejected by the courts. The first requirement for a court hearing
to gain an exemption is that the act be shown to concern
"the interest of the public." It is not enough to simply say that
the matter is related to the public interest. It has been interpreted to mean that a published fact must be "necessary for
or useful to" public interest. The lawyers tend to interpret
public interest in terms of a problem which would affect the
major interest of society, whereas the journalists tend to interpret it to mean a problem which would arose public curiosity
and provoke commentaries.

Japanese newspapers take the position that every article reported in the newspaper is related to public interest. Their
view is that unless it is relevant to the public interest, there
would be no reason for newspapers to carry an item. In actual

19. Ibid., pp. 217-41.

implementation of law, the courts seem to accept the presupposition that the facts covered in the respectable newspapers do have relevance to public interest. They have never challenged any newspapers belonging to the Japan Newspaper Association in this respect.

The second requirement poses a probelm in that a report must show that the objective of the article was one of promoting primarily public interest. According to legal theory and judicial decisions, the work "primarily" (*moppara*) means that it was the "major" (*shuyōna*) objective. The presence of other objectives does not disqualify a newspaper from the application of this principle. However, if it is clear that the major objective is other than public interest, even if some public interest is present, the second requirement is deemed not to have been fulfilled.

When the above two requirements are met, one is allowed to provide evidence to establish truth of the matter. When the reported fact is completely in accord with truth, no problem will arise. The question in most cases is to what extent and in what ways truth and reported facts are expected to correspond. The accepted interpretation is that a major or principal section of the writing must be true. In proving truth, it is sufficient that a major section be validated. What constitutes the major section is not a legal criteron but a problem of social criterion or social evaluation. The meaning of truth of the principal section is whether a story, excluding trivial points, is accurate in major outline.

The case in which the reported fact in question is in accordance with truth poses no problem. However, what if there was considerable reason for believing the fact to be true, even though the truth of the matter could not be completely established? The question of whether one is exempted from responsibility when there was a mistaken belief in the truth of a fact depends on an interpretation of the legal character of the phrase "will not be punished" in paragraph 2 of Article 230. If the wording is taken to mean a reason for dismissing punishment, then the exemption of responsibility occurs only when truth objectively exists. If the phrase is taken to mean a ground for dismissing illegality of acts or at least a reason for dismissing the applicability of the constituent requirement for crime, then a person will be exempted from responsibility even when he has mistakenly believed the fact to be true. The Japanese Supreme Court ruled in 1966 and 1969 that if there was considerable reason in view of available documents and evidence, a person may be exempted from responsibility in the case of mistaken belief. What constitutes "considerable reason" for believing a fact to be true? If news is gathered from a reliable person or organ, for example, an investigative agency, this would meet the criterion of "considerable reason." A report based on an official announcement poses no problem. However, if the report is based on unofficial or private news gathering, most court decisions reject the claim for exemption on the ground of the presence of considerable reason. Unless the report was based on official announcements, the newspapers must establish the truth of the reported facts to claim the exemption. However, there was a case in which news reporting was based, not on information from a public investigating agency, but on a reporter's own investigation, and it won the court's recognition.[20] Because the article was the result of a thorough investigation, the court was ready to recognize that there was considerable reason believing the fact to be true, even if the report turned out not to be consistent with the truth.

The Japanese Constitution does not make specific reference to the freedom of reporting. However, the prevailing interpretation is that the freedom of speech and expression guaranteed by the Constitution does include the freedom of reporting. The Japanese Supreme Court stated in the *Hakata* case (1969) that reporting by a news organization provides the public with important material for making judgments concerning national politics; hence it serves the public's "right to know." Therefore, along with the freedom of expression of thoughts, the freedom of reporting is under the protection of the freedom of expression stipulated in Article 21.

The question is whether freedom of reporting includes the freedom of information gathering. In a sense the importance of accurate reporting of facts presupposes an adequate level of news gathering. On the other hand, it may be argued that the

20. Ibid., pp. 252-79.

freedom of expression refers to the freedom of communicating externally the content which have already been gathered or determined, and that it is distinct from the process involved in determining the contents of expression.[21]

The Supreme Court decision of 1952 in the *Ishii* case appeared to place the freedom of news gathering outside the framework of constitutional protection. According to a decision in 1958, newspaper reporting belongs to the freedom of expression recognized by Article 21. News-gathering activity for that purpose must be recognized. In the 1969 decision the court stated that in order to ensure accurate contents in reporting, freedom of news gathering, together with freedom of reporting, "is worthy of adequate respect in the light of the spirit of Article 21 of the Constitution." At the present time, it cannot be categorically stated that the freedom of news gathering is clearly guaranteed by the Constitution, but it does enjoy a status akin to that of the freedom of expression.

Aside from constitutional interpretation, it is important to note to what extent and in what ways the freedom of news gathering has been challenged. Although news gathering has not been suppressed, specific prohibitions under specific circumstances do occur. Photography and tape recording inside the court room require the permission of the court. A difficult problem arises when the public authorities demand in the name of a fair trial the disclosure of the identity of news sources and submission of notes and newsfilms collected during news-gathering activity. The news organizations have resisted such demands on the grounds that compliance with such a request would deal a fatal flow to the freedom of news gathering and would violate the freedom of reporting. The Supreme Court ruled, however, that compliance with such an order is required because the interest of a fair trial takes precedence.

In view of the fact that there is no law explicitly providing for the protection of news sources or for refusal to submit material evidence, news gathering is generally considered to be more restricted than freedom of reporting. A decision must be made, depending on particular circumstances, weighing the reduction of the freedom of reporting through the limitation of news gathering and the advantage derived from limiting news-

21. *Genron no Jiyu*, pp. 69-70.

gathering activity. The court has followed this rule and tended to give priority to the interest of a fair trial and less consideration to the interest of news organization on the grounds that adverse effect would be confined to the possible impairment of the future freedom of news gathering but would not affect the freedom of reporting itself. From the perspective of the news organizations, news-gathering activity requires cooperation from the objects of the news gathering, and that requires a relationship of trust between news reporters and the objects.[22]

There are some legal constraints regarding the freedom of reporting.[23] Such interests as fair trials, fair elections, and national security compete with the freedom of reporting. The tension between the media and the government arises when the mass media attempt to reveal secrets that the government desires to protect. It is conceded that a government needs to guard certain information for a period of time. Protecting military and diplomatic secrets is generally considered to be a valid reason for restraining the freedom of reporting.

Censorship, an effective method of prior restraint, is prohibited under the Constitution. The question remains whether prior restraint, which would resemble an absolute ban, can be imposed by the court.

Classification of information into various categories of secrecy is another method of restraint. Aside from a host of questions related to this problem, it should be noted that when the leak of classified information becomes an issue in a case, the court is thought to have the power in principle to determine whether information should be so classified.

A method of maintaining national secrets is to impose strict discipline on officials. Government employees have the legal obligation to maintain official secrets, and violations are subject to penalty. Administrative acts punishing those who leak secrets would pose no constitutional question. Another method is to protect secrets by imposing criminal liability. Criminal penalties in regard to the leaking of national secrets are stipulated in paragraph 1 of Article 100 of Law on National Public Employees, Article 59 of Self-Defense Forces Law, and Article 34 of Local Public Employees Law. To impose criminal liability

22. Ibid., p. 71.
23. Ibid., pp. 72-77.

on news organizations for being an accomplice or for the commission of an independent crime under Article III of Public
Employees Law might be a threat to the freedom of reporting.
An example is the *Nishiyama* case, which will be discussed
later.

The protection of a news source is considered to be a supreme professional ethic. Even if arrested and prosecuted, a
reporter is expected to protect professional secrets. This position is accepted among journalists and academic specialists.

The celebrated *Ishii* case involved the refusal of an *Asahi*
reporter to testify. In April 1969 the police in Matsumoto city
sought an arrest warrant from the court for a tax official on
bribery charges. The following day, the *Asahi* (Nagano edition)
carried a story identical to the suspected facts contained in the
warrant. An investigation began on the suspicion that a violation had occurred in the safeguarding of official secrets under
the National Public Employee Law. Ishii's testimony was
sought, but he refused. The Nagano district prosecutor demanded the questioning of the witness under Article 226 of the
Law of Criminal Procedure. Ishii responded to the court's sum-
mons but refused to testify about the source of the information. He was then indicted on the charge of refusing to testify
under Article 161 of Law of Criminal Procedure, convicted, and
fined 3,000 yen. The appellate court upheld the lower court's
judgment on the first instance, and the defendant appealed.
There were two major points in the appeal. First, the newspapers
are society's public instruments that provide materials needed
for judgment by the sovereign people. To enable them to discharge the most important function of expression, the newspapers are guaranteed the freedom of expression. In order to
secure freedom of expression, the method of news gathering
must also be free, and to maintain freedom of news gathering,
it is necessary to protect anonymity of news sources. Therefore,
news sources ought to be protected by Article 21, which
guarantees freedom of expression. To refuse to testify about
news sources in court would constitute justifiable grounds as
specified under Article 161 of the Criminal Procedure Law,
and for this reason the original judgment that ruled otherwise
on the issue was unconstitutional. Second, the interests protected by the right of refusal to testify, as enjoyed by physi-

cians, midwives, attorneys, and clergymen, are private interests. However, security about news sources of newspapermen has direct major influence on public welfare and is guaranteed protection by the state. As in the case of a physician, the newspaperman, too, has a justifiable ground for refusing to testify about news sources.[24]

The Japanese Supreme Court rejected these arguments and delivered the following unanimous decision: Article 21 of the Constitution guaranteeing freedom of expression extend to all people equally; it does not provide a special guarantee for reporters. Article 21 means that what a person wants to say must be allowed to be said. It can by no means be understood to guarantee the right of refusing to give testimony about news sources concerning news gathering. This type of guarantee would sacrifice the obligation to give testimony indispensable for the exercise of fair judicial power, which is important for public welfare.

The law embodies the principle of the citizen's obligation to testify at a court and recognizes exceptional cases in which the obligation may be exempted. The question of whether to recognize the reporter's refusal to testify about news sources has been subjected to policy review, and there has been legislation proposed in this area. However, the current law on criminal procedure does not enumerate the case of reporters and, hence, cannot be applied to them. In short, the Supreme Court's ruling has established that the reporters do not enjoy such a right since the law makes no specific reference to reporters.[25]

The *Ishii* case is the only one involving the right to refuse testimony that has come before the court. Since no court dispute has occurred since then, it may be that the prosecuting authorities do not in fact demand testimony, and that the practice of not demanding it reveals that the protection of news sources has become established.

The *Ishii* decision represented the position that freedom of news gathering is not included in the freedom of expression, and this view is shared by some constitutional scholars. From the perspective of the newspapermen, the freedom of news

24. *Ho to Shimbun*, pp. 283-84.
25. Ibid., pp. 284-86.

gathering is essential for securing freedom of reporting. They cannot quite accept a view that the former is not guaranteed by the Constitution. As has been stated earlier, a subsequent Supreme Court decision of 1969 has somewhat modified the position in this regard. According to the *Hakata* case, "freedom of gathering for the purpose of reporting, too, must be said to be worthy of adequate respect in the light of the spirit of Article 21."

The position that the freedom of expression enjoyed by newspapers is the same as that of the ordinary citizen might be reasonable if the freedom of expression is interpreted to mean only the freedom of the sender of information. The position taken by the newspapers is that freedom of expression is supported by the public's right to know. The value of reporters lies in their contribution on the formation of opinion by accurate and speedy transmission of the many developments in the society, especially in providing the sovereign citizens with materials for judgment as they participate in politics. Thus, the newspaper exists as the champion of the public's right to know. If the freedom of expression is taken to mean not only the freedom of the sender but also as including the receiver's right to know, a different judgment would be possible.

The newspapers take the position that protection of news sources is an ethical practice. The reporters are willing to pay fines for maintaining this position. In a libel case the newspapers occasionally find that they are unable to demonstrate the truth of the matter unless news sources are named. Their choice is to accept a libel judgment or to reveal news sources. They can exercise the right to remain silent under Article 38 of the Constitution and can refuse to testify under Article 146 of the law of Criminal Procedure. Even now under the current law it is possible for the reporters to refuse to testify, but this is not viewed as a desirable method of protecting news sources.

Refusal to Turn over Materials and Newsfilms

In the case of news sources, the usual practice of the newspapers has been to reject in principle a request for disclosure. In the case of a request for materials, the newspapers have dealt with the matter on a case-by-case basis. Under the current Law of Criminal Procedure, the right to refuse confiscation is considered as a parallel concept, so that a person who can refuse testimony can refuse confiscation of articles he possesses concerning professional secrets (Art. 105). Since the news organs are not exempted from the obligation to provide testimony, they are also deemed to be without the right to refuse confiscation.[26]

Prior to the *Hakata* case, news organs were occasionally asked to submit material evidence such as news photos and newsfilms. On some occasions, they voluntarily turned them over at the request of the authorities, but on other occasions they agreed to "submit" in the form of confiscation after negotiation with the authorities. This was to indicate that the newspaper was abiding by the law and at the same time was concerned about the neutrality of the newspapers. Up to 1969, the Association of Japan Newspapers took the position that the provision of news photos should in principle be decided in accordance with the independent judgment of each company, though a newspaper should try to avoid a situation where freedom of gathering might be restricted.

In 1969 the association made its position more explicit in relation to the *Hakata* case.

1. In principle, the newspaper company should not comply with a request from the investigating authorities and the courts to turn over news photos, files, and notes as material evidence, for it might bring about major limitations on the freedom of reporting and news gathering.

2. Whether or not to comply with requests for materials should be resolved case by case on the basis of the relative weights of a fair trial and the freedom of reporting. However, in making a judgment, it is desirable to respect the preceding principle.

The following developments probably contributed to the realization that the use of collected notes and photos for the purpose other than reporting might seriously affect freedom of gathering.

1. There have been a growing number of events with political and ideological ramifications. Unless the newspapers clarify

26. Ibid., pp. 294-300.

their political neutrality, speedy and accurate gathering would be hampered.

2. There is a danger that reporters would be hampered and harassed while gathering news. For example, during demonstrations radical students might attack a reporter who had reported news disadvantageous to the students. In hostile environments reporters must gather news while being watched by both students and policemen. As a result, the reporters feel that their physical safety is threatened. The decision not to use photos and files for purposes other than reporting would reduce the danger.

3. There have been a large number of requests from the investigating authorities for news photos as evidence. Often, these photos are the only available evidence for a court proceeding.

The preceeding paragraphs should not be interpreted to mean that news organizations would refuse to supply materials under all circumstances. When a matter has political and ideological implications, and especially when it is unclear which side is guilty, the newspapers are particularly reluctant to see their photos used in the determination of one side's innocence or guilt.

A brief discussion of the *Hakata* case is now in order. On January 16, 1969, about 300 radical students got off a train at Hakata station on their way to Sasebo to demonstrate against the U.S.S. *Enterprise*'s port call and subsequently clashed with the police. One student was tried on a charge of obstructing the performance of official duty. The Fukuoka District Court acquitted the student, placing the blame for the clash on the overzealousness of the guards and the police. Thereupon, the Japan Socialist party and the National Federation for the Protection of the Constitution filed charges with the Fukuoka District Procurator's Office against 870 officers for their alleged violent and brutal actions.

The Procurator's Office decided not to indict them. The plaintiffs then petitioned the Fukuoka District Court to investigate whether or not there were sufficient grounds to try the suspects under Article 262 of the Law of Criminal Procedure. During the hearing for examining the petition, the Dukuoka District Court issued orders to four television stations demanding submission of their newsfilms of the Hakata incident. A special appeal was lodged with the Supreme Court against the ruling of the Fukuoka High court affirming these orders.

In the end, the Supreme Court reached its decision by balancing the competing interests.[27] The court made reference to the "right to know," although not recognizing it as such. Freedom of gathering was acknowledged to be included in the freedom of reporting. However, it rejected the contention of the four corporations that submission should be done independently and voluntarily by the media. The decision was that it is the court which decides on the basis of relative balancing of legal interests.

Since the news media already had in their possession the films in question, the court order demanding submission had no direct relation to the news-gathering activity itself. However, when the film gathered by news media for reporting are used for other purposes, there can be a fear that future hindrance to the freedom of gathering may occur. The freedom of gathering is not absolute and should be restricted to a certain degree when there is a constitutional requirement such as the realization of a fair trial. A fair criminal trial is one of the nation's fundamental requirements, and when the data collected by news media are necessary as evidence in order to secure a just trial, the freedom of news-gathering activities can be restricted. Even in such a case, the court added, the character, mode, and gravity of the crime, the evidential value of the data, and the necessity for the realization of a fair criminal trial should be considered at first, and then they should be balanced with the degree of the hindrance to the freedom of news gathering that would occur. Even when the use of the data as evidence in a trial is considered to be inevitable, care should be taken lest the disadvantage suffered by news media should exceed the indispensable degree. In the *Hakata* case, news films had a highly important evidential value and were almost essential for deciding the criminality of the suspects. The disadvantage accruing to the media did not relate to the freedom of a news report itself, but only to the possible hindrance in future

27. Ibid., pp. 300-304.

news-gathering activity. This disadvantage was still within the proper limits to be endured by the news media so as to realize justice. Therefore, the order demanding submission of the films was neither repugnant to Article 21 of the Constitution nor even to its purport.[28]

The ruling of the Tokyo District Court on January 31, 1974, in the *Nishiyama* case gives a cogent exposition of the freedom of reporting and "freedom" of news gathering: under Article 21 of the Constitution, news organizations are guaranteed the freedom of expression of opinion and the freedom of reporting facts and other's opinions.[29] The freedom of news-gathering activity—for the purpose of reporting—which in itself is not an act of expression, must be sufficiently respected in the light of the spirit of Article 21. This position is consistent with the action taken by the Supreme Court in the *Hakata* case but is noteworthy in its clear exposition of its rationale. News organizations serve the public's freedom to know, its formation of opinion, and its freedom of expression in the following ways: (1) they provide the people with information through a collection of facts and opinions concerning matters of public concern; (2) they provide speedy reporting; and (3) they form their opinions and express them based on the information gathered by the news organizations themselves. Thus, the opinion of the public is introduced into the arena of public debate, tying together the public and state organs. This emphasis on the public mission of news organizations forms a basis for justifying the constitutional guarantee for freedom of reporting and gathering. In the ruling, the freedom of expression and "freedom" of gathering are linked to the right to know and/or the freedom to know. To the extent that freedom of expression is identified to be a prerequisite for a democratic system, the status of the right to know is secure. Under such a conception the receiver of the communication is viewed as the one who enjoys the freedom of reporting. This in turn links the freedom of reporting to popular sovereignty, making the former an indispensable condition for popular autonomy.

28. General Secretariat, Supreme Court of Japan, *Ruling upon Case of the So-Called Hakata Railway Station Case and a Court Order to Produce Films Collected for News Report*, 1970.
29. *Jurisuto*, April 15, 1974, pp. 97-103.

The emphasis on the right to know is associated with respect for the freedom of distribution of information, thus helping to justify the constitutional guarantee of the freedom of reporting. The court decision tends to support this view. Another implication of the emphasis on the right to know in the constitutional interpretation is that many specific acts which otherwise may be illegal may now obtain legal protection as long as they were enacted for the purpose of serving the right to know.

In this case, Nishiyama, a *Mainichi* reporter, was charged under Article III of the Public Employees Law with having enticed a female employee of the Foreign Ministry to leak an official secret in the form of three telegrams. The issue was the constitutionality of the article in view of the constitutional guarantee of free distribution of information associated with the right to know. The court in the first instance ruled that the article does not contravene the constitution and that the act of Nishiyama did fall under the constituent requirements of the provision. The ruling implies that a gathering of information concerning state secrets would normally require some kind of enticement and that most of such news-gathering acts—at least provisionally—would constitute the violation of the Public Employee Law. Such an interpretation tends to constrain news-gathering activities.

The court ruling is particularly noteworthy on the question of the justifiability of news-gathering activity for the purpose of reporting. The court pointed out that the freedom of gathering is not unlimited, though it deserves to be respected. Without the freedom of gathering, there is no freedom of reporting. When the freedom of gathering is threatened or is severely restricted, news organizations cannot provide the receiver with accurate information. However, news-gathering activity at times comes into conflict with other legally protected interests and may constitute an illegal act. While acknowledging various legal restraints on news gathering, the court ruled that there are some cases in which news-gathering activities may be tolerated as a justifiable act, even if such acts would otherwise constitute a violation of law.

The court provided the criteria for judging justifiability, the lawfulness of the objective of news gathering, the appropriateness of the methods employed, and the relative weights of interest served and interest damaged. Regarding the objective of the gathering act, the court acknowledged that Nishiyama committed an act to realize the collection of information accurately and comprehensively on a matter of interest to the public and reported it through the newspapers.

The court also commented on the question of whether Nishiyama had a private desire to gain fame. Given the profit-making nature of news organizations, and free competition among them, it is not unusual for a reporter to pursue profit for his organization and to seek private advantages and fame by obtaining a scoop. Yet even if such a private end was involved, unless the reporter primarily sought a private end, his act cannot be judged to lack justifiable objective.

Second, even if the method of gathering may be said to be somewhat inappropriate, the degree of deficiency is such that one can still say the method had a tinge of justifiability. It is not so serious as to say that the inappropriateness of the method itself nullifies the justifiability of the gathering act. Another criterion is a balance between the benefit to be derived from enticement and the benefit derived from protecting secrets.

The court opinion was based on the premise that information gathering in this case was necessary to serve the important national interest of democratic control over diplomatic negotiations. The national interest to be derived from gathering activity is thought to be important and suggests that the freedom of gathering information should be respected. In balancing relative benefits, the court stated that before one can judge the benefit of protecting secrets to be greater, the damage from the leakage of secrets must be of such a character that it would exert important and irreparable adverse consequences upon the diplomatic negotiations. Moreover, in comparing the relative interests, the court pointed out that to impose a penalty for an act committed as part of information-gathering activity might dampen future information gathering of all reporters. This position represents a more positive understanding of the freedom of information gathering than the earlier rulings. For example, in the *Hakata* case, the court took the position that the disadvantage to be inflicted on the news organizations by the court order to turn over the television films does not lie in the realm of the freedom of reporting itself but is confined to a concern that information gathering for the future might be adversely affected. Thus, in that case the court accorded the freedom of gathering a lower priority.

The remaining issue was the legitimacy of the official's cooperation with the information gathering. The court pointed out that such an act seems to serve the public mission of news organizations. To that extent, the act can receive protection corresponding to the protection accorded to the freedom of gathering. On the other hand, the public employee's obligation to protect secrets is a duty to the people and its violation at times could damage important interests of the people as a whole. In order for the act of leaking secrets to be considered lawful, it must be done with a positive intent to promote public interests by serving the public mission of news organizations. Leaking secret data in order to win goodwill and to court the favor of a reporter or to promote private interests such as publicity would not constitute a justifiable act. This criterion might facilitate the cooperation of officials toward information gathering and is significant in view of the freedom of reporting and the public's right to know. Apart from the legitimate end, in deciding justifiability, the court took into account the appropriateness of methods and the superior interest of news gathering over the necessity of protecting a secret.

The court ruling acknowledged that Nishiyama's behavior, which took advantage of sexual intimacies with a female employee, constituted enticement as specified in Article III of the Public Employee Law even though there was no persistence or coercion involved. However, when the three criteria are applied, the act of enticement lacks illegality. To use his sexual relations with an informant deviates from the right path of a reporter and cannot avoid social disapproval; it is certainly indecorous. Yet one cannot conclude that Nishiyama's act lacked justifiability on that account alone. When other factors were taken into account, the act was still tinged with justifiability. One can understand a reporter's enthusiasm in seeking more accurate information when easy news-gathering activity cannot ascertain the truth in cases in which secrets are tightly guarded.

Aside from the ethical question regarding the method of information gathering, there was a question of the failure to protect news sources, which is the highest moral norm of journalism. Another aspect of the case was that the reporter transmitted the material in question to a member of the opposition party to have it aired at the National Diet, even though a portion of it was used in Nishiyama's own reporting.

On January 31, 1974, the Tokyo District Court sentenced the female employee to six months of imprisonment with a one-year suspended sentence; it acquitted Nishiyama. The woman chose not to appeal, but the Procurator's Office, dissatisifed with the verdict on Nishiyama, appealed to a higher court. The Tokyo Higher Court announced its ruling on July 20, squashing the decision of the District Court. Nishiyama was sentenced to four months' imprisonment with a one-year suspended sentence.

In the decision the Tokyo Higher Court, citing the Supreme Court decision of 1969, stated that the freedom of gathering in the sense that the state is not allowed to impose unlimited restraint on news-gathering activity belongs to the category of freedom protected by Article 21 of the Constitution. As compared with the decision of the District Court, this phraseology seems to place the freedom of gathering more positively within Article 21 than previously evidenced. This is the first time that the court stated so clearly that the freedom is within the scope of the constitutional guarantee. This language, however, is qualified by the statement that the freedom of gathering remains a passive freedom, and that it does not impose an obligation on public employees who are the targets of news gathering to respond to news-gathering activity.[30] Article III of the Public Employees Law is interpreted as excluding the proper news-gathering activity from the scope of the application of the laws, i.e., news-gathering activities within the proper scope are allowed. The act of enticement specified in Article III refers to the act of suggestion, accompanied by any means that make it impossible for a public official to make a free determination of will as to whether to leak secrets, or to an act of suggestion undertaken by a reporter to obtain a secret. The reporter, in turn, is aware that because of the influence he has exerted, the public official is not in a state to make free determination of will whether or not to leak a secret. Enticement is an act which takes advantage of such a state.[31]

30. *Jurisuto*, Sept. 15, 1976, pp. 33-37.
31. *Asahi Shimbun*, July 20, 1976.

The court decision made the distinction between a "true" secret and a "false" secret. The decision provided a criterion for judging a secret which is worthy of protection, backed up by criminal penalty. A true secret is information classified as secret the leakage of which would be judged detrimental to the interests of the state. False secrets refer to information classified as secret, not for state interest, but to conceal a particular piece of information for the political interests of the government at the time. Regardless of whether the secret in question is true or false, if an act of suggestion occurs with the means and under the circumstances described earlier, the criterion of enticement is met. However, if the secret in question is judged to be false subjectively by the reporter, and it can also be objectively conceded that there was sufficient reason for believing so, then the act of suggestion which otherwise constitutes enticement may be judged not to fall within the criterion defined by Article II and paragraph 12 of Article 109. In the opinion of the court, the act of Nishiyama constituted enticement. The three telegrams concerned were classified secret. But the act of enticement with regard to two of the telegrams did not constitute a crime as there was sufficient reason for believing the presence of false secrets.

The decision faulted Nishiyama for having attempted to obtain information without adequate recognition as to which kind of secret was involved. Practicing journalists are, however, dubious about the distinction between false and true secrets. They argue that it is impossible to distinguish the two as the reporters go about gathering information. News gathering in actual practice begins with the question "What is happening" before making a judgment as to whether it is secret, and whether it is a false or a true secret. A reporter faced with covering negotiations between the United States and Japan for the reversion of Okinawa would naturally be interested in what is happening. Their view is that the court's argument is incoherent and is putting the cart before the horse.

Naito, a veteran reporter, has argued that the reporters do not think, prior to newsgathering, about what kind of secrets are involved or what methods may be legally employed. Moreover, the reporters are interested in exposing any secrets and do not think that there should be any limit to what they can pursue and expose. Hence, it is not realistic to say that one can or cannot commit enticement depending on the types of secrets. The reporters try to gather information using all conceivable means and get at whatever secrets may be involved. So far as his daily gathering activities go, Naito says, what he is doing may be labeled as a kind of enticement or fraud. For news gathering, enticement is indispensable.[32]

The Japanese Supreme Court on June 2, 1978, upheld the decision of the Tokyo High Court, thus reaffirming the position it took in the *Hakata* case. Acts may assume at times the character of enticement or instigation, but they do not at once become illegal just because enticement was made for disclosing a secret. As long as the ways and means of news gathering can be approved in terms of social ideas, viewed from the spirit of the whole legal order, such an act of news gathering is devoid of illegality and constitutes a legitimate act.[33]

The Supreme Court offered the following criterion for judging the question of legality of news-gathering activity. An act would be illegal if the ways and means of news gathering constitute an infraction of general criminal law such as bribe, blackmail, and extortion. Even if no such infraction of laws occurs, if the act cannot be recognized as being consistent with social ideas from the standpoint of the spirit of the entire legal order—such as when the dignity of the target's (news source) personality is violated—then such an act is deemed to have deviated form the legitimate scope of news gathering and assumes the character of illegality.

With regard to Nishiyama's behavior, the court stated that the defendant had sexual relations with the target with the intent to use them as a means to obtain secret documents. Taking advantage of the target's psychological state in which she found it difficult to refuse the defendant's request, Nishiyama caused the secret documents to be taken out. Subsequently, he dissolved the relations and did not take notice of her any longer. This considerably violated the dignity of the target's personality. The act cannot escape illegality.

As for the freedom of reporting and news gathering, the court said that newspaper reports on national government policies provide the people in a democratic society with ma-

32. *Jurisuto*, Sept. 15, 1976, pp. 20, 30-32.
33. *Asahi Shimbun*, June 2, 1978.

terials necessary to make important judgments, thus serving the people's right to know. The freedom of reporting is an especially important element in the freedom of expression, protected by Article 21 of the Constitution. For such reporting to have accurate contents, the freedom of gathering for the purpose of reporting is worthy of due respect in the light of the spirit of Article 21.

Some critics expressed a view that the court decision ignored the actual problems attending news gathering and carried a risk of restricting the scope of freedom of reporting and news gathering. A critic also charged that what constitutes an infringement of the person's personality is not made clear.

CHAPTER VIII

Foreign Constraints:
Japanese Reporting
on China

This chapter is concerned with the various pressures, emanating primarily from external sources, that significantly shape the gathering and processing of news. Because of the newspapers exceptional sensitivity to external sources these pressures may become operative even when they are not overt. The impact of such pressures may be manifested in several forms of self-censorship. They range from acts of omission of otherwise newsworthy facts to avoidance of any critical comments accompanying factual reporting, and to acts of commission such as positive support for pressure-generating groups and individuals.

The sources of the pressures operating on the newspapermen may be divided into two categories: (1) the pressures generated from without, i.e., from foreign governments, and (2) the pressures generated from within, i.e., the political parties, the interest groups, and individual politicians and bureaucrats.

This chapter examines several cases of alleged partial and unfair reporting by a major newspaper with a view toward understanding the nature of constraint arising from external pressure and the manner and degree of its impact on news gathering and reporting. For the purpose of this discussion, the *Asahi* reporting on the China question and the Vietnam War receives primary attention. The *Asahi* is given the primary focus, not just because of the high prestige it enjoys, but also because it is widely thought to be the most partial and unfair politically of all the national dailies. The issues of China and Vietnam were chosen because they were identified by the critics of the Japanese newspapers as the ones where the *Asahi*'s partiality and unfairness were manifested most conspicuously.

The examples of varying degrees of self-censorship abound. A Japanese university student, Araki Mihoko, leaped to her death from the roof of a five-story hotel in Sian on August 25, 1971. Miss Araki was visiting the People's Republic of China (PRC) as a member of the China Visiting Group of the China-Japanese Student Friendship Association. None of the major Japanese newspapers reported the incident. Japanese newspapers would normally carry news about a Japanese committing suicide abroad and pursue the circumstances surrounding the case. Peking showed the family of the deceased special courtesies. On September 1 the father was in Sian, and he was invited to Peking to meet with Premier Chou and other officials. A year later both parents were in Peking to be received again by Chou and other officials.

These activities were fully reported in the Chinese *People's Daily*, yet Japanese correspondents failed to report the incident. Thus, Professor Eto Shinkichi wondered whether the failure to report the indicent was due to simple negligence or to a fear that once this incident was reported, the somewhat mysterious circumstances surrounding the incident would have to be more deeply probed, which might have been contrary to Peking's wishes. Or was there a Chinese suggestion, continued Eto, that the papers should be considerate of the feelings of the parents who had lost a daughter. If so, the Japanese reporters, who normally force their interviews in ruthless disregard of a person's feelings, had become compassionate at the mere utterance of one word by the Chinese.[1]

The *Mainichi* has been alone in expressing its view publicly on the issue of the disputed island of Senkaku. Immediately following the New China Agency report of December 4, 1970, that Senkaku belonged to the PRC, the *Mainichi* asserted in an editorial of December 5 that Senkaku constituted a part of Okinawa. In an April 14 editorial, the *Mainichi* stated that there was no room for argument over the appropriateness of the return of Senkaku to Japan. The United States Department of State announced on April 9 that the administrative rights over Okinawa, including Senkaku, would be turned over to Japan. This announcement drew protests from Peking and Taipei on

1. Miyoshi Osamu and Eto Shinkichi, *Chugoku Hodo no Henko o tsuku* (Tokyo: Nisshin Hodo, 1972), pp. 207-8.

April 10. Whenever Peking asserted its claim over Senkaku, the *Asahi* reported it promptly without indicating its own position. For example, the *Asahi* duly reported the New China News Agency (NCNA) story on Senkaku on April 11. It gave detailed coverage to the article in the *People's Daily* of May 1 which asserted that China would not tolerate a violation of its territorial sovereignty. Japan reportedly planned to expand its Air Defense Identification Zone to include Senkaku upon the reversion of Okinawa to Japan. On June 27 the *People's Daily* denounced the plan as a grave provocation. Again, the *Asahi* promptly reported this to its readers. To a critic like Eto, all this signifies that the *Asahi* plays the role of a faithful spokesman for Peking.[2]

Noting the failure of the *Asahi* to state its views in its editorials, Eto speculated that the *Asahi* must be hesitant about publishing an editorial that runs counter to the reports of its own Peking correspondents. It was not until after an issue of *Bungei Shunju* carrying Eto's criticism appeared on the newsstands and the *Mainichi* and *Yomiuri* published their respective views on March 9 and 10 that the *Asahi* was willing to pronounce its views. Finally, the *Asahi* declared in its editorial of March 20 that Senkaku belonged to Japan.[3]

Another instance in which the *Asahi* maintained virtual silence for a long time involved the so-called Hang Zhou incident. In 1975 a massive riot occurred in Hang Zhou in which about 200,000 workers, in open defiance of the Peking government, occupied factories and fought with troops for several months. On May 19 the *Asahi* introduced a brief Agence France Presse (AFP) report on the political struggle in Hang Zhou. It is significant that no stories by its own correspondent, nor any editorials or commentaries, appeared in the *Asahi*. No other reports appeared from May through July. On August 11 the *Asahi* carried an AFP dispatch reporting the introduction of more than 10,000 Chinese troops into factories for the purpose of increasing production. On August 13 the *Asahi* correspondent in Hong Kong filed a story reporting on strikes underway in China where workers were demanding better treatment and campaigning against the material incentive policy for increased

2. Ibid., pp. 205-6.
3. Ibid., pp. 227-28.

productivity. He also reported the resultant intensification of struggle and work stoppage at factories and the introduction of the People's Liberation Army (PLA) including the air force.[4]

Having examined the *Asahi*'s coverage of the incident, Professor Saga Jun'ichi concluded that the strikes would have received far greater attention if they had occurred in the United States, Western Europe, or South Korea. By his counting, however, the *Asahi*, in the Hang Zhou case, carried only three articles up to that point: an AFP report (28 lines on page 7), a Reuter report (28 lines on page 4), and the Hong Kong correspondent's report (60 lines on page 4).

The *Asahi* carried related stories filed by UPI and Tass on August 15 and August 21. It was not until August 23, 1975, that an editorial appeared in *Asahi* (130 lines on page 7). Yet, it is significant that the editorial was preceded by the NCNA report on August 14 which officially confirmed the incident. After that editorial, no commentaries appeared, although the NCNA introduced an AFP report on September 11. Professor Saga found it incomprehensible that the *Asahi*'s own correspondent ignored the Hang Zhou incident so completely. Upon his review of the stories by the *Asahi* correspondent for the period January through December, he found not a single article which dealt with this problem directly.[5] This demonstrated a self-censorship that involved deliberate omission of materials, disallowing the publication of news or commentaries critical of Peking's interest.

Perhaps the most glaring example of "biased" reporting on China involved the Lin Piao affair. When the news about the downfall of Lin Piao, Mao's designated successor, reached Tokyo, it was through AFP reports. Japanese correspondents in Peking (representing four companies, *Asahi*, *Nihon Keizai*, *Nishi Nippon*, and Kyodo Press Agency) either remained silent or attempted to deny the foreign speculation about Lin's political demise or the implications that foreign observers had drawn from the cancellation of the national day parade. Later on, when the evidence became overwhelming, a Japanese correspondent was reported to have told his Tokyo office that

4. Saga Jun'ichi, *Asahi no "Kiji" wa dokomade shinjirareruka* (Tokyo: Nisshin Hodo, 1978), pp. 145-64.

5. Ibid., pp. 165-70.

there was no doubt about the downfall of the Lin Piao and that the Tokyo office should feel free henceforth to use AFP dispatches datelined Peking without hesitation.[6]

The question is this: if Lin Piao's demise was believed to be true, why did the Japanese correspondents not attempt to write about it themselves, ascertaining the circumstances which led to such an momentous event by seeking corroborative facts? Evidently, Japanese correspondents in Peking consciously refrained from making commentaries on the matter sensitive to the Chinese so that they would not be expelled from Peking. A journalist cherishing freedom and independence of the press, Hayashi Takeski, a commentator, condemned this behavior as being "cowardly, despicable toadyism."[7]

The following is a brief review of the *Asahi* coverage of the Lin Piao affair.[8] On September 22, 1971, the *Asahi* published a Peking-datelined AFP report in which mention was made of a possible cancellation of the annual parade originally scheduled for October 1 at Tien An Men Square. The report also cited an opinion that a major political event might occur in Peking soon. The cancellation of the parade was confirmed by the Chinese authorities on twenty-second and the *Asahi* carried a Reuter report to that effect on September 23.

In the September 22 issues of the *Asahi* another AFP dispatch appeared noting the disappearance of Mao's portraits and books from public places beginning earlier that summer. On the same day a story filed by the *Asahi*'s Paris correspondent stated that the previous day the French National Broadcasting system treated as the top news of the day a report that Mao was possibly dead or in critical condition. A *New York Times* report printed in the *Asahi* of September 23 noted a considerable amount of abnormal movement of the PLA. It further mentioned Western intelligence reports that flights of all military aircraft and almost all civilian aircraft had been halted since September 12.

6. Miyoshi Osamu et al., *Shimbun Bokoku Ron* (Tokyo: Jiyusha, 1972), pp. 274-75.

7. Ibid.

8. Muranaka Kajiro, *Asahi Shimbun no Henko o kataru* (Tokyo: Keiei Mondai Kenkyujo, 1975), pp. 314-26.

It is of interest to note what the *Asahi* correspondent himself wrote during those days. The *Asahi* carried, on September 23, a telephone conversation between its Peking correspondent and his Washington counterpart. The Peking correspondent stated that it would be too much of a logical jump to infer Mao's death and the ongoing power struggle from the cancellation of the parade rehearsals. He added, "Peking's appearance is calm."

The *Asahi* story filed by its Peking correspondent on September 27 said that Peking's general state was "totally serene," a viewpoint contrary to the belief current in certain other countries that Chinese affairs were in an abnormal state. The report went on to say that it would be a mistake to interpret the possible forthcoming major announcement as indicating some unusual developments. Rather, it should be taken as evidence that the political program announced by the joint editorial of the *People's Daily*, *Hurgch'i*, and the *Liberation Army Daily* was progressing smoothly.

The *Asahi* continued to carry the foreign press agencies' dispatches related to China. The November 10 issue of the *Asahi* contained an AP dispatch datelined Washington which reported that according to a State Department source, Lin Piao was ill either physically or politically. On December 1 the *Asahi* carried a Hanoi dispatch indicating that Hanoi had apparently been notified by Peking that Lin Piao should no longer be considered a prominent member of the Chinese leadership.

Meanwhile, the *Asahi*'s own correspondent was still filing stories that contradicted the speculation of the Western press. In his report published on November 25, he told of seeing a huge color photograph of Mao and Lin standing together at the customs office at Shinchon. On February 4 he cautioned against concluding that there was a change in the ranking of the party leadership on the basis of the evidence cited in the foreign press. He pointed out that the *People's Daily* had yet to show any indications of the development of a major intraparty dispute, that there still stood in Peking a huge tower with an inscription "united under the leadership of the party control with Mao as head and Lin as deputy," that a celebrated phrase of Lin Piao was still found on the bulletin board on a main street in

Peking, and that Lin Piao's political reports adopted by the Ninth Party Plenum were still available for sale at a hotel frequented by the Japanese. However, as to "why Lin Piao is not seen," he added, "this certainly is a riddle."

The July 29, 1972, AFP dispatch published by the *Asahi* cleared up the mystery when it disclosed that Chinese officials confirmed that Lin Piao had died the September before while escaping to the Soviet Union after his unsuccessful attempt to assassinate Mao. His plane crashed in Mongolia en route to the Soviet Union. In the same issue of the *Asahi*, a dispatch by an *Asahi* correspondent stated: "We have now reached the stage where the so-called Lin Piao affair can be confirmed. . . . Lin's demise is confirmed at long last." The critics charge that the *Asahi*'s reporting of the China problem went beyond deliberate omission. Its coverage was low-key, hesitant, and excessively cautious in reporting the unfavorable events that were happening. They contend the *Asahi* had not only misrepresented and often manipulated public opinion, but had even actively advocated specific policies on behalf of the PRC.

Yano Ken'ichiro, a journalist with over thirty years of experience, has contended that the Japanese mass media was subservient toward the PRC in relation to the issue of the Japan-China Aviation Agreement.[9] Before the conclusion of the agreement in 1974, the Japanese press in general asserted that the agreement should and could be reached through greater effort on the part of the Japanese government. Familiar themes in the press were that the delay in reaching the agreement was due primarily to Japan's negligence and that the successful conclusion of the agreement depended primarily on Japan's will. The *Asahi*'s editorial of November 8, 1973, deplored the conflict of opinion with the government and the ruling party that was blocking the liquidation of Japanese-Taiwanese political relations. It asserted that the difficulty in the negotiations for the aviation agreement was due to the inability of the Japanese government to reach a definite decision regarding the Taiwan air route. The ediotiral further contended that a recent visit

9. Yano Ken'ichiro, *Shimbun no Kekkan o tsuku* (Tokyo: Nihon Kyobunsha, 1975), pp. 28-30.

by a large contingent of Liberal Democratic party legislators to Taiwan contributed to Taiwan's inflexibility and that the deadlock in the negotiations was caused by the lack of enthusiasm on the part of the prime minister to form a consensus within the government and the party.

The *Mainichi* editorial of December 31, 1973, suggested that the obstacles to the aviation agreement were the Japan-Taiwan air routes and the pro-Taiwan legislators within the Liberal Democratic party. In the same vein, the *Yomiuri* maintained in its editorial of December 14, 1973, that the deadlock in the negotiations was due to the "high-handed resistance" of the pro-Taiwan faction within the party. It called on the Japanese government to take into account the strong dissatisfaction of the Chinese side and to come to a prompt and definite decision on the problem.

Another frequent theme in the press was the suggestion that the aviation agreement ought to be settled along the lines demanded by China. The *Yomiuri* editorial of December 7, for example, noted that while there was no exchange of flights between the PRC and Japan, Japan Airlines maintained thirty-seven flights to Taiwan each week, and Taiwan had twenty-one to Japan. The editorial went on to say that the Japanese government's position was clearly contrary to reason and that the current treatment of Taiwan's planes deviated from the basic principle of the Japan-China Joint Communiqué.

It did not make sense, the *Mainichi* editorial of December 31 asserted, that the Japanese government should declare understanding and respect for the position that Taiwan was part of China in the joint communiqué while trying to preserve the existing Japan-Taiwan air route. China's strong objection to the name and flag of the Taiwanese airline was not a mere technical argument, continued the editorial. In its December 14 editorial, the *Asahi* argued that the solution of the problem was to make the Japan-China air route a major air route, while treating the Japan-Taiwan route as "local." After reviewing the editorials of several papers on the subject published during the period, Yano expressed his amazement that the principles the newspapers insisted the Japanese government implement were the Chinese principles. In his view, the Japanese press talked only of the Chinese principles, advocating Japan's acceptance of them, while refusing to recognize that Japan too had a position that needed to be safeguarded.

The *Sankei* constituted the only exception. In its January 8 editorial, the *Sankei* reminded the reader that the Japanese government had declared at the time of the normalization with PRC in 1972 that it would maintain economic and cultural interchanges with Taiwan even if diplomatic relations were severed. The paper maintained that to revive this realistic attitude constituted the essense of diplomacy. In short, the attitude of most Japanese newspapers was that all of the Chinese demands were just and that Japan had no basis for making any assertions.

The remarkable extent to which a Japanese newspaper extended its support for the PRC can be seen in the following episode. On June 16, 1972, Prime Minister Sato formally announced his intention to step down from office. In anticipation of this move, the succession struggle had already begun among several aspirants: Miki, Ohira, Tanaka, and Fukuda. On June 7 the *Asahi* carried in its column "Zahyo" a story filed by its correspondent in Peking. The article suggested that a new prime minister of Japan must accept Peking's three principles for normalization and must demonstrate, by concrete action, that its pledge to do so was genuine. Then, the article stressed, the Chinese leadership would, at an appropriate time, agree to a new prime minister's visit to China. The article also suggested that Fukuda's assumption of power would make the normalization of relations with China difficult. Muranaka Kajiro, a critic of the *Asahi*, commented with evident exasperation that it was astonishing for a Japanese journalist to suggest that the selection of a prime minister of Japan be carried out in accordance with the wishes of Peking. To him that was an affront to Japan. He felt that anyone of Japanese heritage would be outraged at this lack of national pride on the part of the *Asahi* reporter.[10]

Having reviewed the newspaper coverage of the period 1970-71, Professor Eto criticized the *Asahi*'s reporting of the Japanese-Chinese normalization issue as displaying the manipulation of public opinion and active advocacy.[11] Throughout 1971, major national dailies gave extensive attention to the

10. Muranaka, pp. 309-12.
11. Miyoshi and Eto, pp. 219-24.

issues of China's representation in the United Nations and the normalization of relations between Japan and China. In that year, every major national paper carried an average of forty-seven editorials, or about four each month, on the subject. Of all the papers, the *Asahi* made the greatest effort in this respect. The *Asahi*'s campaign that year began with the January issue, where two entire pages were allocated for the China question. The specific proposal contained in that issue called for a government-to-government contact, in the interest of restoring diplomatic relations. It also contained a call for the termination of efforts to maintain Taiwan representation at the United Nations. The *Asahi*'s position on the China question was unequivocal: the PRC was the sole lawful government of China; Taiwan was included in part of China's territory; and the resolution of the Taiwan question was an internal problem.

Eto pointed out that the poll conducted by the *Asahi* on June 23, 1970, taken about a half year before the *Asahi* proposal, had established that only 19 percent of the respondents agreed with the statement that "in order to establish diplomatic relations, it cannot be helped if the ties with Taiwan are severed." Forty-six percent opposed it. The *Asahi* then apparently decided to "educate" the public. After conducting a press campaign for five months following the January 1971 proposal, the *Asahi* took another opinion poll in which a similar question was asked: "In order to restore diplomatic relations with China, it it necessary to accept the position of 'one China.'" That is to say, the government of the PRC in Peking represents China and Taiwan is part of the Chinese territory. Thirty-three percent of the respondents agreed with the statement while 22 percent disagreed. The *Asahi* thereupon asserted in its editorial of June 23 that while the great majority of the people wanted the restoration of diplomatic relations with China, the government and the ruling party were holding stubbornly to the policy of "one China and one Taiwan." Other newspapers conducted similar surveys about the same time. In all, the proportion of those desiring the establishment of diplomatic relations with China was a majority. However, there was a considerable difference between the *Asahi* poll and the other polls with regard to the proportion of those who accepted the position that Taiwan was part of the PRC and that Japanese ties with it should be severed. Those who desired diplomatic relations with China were asked a follow-up question on what Japan's relations with Taiwan should be. The responses to this question were:

1. Sever relations with Taiwan   9%
2. Maintain relations with Taiwan   68%
3. Others; no answer   6%

The *Yomiuri* polls of June 14, 1971, yielded the following distributions:

1. Peking government represents China.   19.1%
2. Taiwan government represents China.   3.7%
3. Each is an independent government.   40.5%
4. Others   1.3%
5. No answer   35.5%

The results of the *Sankei* poll of July 21, 1971, were

1. Sever relations with Taiwan and immediately establish diplomatic relations with China with relations with Taiwan of secondary importance   10.7%
2. Gradually build up friendly relations with China   19.9%
3. Proceed cautiously to promote friendly relations with China so as not to jeopardize relations with Taiwan 46.7%
4. Wait and see, for the time being   19.1%
5. Others   1.1%
6. Don't know   2.3%

The questions asked by the different newspapers were not exactly comparable. Yet, a gap between the *Asahi* poll and the others is conspicuous. The *Asahi* data alone indicates the relative preponderance of the one-China view, i.e., 33 percent vs. 65.8 percent in the *Sankei* poll. At the least, the *Asahi*'s assertion that the government and the ruling party were alone in stubbornly adhering to one-China and one-Taiwan was inaccurate. Furthermore, the *Mainichi* survey indicated that those who wished to maintain relations with Taiwan were not confined to Liberal Democratic party supporters. Those who wished to maintain Japan's relations with Taiwan constituted a distinct majority from each of the opposition parties.

Until September 1971 the *Mainichi*'s position had been one of recognizing reality. In its editorial of June 14, the *Mainichi* pointed out that Peking governed the mainland but did not rule Taiwan; Nationalist China ruled Taiwan but did not govern the mainland; this was the reality, and a foreign policy must be formulated on the basis of reality. In its editorial of November 11, the *Mainichi* called upon both the governing and opposition parties to adopt the plan for restoring diplomatic relations between Japan and China "out of respect for the will of the people." The *Mainichi* had conducted a poll from September 30 through October 3 which included a question on normalization of relations with China. However, no question was asked about the attitude toward Taiwan. Eto suggested that the *Mainichi* did not wish to see a contradictory result since the editorial position had by then changed to recognize the PRC. Eto lauded the *Yomiuri* for its honesty and definitiveness. *Yomiuri*, in its editorial of March 3, 1971, stated that the poll showed a majority desiring normalization, but that quite a few of those people desired the continuation of diplomatic relations with Taiwan. "Nevertheless," the editorial continued, "relations with Taiwan must be severed."

One of the factors that had significantly shaped the conduct of the Japanese reporters in Peking and at home was the understanding embodied in the so-called three political principles and the Memorandum Trade Communiqué.The first formal agreement regarding the exchange of reporters between China and Japan was adopted in 1964. Before that year, there had been sporadic visits of reporters on an ad hoc basis. Under the agreement as revised in August of that year, the first contingent of nine correspondents arrived in China in September. (This number does not include reporters who visited China for a short-term stay.) The agreement had been negotiated by the representatives of the Liao-Takasaki (L-T) trade offices. For three years the exchange under this 1964 agreement was carried out without much difficulty.[12]

Beginning in 1967 the status of Japanese correspondents in Peking became vulnerable. On September 10, 1967, three Japanese reporters (*Mainichi, Sankei,* and *Nishi Nippon*) were suddenly deprived of their correspondent status and were immediately ordered to leave China. The Chinese official concerned declared that the three newspapers defamed China's Cultural Revolution by carrying an inappropriate cartoon and

12. Ibid., pp. 97-115.

news article despite the strong warning given earlier by Chinese authorities. It was absolutely impermissible, the Chinese continued, for the papers to defame "the leader of the peoples of the entire world, the red sun, the most beloved Chairman Mao." No replacements for the three correspondents were allowed.

On October 12, 1967, the *Yomiuri* correspondent in Peking was expelled on the charge that "the *Yomiuri* conducted vicious anti-China activity in Tokyo by holding an exhibition of Tibetan Treasures." In the meantime, China refused to accept a replacement for a Nihon Television (NTV) correspondent whose stay in Peking had ended abruptly on September 5. This case seemed to have been related to the *Yomiuri* exhibition. A more dramatic event was yet to unfold. On June 5, 1968, Samejima Keiji, a *Nihon Keizai* correspondent, was arrested and confined for approximately a year and a half. When he was released on December 20, 1969, NCNA reported that Samejima had conducted espionage activities for a long time. The report contended that he had stolen a great deal of information concerning China's political, military, and economic secrets and had offered it to United States and Japanese reactionaries. It went on to say that Samejima had admitted his guilt, and that the Chinese authorities had decided to expel him "out of generosity."[13]

In November 1968 an NHK correspondent, Shiojima Toshio, returned home upon the expiration of his initial period of stay in Peking. His application for reentry was denied because of the NHK's news-gathering activity in China and its reporting on Taiwan. After eight months of waiting, he was allowed reentry in August 1969. After he returned home in September 1970, he was again refused reentry. This was apparently because of the NHK membership in the Asian Broadcasters Union, of which Taiwan was also a member.

On September 19, 1970, Nakajima Hiroshi, a correspondent for Kyodo Press, was expelled on the grounds that Kyodo had sponsored, in Tokyo, the Third General Assembly meeting of the Organization of Asian News Agencies. Taiwan was a member of this organization. The *Asahi* was not the only Japanese press represented in Peking. After a lapse of a few months, *Nihon Keizai* and *Nishi Nippon* were allowed to send reporters

13. Ibid., pp. 116-18.

back to Peking. In January 1972 a Kyodo correspondent was granted permission to return to Peking.[14]

When the three correspondents were expelled in 1967, the *Mainichi* alone ran an editorial (September 20, 1967) expressing its regrets about the expulsion, from the standpoint of desiring a free press. The *Mainichi* and the *Sankei* subsequently allowed contributions from their expelled reporters to a series of articles about China for their respective papers. The news of the expulsion prompted a series of meetings among the nine newspapers that had had correspondents in Peking. A conflict of interests developed between the three papers whose correspondents had been expelled and the others whose correspondents remained in Peking. At one point the *Sankei* and the Kyodo supported a proposal that a protest be lodged, or at least a unilateral statement ought to be issued, about the expulsion. The *Sankei* is supposed to have expressed a view that a unilateral deprivation of the freedom of reporting is a matter of concern to all newspapers in Japan. On the other hand, the *Asahi* and Kyodo advocated a cautious approach. The *Asahi* took the position that even if one could not send a dispatch from Peking, for the sake of posterity a correspondent should be placed in Peking to bear witness to the unfolding of history. The *Asahi* said it must withdraw itself if other newspapers insisted upon the issue of a joint statement. It was decided at the final meeting that the six remaining companies would cooperate in providing the three companies with news. As a provisional measure, the Kyodo agreed to distribute its news from Peking to the three papers.[15]

The expulsion of the three reporters in the fall of 1967 indicated the application of a political rule. According to Miyoshi Osamu, in the understanding reached in 1964, known as the Trade Conference Memorandum, there was not included an explicit provision regulating the political stance of newspapers toward China. On the other hand, the same officials of the *Asahi* and *Nihon Keizai* maintained that an informal understanding had been operative since 1964. It is not clear whether the understanding was ever documented. Samuel Jamieson has formally reported the existence of a written document.[16]

14. Ibid., p. 120.   16. Ibid., pp. 124, 132-73.
15. Ibid., pp. 146, 121-24.

In 1968 the agreement of 1964 was dissolved together with the L-T trade. In that year, the so-called Memorandum Trade was instituted. The activities of Japanese correspondents in Peking were expected to be consistent with the purpose of the Joint Communiqué on Memorandum Trade (March 1968) and with China's three political principles. Unless a newspaper signed a pledge to abide by the three principles and the spirit of the communiqué, it was not permitted to send a correspondent to China. This political restraint was to be applied not only to a correspondent's activities in Peking and the content of his dispatches but also to the fundamental attitude the newspaper took toward the PRC.

Miyoshi's inquiry established that Japanese newspapers had accepted a political condition imposed by the PRC government in order to maintain a correspondent in Peking. Thus, Japanese journalists were forced to practice self-restraint in the process of editing and writing on the China issue. This, Miyoshi contended, led to distortion in reporting and commentary.[17]

It should be noted that the arrest of Samejima of *Nihon Keizai* and the denial of a reentry visa to Shiojima of NHK occurred after the institution of the Memorandum Trade. The Shiojima case was the result of Peking's displeasure toward NHK's news gathering in Taiwan and its subsequent showing of a film with a poster emblazoned with "Return to the Mainland" depicted on the wall. An *Asahi* reporter's return to China was delayed, at the same time, because the Chinese perceived that the *Asahi*'s coverage of a particular NHK program constituted "an act of praising" Chiang Kai-shek and Taiwan. The *Asahi* was reported to have written a note of apology promptly which was satisfactory to the PRC, and obtained permission to send its reporter back to China. The NHK's reluctant and delayed response in expressing its regret caused a further delay in its obtaining entry permission from China. The *Yomiuri* is also reported to have written a letter of apology to China regarding the exhibition of Tibetan Treasurer.[18]

Whether or not a political regulation was in existence came to question when the Chinese authorities delivered a written note

17. Ibid., p. 40.
18. Ibid., p. 124.

to Kyodo at the time Nakajima was expelled. The note stated that the Kyodo sponsored the Third General Assembly meeting of the Organization of Asian News Agencies. The political objective of this conference, according to the note, was to create two Chinas, to facilitate actively the new Asian policy of American imperialism, and to implement the expansionist policy of Japanese militarism. The Kyodo was accused of having opened the way, with United States support, for the establishment of a new Asian counterrevolutionary military alliance, with Japan as the leader. Most importantly, the note went on to state that such actions constituted a gross violation of the three political principles and the principle of the Memorandum Trade Joint Communiqué which both parties had to observe without fail in their exchange of reporters.[19]

In the Memorandum Trade Joint Communiqué of March 6, 1968, China made the following point: the obstacles that had existed in China-Japan relations had been brought about by the anti-China policy pursued by American imperialists and Japanese authorities. A Japanese aide expressed a deep understanding for the Chinese position and declared that the newspapers would further exert themselves to remove such obstacles and promote normalization of Japan-China relations. Both sides were to observe the three political principles and the principle of nonseparation of politics and economics in Japan-China relations. They agreed that they would continue to make efforts to lay the political foundation for these principles to be upheld.[20]

The three political principles called for (1) an end to the policy of hostility toward China, (2) a pledge not to participate in the plot to create two Chinas, and (3) an agreement not to obstruct normalization of relations between the two countries.

These principles may appear innocuous at first glance, but when applied to press activities, they constituted severe restraints. The application entailed, at least as interpreted by the Chinese side, the adherence of the Japanese press to the following guidelines: no news-gathering activity in Taiwan as well as the suppression of news about Taiwan, withdrawal from all

19. Ibid., p. 126.
20. Ibid., pp. 135-36.

international organizations of which Taiwan was a member, and acceptance of the principle of the abrogation of the Japanese-Republic of China Treaty.

The three principles were interpreted to mean that the newspapers had to refrain from expressing any disapproval or opposition, however implicit, to the policies and activities China was pursuing. Since there was no consistency in the content of the three political principles, the newspapers were forced to adjust their editorial policies as China's policies changed.[21] This led to self-censorship in anticipating the Chinese intention. The application of the principles occasionally led to the glorification and mystification of China. News about Taiwan was excluded from the newspapers while the events and culture of mainland China were glorified.

Miyoshi's findings, originally published in the April 1972 issue of the *Keizai Orai*, were challenged by Tagawa Seiichi, a Liberal Democratic party member of the Diet who participated in the 1968 negotiation on memorandum trade. Tagawa's rebuttal to the Miyoshi report, containing the remarks he made to a *Los Angeles Times* reporter, and Miyoshi's rejoinder establish a few points of fundamental importance. The exchange of reporters between Japan and China was indeed regulated by China's three political principles. Tagawa unequivocally stated that when he had negotiated with China on the exchange of reporters in March 1968 the Japanese side simply confirmed that they would observe the principle of the Joint Communiqué on Memorandum Trade. In his interview with a *Los Angeles Times* reporter, Tagawa acknowledged that the political principles were supposed to govern completely the editorial policy, with regard to news commentaries and editorials, of the newspapers that maintained correspondents in Peking. The then foreign news editor of the *Asahi*, Kawamura Kinji, and the managing editor of the *Nihon Keizai*, Arai Akira, concurred with Tagawa's view that the political principles had been implicitly accepted by the Japanese newspapers since 1964, although there had been no written agreement to that effect. They stated that their acceptance of the political principles had not posed a problem to their newspapers, because they had already indicated in their editorials their agreement with

21. Ibid., pp. 136-37.

the principles. Miyoshi pointed out in this connection that it was one thing for an editorial to voice its support for the political principles of a foreign government yet it was quite another matter to accept the political principles as a basic principle governing editing, allowing it to impose self-restraint on news and to destroy objectivity, fairness, and balance in reporting. Kawamura told Jamieson that the vigorous news-gathering activities of Japanese reporters which had won international acclaim came to an end when the Chinese authorities warned the Japanese correspondents to stop anti-China activity. Both Kawamura and Arai conceded that their correspondents had avoided sending any dispatches that might contravene the three political principles.[22]

A primary motive for this self-censorship on the part of newspapers was to obtain an entry permit for their correspondents. A *Los Angeles Times* editorial pointed out that intense competition among Japanese newspapers and the traditional Japanese emphasis on formality accounted for the acceptance of China's terms. It meant a great deal for a newspaper to be able to carry a story, filed by its own correspondent, datelined Peking. The struggle to station a resident correspondent in Peking apparently outweighed the concern for substance in reports coming from Peking, the ethical aspect of the problem, the sense of public service, and freedom of the press.[23]

22. Ibid., pp. 150-70, 233-52.
23. Ibid., p. 253.

CHAPTER IX

Domestic Constraints: The Government and the Ruling Party

This chapter begins with a discussion of the various ways and channels the government employs to influence news gathering and reporting. Following this discussion there is a brief review of selected cases of government-press relations. The final section deals with the influence of interest groups on newspaper making. The question of how individual politicians as factional leaders influence the reporters will be examined in the succeeding chapter.

Influence Attempts by Government and Party Leaders

Periodic contacts between the government and the ruling party leaders with the representatives of the mass media constitute an important channel through which government influences can be brought to bear upon the mass media.[1] The prime minister maintains personal ties, frequently dining and conferring with newspaper presidents, managing editors, and editorial writers. During the course of such contacts, the prime minister seeks the understanding and cooperation of media representatives toward major policy concerns of the government.

A more institutionalized contact takes the form of media representation in various government commissions and deliberative councils. Editorial writers usually represent the media. Sometimes, presidents or vice-presidents of newspapers participate in such councils. Mass media representation gives a sem-

---

1. Nihon Janarisuto Kaigi, ed., *Masukomi Kokusho* (Tokyo: Rodo Jumposha, 1968), p. 97.

blance of fairness of policy output, ensuring a degree of media support. After leaving the post of chief editorial writer of the *Asahi*, Ryu Shintaro made a rather telling remark: If a newsman participates in government commissions indiscriminately or excessively, he runs the risk of losing the critical attitude needed for obtaining information, and in the end, it may be impossible to distinguish him from a government employee.[2]

The government affects mass media by providing them with preferential treatment in the area of business management. The newspapers and private television networks are exempted from regular corporation taxes. Sales and advertising agents for the newspapers enjoy the same privilege. Special postage rates and railroad fares are made available to the newspapers. For the construction of their office buildings, major newspapers, such as the *Mainichi* and *Yomiuri*, received an allotment of state-owned land at moderate prices. These measures may be said to reflect the government's enlightened cultural policy, but they provide the government with leverage vis-à-vis the mass media.[3]

The government influences the newspapers through its provision of facilities for news gathering. First of all, as indicated earlier, each government agency provides a reporters' club room, together with the necessary equipment for use by the members of the club. The reporter there has access to briefings and lectures by government officials and is supplied with written materials prepared by the government.

Second, special favor may be bestowed upon particular reporters. For example, the use of military aircraft may be granted so as to help certain reporters publicize selected information on behalf of the Defense Agency. One is reminded of an old tale of the late 1950s involving the members of a reporters' club attached to the main office of the Japan National Railways. The reporters were occasionally taken on field trips by a special carriage linked to the regular train service. Annual dues paid by each newspaper constituted a fraction of the actual expenses incurred. The National Railways bore the expense for these field trips, food and sake consumed on the train, lodging, and entertainment. As one journalist put it, the reporters then were practicing, in a sense, blackmail and extortion.[4]

2. Ibid., p. 98. 4. Ibid., pp. 100-101.
3. Ibid., p. 99.

Nowadays, the degree of reporters' dependence on conveniences and courtesies provided by a government agency appears to be considerably less than it once was. However, this may be due to the government's provision of press facilities and, especially, briefings and written materials. Such services by the government give it an institutionalized means of exerting influence on press activities.

The government itself is actively involved in the dissemination of information to win the public's support for government policies. For this purpose, the government agencies periodically place advertisements in the newspapers. The Cabinet Research Office of the Office of the Prime Minister regularly monitors the newspapers and magazines. It provides financial support for specific research projects and public relations projects by external research and news organizations. The Office of the Prime Minister provided part of the funding for the establishment of the Japan Information Center in 1967. The center's board members include the major figures of the business and mass media communities. It is designed to conduct effective public relations activities and to obtain the public's trust and support for government policies. For this purpose, in addition to the government's own information activity, the cooperation of government specialists in the news and public relations field is elicited. The center provides television programs, conducts research, prepares materials necessary for public speeches, and edits magazines published by the Section of Information within the Office of the Prime Minister.[5]

The chief responsibility of the Section of Information is to produce public relation programs for the use by television and radio, place ads in dailies and weeklies, and produce various information pamphlets. The budget for Fiscal Year 1972 was in excess of two billion yen. Of this sum, 830 million yen were allocated for placing advertisements in newspapers and magazines. For example, in 1965 advertisements were placed four times during the year in six major papers. Since 1966, other newspapers, so-called bloc newspapers and major local newspapers, were included among the targets. There has also been an increase in the frequency of ads in major national dailies.

5. Ibid., pp. 103-6

Opinion advertisements placed by the Office of the Prime Minister included those which are designed to bolster the government's position on the northern territorial issue and anti-Soviet propaganda and those designed to emphasize the necessity of Japanese-American cooperation. These ads often take the form of conversations or interviews involving cabinet ministers and influential financial figures on the one hand and commentators on the other. The government advertisement fees prove a welcome source of revenues for the newspapers.[6]

The Cabinet Research Office contributes about a billion yen a year to media organizations such as NHK, Kyodo, and Jiji under the label of information and research contract expenses. Other government agencies also have funds for information activities. For example, the Defense Agency's information budget for 1972 was 317 million yen. Emphasis was on the buildup of the Self-Defense Forces' image, recruitment of Self-Defense Forces personnel, and the enhancement of national defense consciousness.[7]

Attempted Government Influence: Case Studies

The government occasionally intervenes, overtly or directly to influence the operations of the mass media. This takes the forms of expression of dissatisfaction, issuance of warnings through phone calls, or direct meetings with media representatives. These may occur after deliberations in committees of the Liberal Democratic party, various government agencies, and, at times, cabinet meetings.[8]

An overt government campaign to mobilize and elicit media support for its program occurred in relation to the Japan-Korea Treaty of 1965.[9] As Diet deliberations on the treaty approached, the ruling Liberal Democratic party allocated 500 million yen for information activities. On September 1, 1965, a conference of national representatives of the party, held for the purpose of conducting a nationwide campaign on the ratification, established the National Council on Promotion of Rat-

6. *Gendai Janarizumu* 2: 154-55.   9. Ibid., pp. 85-86.
7. Ibid., pp. 155-56.
8. Ibid., pp. 102-3.

ification of the Japan-Korea Treaty. On September 8, 1965, ranking officers of the thirteen provincial/local newspapers, including *Hokkaido, Chubu Nippon,* and *Nishi Nippon,* were invited to a luncheon with Prime Minister Sato. On September 14 ranking officers of the major newspapers in Tokyo (*Asahi, Mainichi, Yomiuri, Nihon Keizai, Sankei, Tokyo,* and *Tokyo Times*) along with the leaders of Kyodo, Jiji, and NHK were similarly invited. At these sessions Sato requested the cooperation of media officials in ratifying the treaty.

On October 6 the Broadcasters' Deliberation Council on Politics was formed by pro-Liberal Democratic party media personnel. In attendance at its opening ceremonies were Prime Minister Sato, the chief cabinet secretary, and the minister of postal service. On October 19 the director of information of the party criticized specific television programs as being unfair on the Japan-Korea problem. Subsequently, various television program that tended to favor ratification were aired. Major newspapers had circulated an internal memorandum urging a cautious attitude toward the Japan-Korea Treaty. The party's Committee on Information monitored the television and radio programs in Tokyo, exerting influence on the officers of the television and radio stations.

One day immediately before a vote at the Special Committee on Japan and Korea of the House of Representatives (November 4, 1965), ranking party officers paid visits to major newspapers. Most papers reportedly established an editorial policy under which no opposition would be voiced and little coverage would be given to the demonstrations opposing the treaty. In February 1968, when a controversial statement by Kuraishi led to parliamentary paralysis, Hashimoto, chairman of the party's Board of General Affairs, and other party officials met with editorial writers and ranking editorial members of major newspapers and requested their cooperation. The party reportedly played a role in replacing the managing editor of Kyodo Press Agency, which had scooped the news of Kuraishi's remarks.

The extent of the government's active attempts to influence the mass media can be seen in the case of the revision of the Security Treaty in 1960.[10] Prime Minister Kishi conferred

10. Ibid., pp. 144-47.

frequently with heads of the Political Affairs Departments of various newspapers. Toward the end of 1959 Kishi dined with the leaders of different media firms separately, asking for their cooperation. Kishi scheduled three separate meetings with the *Asahi*'s president, ranking board members, managing editors, and heads of the political, economic, and social affairs departments. At the time these activities seemed to have had a favorable effect on the mass media.

After Kishi's government rammed the treaty through the Diet in an arbitrary manner, and as massive demonstrations surrounding the Diet building occurred, the newspapers began to demand Kishi's resignation and the dissolution of the Diet. This, in turn, made the government and the Liberal Democratic party intensify their efforts to influence the mass media. At the meeting of the Council of Secretary General of the Liberal Democratic prefectural parties, it was decided on May 27 to launch a systematic campaign of protest against the bias of the media. On May 31 several Liberal Democratic dietman personally visited the newspapers, lodging a protest. The June 3 cabinet meeting considered a measure of warning to NHK. On June 7 Kishi again invited the presidents of the major newspapers to his official residence, asking their cooperation. At the same time, United States Ambassador MacArthur invited managing editors of major newspapers to his residence, requesting their support for President Eisenhower's proposed visit to Japan. These efforts led to a media campaign for welcoming President Eisenhower. Two days following the bloody incident of June 15, seven major newspapers issued a celebrated joint declaration urging the return to normalcy. This was subsequently carried by forty-eight papers throughout the country.

Sensitivity of the Liberal Democratic government to the mass media and its desire to tame them are clearly set forth in numerous party documents. For example, a series of study reports prepared by the Research Council on National Security, a party unit, pointed out the crucial importance of taking "countermeasures" toward the mass media. A report entitled *Far Eastern Situation and Our National Security*, dated May 1965, identified as of primary importance the task of acquainting the people with the Far Eastern situation and urged that "great effort be made vis-à-vis mass media." Another report prepared in June 1965, under the same title, dealt with the crucial role of the mass media in enhancing national security. It stated: "It is only through the mass media that a majority of the people learn of the situation in the surrounding areas. This is the only material on the basis of which the people make judgments on politics and diplomacy. Mass media have shown bias. If . . . mass media reports are biased, this would prevent correct judgment on the part of the people, and thus may inflict grave damage to our nation. For this reason, we should demand that the mass media present . . . objective reporting."[11]

Sato and the Press

Government leaders comment frequently in their public speeches on the role of mass media. For example, in his speech before a general meeting of the Japanese Association of Newspapers in June 1969, Prime Minister Sato observed that "the newspapers and broadcasters should go beyond a mere reporting of facts. More than ever before, emphasis should be placed on the pursuit of national interest. For example, whether the issue is one pertaining to national security or education, we will be able to achieve national consensus on the issue if the media make an effort to form fair public opinion." At a luncheon sponsored by Japan Press Club in April 1970, Sato reiterated his criticism of mass media, urging the media to correct their posture: "Last year I put forward a wish at the general meeting of the Japan Newspaper Association. In view of the recent developments, I cannot help but express the same proposal. Lately, mass media seem carried away too much in their appeal to human interests. 'New Politics' is inconceivable without a rational cooperation of mass media." Araki, director of the National Public Safety Commission, expressed blunt criticism when he asserted on January 6, 1971, that the Federation of Newspaper Workers was under the influence of the Communist party. He said that there was something strange, improper, suspicious about the reporters, and it was because of the federation. The position that the government took in the *Nishiyama* case and at the time of the *Asahi*'s inaccurate reporting on the Supreme Court

11. Ibid., pp. 148-49.

decision reveals a great deal about the government's attitude toward the mass media.[12]

A most dramatic incident occurred on June 17, 1972, in which Sato's hostility toward the newspapers was revealed in a stark fashion. The prime minister had just expressed his intention to retire at the general meeting of the Liberal Democratic party Diet members and was scheduled to appear before a press conference.

Sato entered the conference room hoping to speak to the people directly. When he saw the reporters sitting in the front row, he burst out: "Where are the television cameras? You must have a regard for television. I am asking where they are. Please come forward. I want to talk to the people directly. When things appear in the newspaper . . . when printed, things are different. I regret to say this, but I dislike the newspapers which . . . biased newspapers. I dislike them greatly. Therefore, I would like to talk to the people. . . . I have high regard for television. So you reporters, please step aside a bit and let television move into the center." Then he walked out of the room. After a while he returned to the room and began, "Well, since I am weak in science, I have misjudged . . ." he was interrupted by the representative of the reporters' club who delivered the following protest: "The prime minister is distinguishing newspapers from television and criticizing the newspapers while demanding preference be given to television. We cannot tolerate this." Sato countered by saying, "If you feel that way, please get out, I don't care, let's go. Please get out. Please get out. It's all right to get out." Sato was pounding on the table. The press corps walked out of the room en masse. Then, Sato spoke to the television camera for fifteen minutes in the empty conference room.[13]

The reaction of the newspapers was swift. In the evening edition, the newspapers published a joint statement of protest signed by nine media organizations. The joint statement asserted that "Sato's remarks cannot be tolerated, for they constitute an improper and misdirected challenge to the mass media and trample on the Constitution, which recognizes freedom of the

12. Ibid., p. 152.
13. Ibid., pp. 144-45; Kusumoto Mitsuo, *Shimbun no Sugao* (Tokyo: Kobundo, 1976), pp. 117-18.

press. Sato's remark that he wanted to talk to the people directly through television and that one must be of service to television reveals Sato's intention to convert television into his personal possession." Sato was severely denounced by the press for his "abusive" language and for being "out of his head."[14]

Sato's explosion was in a sense a culmination of years of frustration and anger. The newspapers had not been very kind to him. They had frequently been opposed to his policies and had often denounced him as a reactionary figure. Sato had been condemned as being the incarnation of Japanese militarism. (It is ironic that he was to receive the Nobel Peace Prize in November 1974.)

Tanaka and the Press

Few prime ministers received such a positive and high rating by the press than Tanaka. From the outset the newspapers, in general, greeted Tanaka's arrival with enthusiasm and much expectation. The adjectives used by various newspapers to refer to the new prime minister in 1972 included "a man of determination and action," "a computerized bulldozer," and "cheerful and folksy."[15]

On the afternoon of July 5, 1972, when Tanaka was selected president of the Liberal Democrats, he met with the heads of the Political Affairs Departments of the various newspapers in Tokyo and stated: "However wonderful a policy may be, it will be meaningless unless it receives the understanding and support of the people. It is natural to seek the understanding and support of the people. It is natural to seek the understanding of the people through the mass media. I will show respect for the newspapers."

While in office, he kept declaring publicly that "the mass media represent the people and we must be respectful toward them." However, what appears to have been his real attitude toward the press came to light when a weekly magazine, *Shukan Gendai*, exposed startling remarks attributed to Tanaka. On August 20, Tanaka was in the company of nine reporters at

14. Kusumoto, pp. 118-20.
15. Ibid., p. 122; *Gendai Janarizumu* 2: 145.

a restaurant in Karuizawa and talked among other things about his alleged control over newspapers. He offered the following pieces of advice to the reporters.

When you write a brief column (such as "Kishaseki" or "Seikai Memo) I hope you will stop foolish things such as twisting or teasing. Don't write things such as that I am playing golf.

Since I am thoroughly familiar with the internal affairs of newspapers, there is nothing I cannot do. If I wanted, I could do this [gesturing with his hand at his neck] I can suppress or do anything else I want to do.

It is easy to stop a story in the newspaper. I won't telephone the mass media as Sato used to do. It has already been arranged to stop it.

What I fear most is you—front-line reporters. I can easily deal with the president and the department head.

Don't pursue any trivial matters. If you don't cross a dangerous bridge, I will be safe. So will you. If I think a particular reporter is dangerous, I can easily have him removed.[16]

Subsequently, a member of the Communist party pursued Tanaka's remarks in the Diet, which led to newspaper coverage. Tanaka reportedly ordered a deputy cabinet secretary to identify the person who leaked the story and pressed the magazine concerned to reveal the news source.[17]

Tanaka's cabinet lasted two years and four months. It collapsed following the exposé about his corrupt dealings in the magazine *Bungei Shunju*. It is significant that it was a monthly magazine and not a newspaper that exposed Tanaka's apparently shady financial dealings.

Interest Groups as a Constraint

By spring 1946 the American occupation authorities in Japan embarked upon a policy designed to exclude the participation

16. *Gendai Janarizumu* 2: 145-46.
17. Ibid., p. 153.

of the unions and workers in the management and editorial policy making of the newspapers. This policy helped establish in Japan the concept of "editorial right" (*henshūken*), and it became systematized in the "Declaration on Safeguarding Newspapers Editorial Rights" announced by the Japan Newspapers Association on March 16, 1948. This right has been interpreted to mean, in actual practice, that no one but the management is allowed to participate in the process of editing and no criticism is allowed concerning the newspaper's assertions and contents of pages. It provides the management with a leverage to block criticism of editorial policies and tends to favor the employer in the resolution of labor disputes. Except for a brief period in 1950, editorial rights have not been abused, and the declaration has actually functioned to regulate the activities of the newspaper workers. It has been invoked as a norm in relation to the establishment of editorial policies on important social and political problems.[18]

Aside from the legal interpretation of the editorial right regarding specific court cases such as that of *Sanyo Shimbun* of 1963, a new development has occurred in recent years involving the participation of the workers in the editorial process. Several newspapers have had instances of discussion between the employer and labor on editorial policies. These developments do not constitute a formal challenge to the management's editorial right and therefore do not constitute a formal recognition of the right of workers to confer with the management of an equal footing. However, they present a significant departure from the previous status of the workers with respect to editorial policies. In April 1971, following the *Asahi*'s expressed sense of regret to the Supreme Court over its inaccurate reporting, the *Asahi* held a "teach-in" on editorial guidelines between the management and the labor union. Another example is the case of the *Mainichi*, which held a series of discussions between the management and labor union on fundamental guidelines on reporting on China resulting in a change in the *Mainichi*'s editorial position on the China issue in 1971.[19]

18. Inaba Michio and Arai Naonori, *Shimbun Gaku* (Tokyo: Nihon Hyoronsha, 1977), pp. 115-18.
19. Ibid., p. 119.

Despite the supposed right of management in matters of editorial policy, it finds frequently that it cannot compose pages at will. The influence of young reporters exert a strong influence on editorial policy. The management naturally wants to concentrate on managerial problems, trying to avoid difficulties with employees. This often leads management to seek compromises on editorial policy. This is attested to by Hayashi Saburo, a former *Mainichi* deputy chief of editorial writers. He suspects that it is also true of other newspapers. The young reporters to whom he refers are members of the labor union. The labor union of each newspaper belongs to the Federation of Newspaper Workers Unions, which in turn is a member of the Sohyo, the General Council of Labor Unions. The hierarchy of labor unions exerts considerable influence on each newspaper. Hayashi contends that this is perhaps what makes all newspapers look alike so far as the expressions of opinion are concerned.[20] The incoherence of the statement issued by *Mainichi*'s managing editor at the time of the Nishiyama affair was said to be due to last-minute additions and deletions following the labor union's objection to the galley proof of the statement.[21]

It will be recalled that the *Sankei* and *Nikkei* printed an opinion advertisement by the Liberal Democratic party in December 1973. One of the attacks on the ad in the *Akahata*, the Japan Communist party organ, declared that the Federation of Newspaper Workers Union had issued a statement of protest to the two newspapers and that a series of protests by various mass media labor unions and cultural groups were underway. A day after the Tokyo District Court ruled in support of the *Sankei*, upholding the freedom of opinion advertisement, the *Akahata* carried the statements by the chairmen of the labor unions of the *Asahi*, *Mainichi*, and *Yomiuri* supporting the Japan Communist party's position in denunciation of the court ruling. According to the veteran reporter Yano Ken'ichiro, there is an indication that the Communist party pursued a strategy of

20. Hayashi Saburo, *Shimbun to wa Nani ka* (Kyoto: PHP Kenkyujo, 1978), pp. 153-54.
21. Fukuda Tsuneari, *Shimbun no Subete* (Tokyo: Takagi Shobo, 1975), p. 247.

penetration into various newspapers through the Federation of Newspapers Workers Unions in order to influence the tone of arguments in the newspapers. Such a strategy, Yano argues, has exerted considerable psychological pressure on the management, who fear strikes and other harassments. That the Japan Communist party was able to demonstrate the support of the federation in the *Sankei* case was perhaps indicative of the party's influence over the federation.[22]

22. Yano, p. 107.

CHAPTER X

Domestic Constraints:
Factional Political Leaders

This chapter is concerned with the constraints imposed on news gathering and reporting by using politicians as a news source.[1] For the political reporter in Japan, the leading politicians, especially those of the Liberal Democratic party, constitute the major news source. The officers of the Liberal Democratic party without portfolio as well as those with cabinet assignment become the focus of news-gathering activity. The following discussion is devoted to the relations between the political reporter and the leading politicians with special reference to those factors that tend to constrain the reporter's activity.

The degree of constraint varies with the types of news sources. As has been described earlier, the relationship between a reporter and a politician who heads an economic ministry such as MITI is somewhat different from the relationship held between a reporter and an official from the Ministry of Foreign Affairs. In understanding the peculiar problems faced by the political reporters, it is useful to compare his job with that of the social affairs reporter in regard to their respective relationships with news sources.

The relationship between a social affairs reporter and his news source is usually a one-time occurrence. For example, a crime occurs; then and only then does the social affairs reporter become interested in the subject. When the event is over, e.g., the suspect is convicted, the reporter's relationship is terminated; he pursues other stories. A political reporter assigned to

---

1. This chapter is largely based on the following works: Kato Kazuo and Kiuchi Hiroshi, *Shimbun Kisha* (Tokyo: Godo Shuppan, 1979), pp. 161-75; Honda Yasuharu, *Taikenteki Shimbunshi Gaku* (Tokyo: Ushio Shuppansha, 1976), pp. 30-49, 50-80; Nihon Shimbun Rodo Kumiai Shimbun Kenkyubu, ed., *Shimbun ga Abunai* (Tokyo: Banseisha, 1977), pp. 38-51, 66-80.

cover a particular politician encounters a different set of requirements. His interest in a politician by necessity is not
transitory. The politician, especially one in a leadership position,
is in public view for a long period of time. For the reporter to
fully understand and interpret political actions he must culti-
vate the friendship of his news source.

A social affairs reporter can usually deal with news sources
after an event has taken place, whereas a political reporter is
expected to go beyond the reporting of an event after it has
happened. He must be able to anticipate or predict a development. For example, as a political reporter he is expected to
anticipate if and when a dissolution of the House of Representatives will occur. Likewise, he is expected to guess who will be
the members of a new cabinet when a cabinet reshuffle is
imminent. It is not enough to give a simple reporting of facts
after the dissolution is announced or after the members of a
new cabinet are appointed. He must be able to speculate intel-
ligently before an event, and after an official announcement he
must provide an analysis of why such a decision was made.

All this presupposes a close relationship between the political
reporter and the politician. To have this relationship, a reporter
must have the confidence of the politician he is assigned to
cover. Without this trust a politician simply would not reveal
his true feelings or intentions on anything that might be newsworthy. A politician certainly would not provide a reporter
with a potential scoop. And yet, a reporter is expected to
provide scoops for his paper. To write more than superficial
story, it is essential that a reporter be accepted by his news
source as friendly, loyal, and trustworthy. This need for winning the confidence of the news source is reinforced by the fear
that other reporters might gain better access to the politician,
which might result in a scoop by competing newspapers.

Also, this need for a close relationship with the individual
politician is reinforced by the conviction of the political reporter that politics is shaped to a significant degree by the interplay
of fortuitous circumstances and the nonrational relationships
among politicians, which can only be uncovered by close
observation and access to these egocentric personalities.

This reporter's need is reciprocated by the politician's need
to win the friendship and goodwill of the political reporter

assigned to him. Such a good relationship ensures a neutral stance, if not overly favorable publicity for a politician.

By the very nature of the job requirements, then, the political reporter is under pressure to develop intimate ties with his target. And for this reason, the reporter is vulnerable to the pressure, enticements, rewards, and punishments by the politician.

The offer of gifts (cash, valuable coupons, merchandise, etc.) must be viewed not so much as an attempt to corrupt the reporter. Rather, from the politician's point of view, the reporter's acceptance of such gifts signifies that the reporter will abide by the unwritten rule of conduct and that he will not intentionally damage his patron. To share a certain secret—giving and taking a gift—tends to solidify a trusting personal relationship between the two. Rejection of such gifts would jeopardize a reporter's standing in the eyes of the politician whom he is supposed to cover.

Likewise, the reporter's acceptance of a gift does not necessarily signify that he has succumbed to a politician's attempt at bribery. A reporter realizes that he must win the confidence of the politician by writing unusually favorable reports about his patron, refraining from making critical comments, or remaining reticent about confidential information he may have come to acquire about his patron.

To borrow the colorful language of an experienced reporter, a news reporter is expected to dive into muddy water and stay there to observe the real world of politics. He is reminded, however, to emerge from the water once in a while to see where the muddy stream is heading.

A novice reporter is expected to go through three stages, each signifying an advance he has made toward gaining the confidence of a politician. First, he is allowed to go as far as a guest room near the entrance to the politician's house; as he gains a politician's confidence he may be allowed to enter a living room to talk informally with his news source; and, finally, after a prolonged period of trial he may be allowed to roam around a kitchen to open up a refrigerator at will. Reaching the third stage signifies that he has finally made it; i.e., the politician considers him as one of his men.[2]

2. Honda, *Taikenteki Shimbunshi Gaku*, p. 35.

In order to obtain the confidence of the subject politician he is assigned to cover, the political reporter feels psychological pressure to exercise self-censorship. The intimacy that develops between the reporter and the target politician may be due to considerations other than the ones mentioned in the preceding paragraphs. Some reporters are attracted to the magnetic and charismatic personality of the politicians they cover. It is not surprising that the politicians who have made it to a leading position within the party hierarchies have qualities that inspire respect, admiration, and loyalty. These qualities may pertain to personality traits, policies, or ideologies.

By gaining trust, a reporter becomes privy to the inner thoughts, moves, and tactics of the subject politician. At times, he can use this information selectively in reporting to meet the expectations of his superiors at the editorial office. Even if he cannot use such information in his own writing, he can provide the desk with the useful background insights. With the assistance of his patron politician, he may even achieve a scoop someday. Moreover, he derives a sense of satisfaction and heady feeling of importance from observing at a close range, or being involved in, the unfolding high drama of politics. This may in part compensate for the dissatisfaction arising from the constraint a close relationship imposes on his writing.

Intimate relationship brings with it an encumbrance; that is, it constrains a reporter's zeal to report. It dulls his sense of commitment to the profession to report all newsworthy information. The closer a reporter feels toward the subject politician, the greater the constraint he feels in reporting the information disadvantageous to his patron. Under such circumstances, he can either remain reticent or can go on to write only favorable stories promoting the political interest of his patron. Reinforcing a reluctance to write stories detrimental to one's subject politician is a cultural norm of the sense of obligation. Moreover, a reporter must reckon with the reception he would get from other political leaders, whether of the Liberal Democratic Party or opposition parties. A reporter's exposé about his politician would be in violation of the unwritten code of conduct, and might jeopardize his future access to other politicians. It is significant to note that a veteran reporter of more than twenty years of service hesitated and was acutely conscious that his life as a political reporter was over when he decided to write critically about political leaders he used to cover.[3]

Another major deterrent to uncomplimentary reporting on an individual politician is the fear of a defamation suit.

There are several norms that reporters can invoke if they feel the need to rationalize their practice of self-control. The norms of objectivity, neutrality, nonpartisanship, and nonpartiality can be and are at times invoked to justify their timidity or reluctance.

The norms as well as the customary practice associated with news reporting in Japan make it impossible to publish information about irregularities and improprieties committed by individual politicians unless there is evidence or "objective fact" to support it. When police or prosecuting authorities initiate actions against certain individual politicians, this becomes an objective fact, enabling the press to carry the news. Otherwise, the newspapers refrain from reporting allegations due to the lack of evidence to substantiate the charges. Another practice often discouraging the reporting of improprieties of individual politicians is the system of the reporters' club mentioned in an earlier chapter. Individual reporters feel greatly constrained to act independently of the other club members. It is in this light that one can understand why the newspapers did not pursue the corruption charges against Prime Minister Tanaka with vigor. The following considerations appear to have been operative at that time. The absence of reporting may have been in part a function of intimate personal relations Tanaka had built up with a group of reporters over the years. The sense of obligation to Tanaka may have played a part. The reporters who had known about the irregular financial dealings may have thought there was nothing unusual or extreme about the kind of corrupt practices in which Tanaka was rumored to have been involved; all politicians are alike, to a varying degree. The reporters may have felt that these practices are unavoidable given the nature of politics in Japan. Besides, they may have reasoned that the political reporters should be concerned with more important questions than investigative reporting on corrupt practices. It is possible that the newspapers and individual reporters were

3. Ibid., p. 32.

afraid of retaliation and difficulties they might encounter, not the least of which was the threat of a defamation suit.

Much of what the *Bungei Shunju*'s exposé included had been already reported in piecemeal news items over the years when the opposition parties pursued these allegations in the Diet. Indeed, when the *Bungei Shunju*'s article appeared, some embarrassed newspapermen commented that they had known these details all along and that much of what the exposé said was based on their own legwork which had been published in bits and pieces.

Whatever the reasons for the newspapers' long silence on the question, it is significant that they failed to give the matter vigorous and sustained attention. The newspapers maintained silence even after the appearance of the *Bungei Shunju* article. It was not until after the Foreign Press Club in Japan took the matter up that the Japanese newspapers gave it the serious attention, which ultimately led to the arrest of former Prime Minister Tanaka.

In considering the role played by the newspapers in the celebrated Lockheed affair, several things should be borne in mind. The affair first came to surface in the United States Congress. If the story had not been generated by a United States congressional investigation, the Japanese authorities would not have begun an investigation. Second, if Tanaka or one of his close associates had been the prime minister, the Japanese official investigation might not have proceeded as far as it did. It should be noted that Miki was prime minister at that time, and with his precarious hold on power in the midst of fierce intraparty factional politics, his only defense against an intraparty coalition's attempt to unseat him was to pursue the investigation vigorously with the apparent support of the mass media and the people. The overt attempt by the political forces to overthrow Miki's cabinet seems to have prompted a vigorous investigation.[4]

A former political reporter likened the reporters' club at the headquarters of the Liberal Democratic party, *Hirakawa Kurabu*, to a brothel. And yet, he added, no one at the Political Affairs Department feels sorry to see his colleague assigned to the

4. Ibid., pp. 51-52.

Hirakawa Kurabu. A reporter who has just received the assignment to the party headquarters is said to be excited over the work as if he were a high-class prostitute. In the words of Honda, a shortcut to a successful career as a political reporter is to get to *Hirakawa Kurabu* first of all, and once there catch a particular *danna* (patron). This attitude is related to a certain expectation the newspapers have of a political reporter: to obtain information by any means. Anger at corruption in the political world or a vision of a more desirable future are evidently not among the high-priority expectations. According to Honda, it matters little if a reporter has been a social affairs reporter. When a reporter is assigned to cover the *Hirakawa Kurabu*, he acquires the characteristics after he associates with political reporters. If he lives in the world of dirty politics, dirty politics is reflected in his writing. If he lives in Peking, he reflects the virtues of a "clean" society. After all, a political reporter is expected to have intimate ties with the subject. A political reporter becomes plutocratic, Honda maintains, because he dines at an expensive Askasaka restaurant sipping Scotch and water, discussing high politics with the politicians. A social affairs reporter is oriented toward the common people because he visits a squalid shack drinking second-class sake.[5]

Self-Censorship

Restraint on reporting sometimes arises from the reporter's decision to show deference for the demands and wishes of certain groups and individuals when he otherwise would have acted differently with particular information.

Self-restraint may occur at the level of the editorial office or the front-line reporters. The reporter's self-restraint may occur at the specific request of a news source or even in the absence of any attempt at influence by groups or individuals. Self-restraint may range from complete omission of newsworthy items to the modification of relevant items.

Self-censorship is not confined to the China problem as examined in chapter 9. The newspapers were for a long time

5. Ibid., pp. 68-79.

extremely reluctant to report any news critical of the Soka
Gakkai and Komeito. The press used to employ the phrase
"certain religious group" to refer to the Soka Gakkai. Thus,
a violation of electoral law by the Soka Gakkai was reported in
the press as a violation by a "certain religious group." This self-
imposed restraint about the Soka Gakkai was removed in 1969
when the *Red Flag*, the organ of the Communist party, mounted a campaign against the obstruction of freedom of speech by
the Soka Gakkai and Komeito. The issue was subsequently
taken up by the NHK. The primary reason for self-restraint was
financial. There was a fear that if a newspaper carried information damaging the Soka Gakkai, the newspaper might have to
face a boycott by about 200,000 or 300,000 members of the
Soka Gakkai.[6]

The case of the Japan Communist party versus the *Sankei* is
pertinent in this connection. The *Sankei* and *Nihon Keizai*
carried on December 2, 1973 an advertisement of approximately half a page by the Liberal Democratic party. This ad
took the form of a letter addressed to the Japan Communist
party and began with the statement "Please make it clear." It
identified contradictions with respect to five points between the
Program on Democratic Coalition Government published by the
Japan Communist party and that party's platform. In view of
the fact that the party had enunciated both programs, the
advertisement asked the party to clarify whether its program on
a coalition government was "nothing but a stepping stone" for
a proletarian dictatorship and revolution. For example, the
party's program on a coalition government spoke of safeguarding Articles 4 and 7 of the Japanese Constitution. This amounts
to a recognition of the emperor. and Yet, the party platform
declared the intention to abolish the monarchy and establish a
People's Republic.

The Japan Communist party lodged a strong protest to the
Sankei and *Nihon Keizai*. The substance of the protest was:

1. The slanderous ad of the Liberal Democratic party could
not be simply characterized as "an opinion ad" containing that
party's political views. The ad constituted arbitrary criticism
and attack on the Japan Communist party.

6. Miyoshi et al., *Shimbun Bokoku Ron*, p. 197.

2. The ad turned newspaper pages, the public instrument of society, into a private possession of the moneyed and privileged groups.

3. Since the newspapers inflicted damage to the party by printing such a slanderous document, they should compensate for damage by printing on their own responsibility, and not in the form of an opinion advertisement, a rebuttal as the Japan Communist party deemed necessary.[7]

The *Sankei* responded: The entire responsibility regarding the contents of the ad lay with the Liberal Democratic party. If the Japan Communist party felt it necessary to ascertain the real intention regarding the ad, the party should directly obtain a formal reply from the Liberal Democrats. If their formal reply called for a rebuttal on the *Sankei* pages, the *Sankei* would provide space for such an ad with its expenses to be collected from the Liberal Democrats. Alternatively, the *Sankei* would print a rebuttal in the form of an ad with the Japan Communist party paying the necessary fees. The party rejected the *Sankei*'s offer. As for the *Nihon Keizai*, it rejected the party's protest but agreed not to print mutually critical ads from the five political parties in the future.[8]

On the ground that the two newspapers rejected its demands, the Japan Communist party refused, thenceforth, to cooperate with the reporters of the two companies regarding news-gathering activities and mounted a severe attack on the *Sankei* in the *Red Flag*. The December 5 issue of the *Red Flag* asserted that the method of propaganda called an opinion advertisement was available only to such groups as the Liberal Democratic party as it enjoyed the full financial support of big business and big financial capital. The December 13 issue stated that the advertisement, cast in the form of an opinion advertisement, was especially pernicious because the question was asked in such a way to call for a response. And yet, a response would require enormous advertisement fees.[9]

Yano has pointed out that about four years before this incident, the Japan Communist party itself printed an opinion

7. Yano, p. 102.
8. Ibid., pp. 103-4.
9. Ibid., pp. 104-5.

advertisement of sorts in the major dailies. It placed a full-page ad in the December 21, 1969, issue of the *Mainichi* and a half-page ad in the December 24, 1969, issue of the *Yomirui*. The advertisement expressed the views of Communist party leaders in the form of a conversation with the questioners. These ads were evidently part of the election campaign for that year. According to Yano this was indicative of the party's financial resources and of its willingness to pay for such an ad in the newspaper. Yano argued that the party's contention that the Liberal Democratic ad in question was slanderous and false in character was absurd. The Japan Communist party's ad in the *Mainichi* was no better. It characterized Japanese politics under the Liberal Democratic in a variety of ways. The ad asserted that the leadership was one which did nothing to eradicate the sufferings of a million Okinawa residents, one which trans-formed the United States Security Treaty into an aggressive instrument, one which rounded up the people into a battlefield, one which produced high prices, shortage of housing, contami-nated food, pollution, traffic accidents, and politics at the mercy of American financial circles. Yano maintained that these characterizations were far from being fair.[10]

What is also significant about the *Sankei* incident is that four other papers refused to run the Liberal Democratic ad. A *Red Flag* article points out that the Japan Communist party learned in advance of the Liberal Democratic party's approach to six major newspapers and warned them not to carry the ad. For whatever reasons, four of the newspapers refused to run the ad. The *Mainichi* and *Yomiuri*, which had run the Japan Com-munist party's ad, were among these. It is significant also that none of major newspapers with the exception of the *Sankei* reported this incident initially. Yano argued that the silence was probably due to its sensitivity in relation to the Japan Com-munist party and to the affairs of other newspapers. In his view, this was a disgrace for the newspapers, which so often loudly invoke the people's right to know.[11]

The so-called Takasugi affair provides an example of another type of self-restraint. On January 7, 1965, a day after his appointment as chief delegate from Japan to the Japan-Korea

10. Ibid., pp. 106-7.
11. Ibid., pp. 109-10.

Conference, Takasugi Shin'ichi faced a press conference at the Foreign Ministry. Commenting on the view that Japan should apologize for its thirty-six years of ruling Korea, he stated that he disagreed with the people who claim that Japan exploited Korea during that time. Japan's intentions toward Korea were good. He asserted that it would have been to Korea's advantage if it had stayed in the possession of the Japanese for twenty more years. At the end of his talk, he remarked that he had talked with much candor, perhaps with indiscretion, and might have said some inappropriate things. He asked the reporters to take this into consideration in preparing their reports. At the conclusion of the press conference, the director of the North East Asia Division of the Foreign Ministry requested that Takasugi's remarks be made off the record. The reporters' club agreed.[12] Takasugi's remarkable comments glorifying Japanese colonial rule of Korea did not appear in print in any major newspapers. A few days later, his statement was denounced by the *Red Flag*. The North and South Korean press followed with their denunciation.

On January 18, the *Asahi* reported that the North Korean *Worker's Daily* carried a denunciation but added that "it was not clear when and where Takasugi made the statement as reported in the *Worker's Daily*." The *Mainichi* and *Yomiuri* in their January 21 issue carried Takasugi's clarification that the statement attributed to him was contrary to fact. These papers were so meticulous as to add an explanatory note saying that the Takasugi statement referred to that which was reported by the *Red Flag* and the South Korean newspaper *Tonga Ilbo*.[13]

Self-restraint at times is exercised by the front-line reporters even without any request by a news source. A celebrated example is the so-called Kuraishi incident. On February 6, 1968, Kuraishi, then the minister of agriculture, made the following observation in his meeting with the members of the reporters' club: "At today's cabinet meeting there was not time for me to speak about the problem of safe fishing in the Japan sea. It is helpless . . . unless Japan has warships and guns. A constitution which depends on the sincerity and trust of other countries is akin to salvation by faith through the benevolence

12. *Masukomi Kokusho*, p. 121.
13. Ibid., p. 122.

of Amida Buddha. Even though the prime minister speaks approvingly of the present constitution, he must feel ticklish in his heart. Japan, which is in possession of such an absurd constitution, is like a concubine and has no basis for independence. It may be all right for us, but we must reconstruct it for those young people who will follow us. . . . If only Japan has atom bombs and an army of 300,000." The Kyodo News Agency distributed the news, as did some local newspapers. So did the Tokyo Broadcasting System (TBS) network. The news was taken up by the Socialist party at the Diet the following day; this led to the disruption of parliamentary proceedings and eventually to Kuraishi's resignation.[14]

Kuraishi's controversial statement was not designated by the news source as being off the record, and therefore any reporter who was present at the meeting could have written a story. What is significant is that initially most newspapers had decided not to print the story. A possible explanation may be that his remarks were not newsworthy and besides Kuraishi said nothing new and had always been saying things like that. Even if the story was filed by a reporter, he may have reasoned that the editorial office would kill the story. Whatever decisions were made, it illustrates a defacto self-censorship by the newspapers. This practice explains why Kuraishi was able to make such a politically sensitive statement without hesitation. It is probable that most reporters present felt intuitively that Kuraishi's remarks would not make news.[15]

Although there were thirteen reporters at the press conference, representing thirteen newspapers and television networks, only one reporter from the Kyodo News Agency wrote a story for circulation. It was done shortly after 11:00 a.m. The same day in Tokyo, the *Naigai Times* alone carried the story in its evening edition. The following morning the *Ashahi*, *Sankei*, and *Tokyo Times* gave a cursory treatment to the story in their gossip columns. The *Mainichi* and *Nikkei* ignored the story completely. It was not until after the opposition parties took up the matter at the Diet that the incident was covered in earnest by the major dailies.[16]

14. Ibid., pp. 123-24.
15. Ibid., p. 125.
16. Den Hideo, *Masukomi no Kiki* (Tokyo: Shimin Shobo, 1972), pp. 60-63.

Among the broadcasters, the TBS reported the incident as top news both at 11 p.m. the same day and on its morning news broadcast. The TBS could have carried the news at noon the same day, but it did not. A TBS reporter had been present at the press conference and consulted with the desk at the home office about Kuraishi's statement. Initially, it was decided not to broadcast it. At a meeting of political and economic reporters, which happened to be scheduled for 7 p.m. that day, some reporters argued for using the story on the grounds that a statement made at a press conference was tantamount to a statement issued to the entire people, and that the matter was serious as it was made by a minister who was under obligation to uphold the Constitution and he had made derogatory and negative comments about it. The opponents took the position that Kuraishi's remarks were probably meant to be "light chit-chat at tea-time" and it was unnecessary to broadcast them. After one hour of heated debate, it was decided to broadcast the story. It was also decided at the meeting to add a comment from an opposition party. The chairman of the Japan Socialist party committee on Diet policies was contacted by phone. Yanagita, upon hearing the story filed by the Kyodo, responded that coming from the minister, this was an important statement that could not be ignored. He said that he would pursue this matter at the Budget Committee meeting the following day. Yanagita did indeed pursue this question at the Diet, and as a result, Diet proceedings were halted until Kuraisi was dismissed.[17]

Another instance of self-censorship by the press occurred on October 26, 1971, the day when a historic vote on the question of the Chinese representation was to occur at the United Nations. Following a cabinet meeting, as is customary, the director general of the Defense Agency met with the reporters assigned to his agency. When asked if the cabinet meeting touched on the question of the PRC admission to the United Nations, Nishimura responded: "No, nothing was said about the topic. The admission of Communist China into the United Nations would further worsen the situation there. Both small and big countries have the same vote at the United Nations. In a way, it is something like a credit union in the countryside. At

17. Ibid.

a credit union anyone who pays 10,000 yen can be a member. Everyone receives one vote. When something bad happens, there occurs commotion, each insisting that he too has his right, leading in the end to a brawl in which everyone exchanges blows with an abacus." There were four reporters present that day, though forty-one reporters were assigned to the reporters' club of the Defense Agency. None of the four reporters prepared a news story on Nishimura's remarks. Later on, other reporters who were absent at the press conference heard the tape recording of the press conference. Some of them thought Nishimura's statement should be taken up as news. However, a senior reporter apparently dissuaded them from doing so on the grounds that publicizing it would cause a major political controversy. The chief of the Secretariat of the agency, too, asked several reporters to handle the matter with due discretion. During the same evening, Director Nishimura himself met again with twelve reporters and asked that his remarks of the morning be kept off the record. Everyone there agreed, and consequently no paper carried the story. About a month later the Japan Socialist party took up this question at the Diet. Only then did the incident become known to the public.[18]

It should be noted that approximately ten hours had elapsed since the morning conference before the director requested an off-the-record treatment. Any reporter could have reported a story and the editorial office could have used it in the evening edition. It should also be noted that the reporters at the agency complied with a government request for quickly killing a story. One may question the propriety of the behavior of these reporters.[19]

Taboos

One of the taboos constraining freedom of reporting is inherent in the nature of a newspaper as a commercial enterprise. A most direct souce of such constraint is the sponsorship of advertisements by leading business concerns. Unfavorable publicity involving major advertising clients, creditors, and sponsors is

18. Ibid., pp. 56-58.
19. Ibid.

shunned. Thus, accidents involving a department store's elevators, cases of pickpocketing, or massive food poisoning arising from eating at a department store's restaurant go unreported. A case of embezzlement at a major bank is ignored. To this one must add another operative taboo: the newspapers do not criticize other newspapers and they do not report irregularities within their own organizations.[20]

In postwar Japan the taboo of Chrysanthemum (the emperor) has continued though much attenuated and abated. As compared with pre-1945 days, the newspapers have felt much freer to write about the emperor. However, they still operate with the consciousness that critical comments on the affairs of the imperial household would likely bring about threats and pressure from the right-wing forces. They remember vividly the incident of "Furyu Mutan" involving the president of the monthly magazine *Chuo Koron*. He was physically assaulted by a youth for publishing a fictional story in which the imperial family was decapitated in a grotesque fashion. Conservative political leaders have allegedly attempted to utilize the aura of the imperial household to their political advantage. The emperor's European tour in the fall of 1971 is often cited as an example. The newspapers gave the trip extensive coverage by allocating a tremendous amount of expenses for personnel to travel on the tour. Seventy-one reporters accompanied the emperor, arriving in a city en masse "like a large flock of little birds and passing like a typhoon." Most newspapers gave the trip major coverage but on an emotional and "flunkyist" level. Some critics charge that by emphasizing the human emperor, the press coverage of the trip contributed to the glorification of the emperor, perhaps unwittingly expanding the scope of the taboo. The question of the responsibility for the war, raised by the Europeans and reflected in their cold reception, was all but ignored or given insignificant treatment.[21]

Taboo requires that the emperor and his actions be described with polite expression and using the proper honorifics. Honda Katsuhito recalls what happened to the articles he submitted to his newspapers during the first month of his career as a reporter in Hokkaido. He was to report on the visit of the emperor and

20. *Gendai Janarizumu* 2: 54-55.
21. Ibid., pp. 56-57; *Shimbun ga Abunai*, pp. 158-59.

his wife to his locality. He said he was looking forward to the assignment, thinking that he would write a thoroughly critical article about the emperor. He reported "objectively" of what he saw but avoided the use of honorifics. He did not understand why honorifics should be used and thought the use of them would imply an abandonment of the neutral stance expected of a reporter. Thus he wrote, "the emperor arrived [*tsuita*]" at a meeting hall; but his desk changed his sentence to read "His highness arrived [*otsuikininatta*]" at the meeting hall. His phrase "the emperor seems to know [*shitte irurashi*]" was changed to a polite expression, "the emperor seems to [*gozon-jirashi*] know." As Honda himself indicates, this practice is not confined to the press but is widely shared by the Japanese people.[22]

22. Honda Katsuhito, *Janarizumu Ron* (Tokyo: Suzusawa Shoten, 1975), pp. 229-31.

CHAPTER XI

Ideological and
Normative Constraints

The first part of this chapter deals with the question of whether ideological tendency shapes newspaper reporting. This is followed by a discussion of the impact on press activities of major norms such as objectivity, nonpartisanship, nonpartiality, and neutrality. Ideological tendency is defined as a set of interrelated political values, beliefs, and attitudes loosely associated with "conservative" or "progressive" forces in the context of Japanese politics. The *Asahi*'s editorials on the Vietnam War are examined to assess the impact of ideological tendency. Several considerations led to the selection of this particular issue.

1. The Vietnam War was an intrinsically important political issue, important for Japanese domestic politics as well as for international politics.

2. The war was a highly controversial issue in Japanese politics, one on which persons with different ideological tendencies held sharply differing opinions.

3. The long duration of the war occasioned numerous editorials. During the sixties and seventies, several hundred editorials on the war appeared in the *Asahi*. And more significantly, one writer wrote practically all of these editorials.

4. Direct testimony is now available by the writer mentioned above on why he wrote that particular kind of editorial. His recent book contains a most extraordinary and candid exposition of his ideological tendency relevant to the understanding of the views he expressed in the editorials. He gives a detailed explanation of the perceptions, beliefs, values, and attitudes he had toward the various aspects of the Vietnam War. His account is at times moving, passionate, and eloquent.

Characteristics of the Asahi Editorials on Vietnam

Before we examine his ideological tendency, however, a brief account of the characteristics of the *Asahi* editorials on the Vietnam War is necessary. The book entitled *Shimbun Roncho e no Hanron*, by Urushiyama, formerly a reporter for twenty years, is devoted almost exclusively to a critical analysis of the *Asahi*'s editorials on the Vietnam war. What follows is a partial list of the major themes and assumptions Urushiyama identified as underlying the *Asahi* editorials.

1. The *Asahi* editorials maintained that the Vietnam War was a civil war inside South Vietnam. They supported the view that even if there had been assistance from North Vietnam, fundamentally speaking the explosion of frustration and anger of the South Vietnamese people was the cause of the war.[1]

2. In the initial period of the war, the *Asahi* editorials on occasion seemed to accept the existence of two Vietnams. This notion, however, gradually disappeared toward the end of the sixties. By the early seventies, the *Asahi* took the position that an independent and unified Vietnam was desirable. Moreover, the unification was not to be achieved by South Vietnam but on the initiative of the communist side.[2]

3. The editorials suggested that communism was preferable to freedom or a war by saying that even if freedom is protected, it is meaningless if the land is devastated by war.[3]

4. The editorials contended that if one believed the Liberation Front in Vietnam to be communist, it was a reflection of the anticommunist cold war mentality. The editorials maintained that there was the element of nationalistic aspiration to the Vietnam War, and that judgment on the basis of ideological standpoint alone was inappropriate. The *Asahi* argued that in Asia a nationalistic movement was happening by the collaboration of nationalism and communism. The implications were that nationalists were communists and that communists were

---

1. Urushiyama Shigeyoshi, *Shimbun Roncho e no Hanron* (Tokyo: Nisshin Hodo, 1975), pp. 13-16, 49.
2. Ibid., pp. 53-59.
3. Ibid., pp. 90-91.

nationalists, and that those who opposed the Vietcong were antinationalistic as well as anticommunist.[4]

5. The *Asahi* harped on and condemned the severity of oppression by the South Vietnamese government and the barbarity of American and South Vietnamese troops. Editorials were hostile toward the South Vietnamese government. There were many editorials which justified the actions of the communist forces, but very few which defended that actions of the South Vietnam government. There were no editorials voicing criticism of the communists from the standpoint of freedom. The editorials demanded that freedom of the European standard be practiced in South Vietnam, denouncing the South Vietnamese effort to resist North Vietnam's aggression as being anticommunist. From the mid-sixties on, the application of the humanitarian criterion became particularly severe toward South Vietnam and the United States. Denunciation of atrocities was exclusively directed toward the American and South Vietnam troops. Barbarous acts committed against the Sommi village in 1968, which came to light in late 1969, received sensational treatment, whereas the Hue incident involving a systematic massacre of civilians by the communist side was ignored.[5]

6. During the initial period, the editorials tooks a relatively neutral position on the arrangements for terminating the war. During the mid-sixties the editorial position became increasingly pro-North Vietnam. Initially, the editorials had called for mutual observance of the Geneva Agreement, mutual reduction of war efforts on both sides, and localization of the Vietnam War. Underlying this position was the idea of neutralization. Advocacy of neutrality faded away after the mid-sixties. Emphasis began shifting from the notion of mutual reduction of the war effort to the unilateral reduction of American war efforts. A shift also occurred from the position in favor of mutual respect for the Geneva Agreement to the position that the United States was first in violating the Geneva Agreement. Advocacy of neutrality gave way to an emphasis on the justice and validity of the communist position. By the Tet offensive of spring 1972, the *Asahi* position close resembled that of the

4. Ibid., pp. 94, 110-12.
5. Ibid., pp. 115-22, 139-44, 146-49.

communist side with an increasingly critical attitude toward the United States.[6] By 1972 the *Asahi* supported national self-determination and a coalition government as advocated by the North. The United States was being urged to accept those same conditions.

7. The Vietnam War was severely condemned by the *Asahi* as being a manifestation of the "logic of force" of a big state vis-à-vis a small state. The complete withdrawal of American troops, as stipulated in the Paris agreement, was not enough. The *Asahi* suggested that both civilian and military personnel in Saigon must be withdrawn, together with a termination of the military assistance to the South Vietnamese armed forces and the United States air control command in Thailand. The "logic of force" allegedly underlying the United States military involvement was criticized, whereas the withdrawal of the North Vietnamese military was not advocated.[7]

We shall now return to the testimony of Maruyama Shizuo, who served as editorial writer for the *Asahi* from August 1962 to December 1974. It should be noted that during the twelve-year period 270 of the 280 editorials that appeared on Indochina were written by Maruyama. An *Asahi* column called "Konnichi no Mondai" (Today's Problem) discussed the Indochina problem forty-two times during the twelve years. Maruyama wrote thirty-two of those articles. Technically speaking, an editorial writer drafts an editorial in accordance with the wishes of the chief editorial writer, who assumes the official responsibility for any editorial. As discussed in an earlier chapter, an editorial is prepared following a group discussion. Accordingly, an editorial is a group product. However, the creativity and ability of an individual writer have considerable impact. Maruyama states that it was he who wrote all editorials on the Vietnam issue and the contents were exactly what he had in mind; i.e., he was solely responsible for the substantive contents of his articles.[8]

6. Ibid., pp. 165-75, 180-83, 186.

7. Ibid., pp. 198-99.

8. Maruyama Shizuo, *Ronsetsu Iin* (Tokyo: Tsukuma Shobo, 1977), pp. 5-8.

An Editorial Writer's Ideological Tendency

An examination of Maruyama's ideological tendency is pertinent in order to assess its impact on his editorial writing. His basic attitude toward the American involvement in the war was unequivocally expressed when he stated that "I thought that America should not be allowed to win the war." Such was his personal view, and he added that this view could not appear openly in an editorial. Maruyama's drafts were reviewed by such institutionalized checkpoints as chief and deputy chief editorial writers and his editorial advisor. "However, the writer's point of view comes to the surface in some form, even if suppressed. My wish was incorporated in the editorials in such a form."[9]

Maruyama's perception of the nature of the war and his attitude toward American conduct of the war were clearly revealed in his book. What follows is a series of quotations from his own writing, the totality of which attests to a particular ideological tendency which affected the author.

"The American intervention in Vietnam constituted an imperialistic, aggressive war. U.S. actions were logically contradictory and were in disregard of the law, morality, and customary [international] practices. There was an essential difference between American assistance to Saigon and North Vietnamese support for the liberation forces. . . . The war by the Liberation Front and Hanoi was a desperate struggle to safeguard the independence and sovereignty of the nation and was the last fight to survive as a nation. . . .[10]

From whatever standpoint, America's bombing of the North was an unjustifiable military action. . . .[11]

If the mission of the newspaper is to dig out truth and to report it, one could not naturally have overlooked America's falsehood. . . . This was particularly so since it was the war where a big power attempted to "conquer" a small country. . . . Therefore, I felt indescribable anger at the fact that America began a war without justifiable reasons and without justice capable of winning popular assent, and that it continued the war ruthlessly. . . .[12]

9. Ibid., p. 167.
10. Ibid., p. 170.

11. Ibid., p. 172.
12. Ibid., p. 173.

To be sure, we criticized America severely. But the criticism was directed against falsehood the United States possessed rather than America itself. America's falsehood was formed by its aggressive nature, policy of strength, and discordance between its words and actions. That America was the aggressor was clear in view of the fact that none of the objectives cited by America to justify its expedition to Vietnam holds good in terms of domestic law, international law, and international customary practices. The policy of strength was being pursued because of its overconfidence in the dollars and bombs. Behind this, it could not be concealed, there was a sense of contempt for Asia.[13]

In nearly all cases, there was no consistency in what America did and said. America talked of justice and humanity but beneath its words, it was expanding a war of massacre. . . .[14]

The statements of the generations of American presidents consisted of a collection of lies. Our conscience could not endure the two faces of the United States. My passion as a journalist was devoted to the task of unmasking the mask of justice worn by America. . . . As the war went on and about the time the bombing of the North was intensified, I came to have doubt whether it would be enough merely to attack falsehood and to point out deception. Having observed America's policy of strength at great length, I wondered if international peace could be established at all in the world when a superpower was arrogant about its power, ignoring international agreements, promises, and practices. Will national rights be respected where a big nation-ism stalks the street? A nation should have a right to determine its own destiny, and its independence and sovereignty must be recognized by all the countries in the world. However, if such inherent rights of a nation are denied by a big nation's wanton will, nonbig nations would again be placed in the position of subjugation and exploitation of the seventeenth and eighteenth centuries. . . . If such lawlessness is permitted in the international society, someday such a lawlessness may be brought into a domestic society in the same form. If the powerful and wealthy are allowed to do anything they like to do, what shall the powerless and the poor do? If promise is discarded just as worn-out sandals are thrown away, the social order cannot be sustained. If such a situation comes to pass, the values and principles of living in a human society such as integrity, goodwill, and compassion would be lost. What in the world can we turn to as

13. Ibid., p. 177.
14. Ibid., p. 179.

authority and purpose for going on living? We were afraid that we would lose a hope and the meaning for living. Therefore, we thought that America should not win the war, that America should not be allowed to win the war. . . .[15]

However, we cannot be so candid as to write in the editorial of a commercial newspaper that "America should not win the war." Even if I wanted to write that, there would be an objection at the time of the round table discussion and will not probably be printed because of the objection of the desk and chief of the editorial writers. All I could do was to condemn ever more severely the injustice of America's policy of war and the act of war, to explain ever more objectively the reason why international agreements need to be observed, and to appeal more logically to the reasons of dignity of nationalism. . . .[16]

In fact, as I myself read the editorials over, I realized that in the latter period of the war America is criticized sharply to a degree that surprises even myself, making me wonder how I was able to write that far. For example, in the editorial of December 28, 1972, entitled "American Bombing of the North Is a Challenge to Civilization." I condemned [America] thoroughly for the massive bombing of December 72 on North Vietnamese cities. I wondered, "whether there are any other acts by a state more unethical, nonlogical and more anticivilization" than the bombing of cities, and I went so far as to write, "What President Nixon is pursuing in Vietnam is, I think, the act of imperialism and colonialism and is nothing but genocide." I think that was closest to the limits one can come to in an editorial of a commercial newspapers. It probably exceeded the boundary. As I think about the matter now, at that time my position was not just to report facts. If that is all I had sought, I would not and could not have been that daring in condemning "America's war" that "tenaciously." I approached the war as involving the question of a way of life which holds that the lawlessness cannot and should not be tolerated. . . . Drawing on my conclusion, derived from many years of experience as a correspondent in Asia, that nationalism must be accepted, I hated colonialism and imperialism and entrusted my pen with these thoughts. . . .[17]

. . . throughout twelve years, what I have emphasized consistently in my own words and asserted passionately are the evils of colonialism, [the need for] eliminating colonialism, [the need to] understand, recognize, and accept nationalism.[18]

15. Ibid., pp. 180-81.
16. Ibid., pp. 181-82.
17. Ibid., p. 182.
18. Ibid., p. 220.

The liberation of Saigon on April 30, 1975, was nothing but a proof of the justness of Vietnam nationalism. I rejoiced at the liberation of South Vietnam as it demonstrated that my view of nationalism was not wrong and what I had been maintaining in the editorials was right. Beginning on April 30, through the first and second of May, I received calls from many friends and acquaintances, saying "congratulations." They telephoned me as though I had been elected in the general local elections of April 30. It is certainly wonderful that they [the liberation forces] won, that they persistently fought to the victory.[19]

The passages quoted above were written by Maruyama about his life as the editorial writer reponsible for the *Asahi*'s editorials on the Vietnam War. They constitute an eloquent testimony of how his perceptions of the nature of war, his political values, beliefs, and attitudes affected his writing of editorials.

In the same book, he writes of the numerous criticisms he was subjected to and the difficulties he encountered in carrying out his task. His observations in this regard are quite revealing. Maruyama paid meticulous attention to the expressions he used in his editorials. His basic posture was that he could not yield on his assertions or alter the contents. He tried to make sure he had a firm grasp of the facts so as not to be caught at a disadvantage. At times, he avoided the use of the subject in a sentence in order to conceal where the responsibility rested. By using mild expressions, he sought to divert the attention of the critics and to avoid unnecessary friction while he tried to say clearly what needed to be said. He was quite conscious of the "malicious and spiteful gaze of his opponents." He was aware that the expression "Vietcong" carried an unfavorable connotation of contempt and felt he should use the term "Liberation Front." However, in view of the fact the *Asahi* editorials were the target of attack, he deliberately used "Vietcong" so as to give, however slightly, the impression of a conservative tinge, using this "invisible cloak" in order to say what he felt necessary.[20]

19. Ibid., pp. 234-35.
20. Ibid., pp. 160-61.

Upon reflecting on the question of why he denounced the United States so severely, he offered a few additional observations.[21]

1. It was comparatively easy to criticize the United States since it did not intervene too openly or take retaliatory measures against foreign correspondents whose newspapers were critical toward it.

2. The United States is a major power and as such has a major responsibility. To that extent, it was easy to criticize, expecting it to make concessions. Any man has a feeling of partiality for the weak. He concedes that his support for the Liberation Front may in part have stemmed from this feeling.

3. He had seen a series of Japanese wars, and watching American involvement in a war similar to the Japanese army's aggressive wars, he did not want the United States to repeat the same mistake.

Impact of Major Norms

Major norms presumably shaping newspaper activities in Japan are epitomized in such expressions as "objectivity," "nonpartiality-nonpartisanship," "neutrality," "fairness," and "accuracy." The media profess to adhere to these and pledge to uphold them as guiding principles. In fact, these norms are explicitly codified in the form as the Fundamental Canons of Editing.

The implications of strict adherence to these norms should be noted. The adherence to the norms of objectivity and accuracy may unwittingly result in a de facto concealment of the truth regarding the nature and significance underlying the act of reporting of a particular fact. Suppose the police authorities wanted to influence the public image of a foreign country by releasing facts about a series of activities by espionage agents of that country. News about such activities would be duly reported as "fact" as released by the police authorities. Even though such a report would be prefaced by a statement "according to the police authorities" and the substance of the

21. Ibid., pp. 168-70.

reporting meets the requirements of accuracy and objectivity, the nature and significance of the reported facts, i.e., a political motive of the police authorities, would be concealed.[22]

It is often suggested that these norms are frequently used to criticize the reporting sympathetic to the progressive political forces. The allegation is that the government, the Liberal Democratic Party, and their supporters condemn any embarrassing news reports as being biased or lacking in objectivity.[23]

A veteran reporter of twenty years' service with the *Mainichi* observed that he has been bothered by the realization that the emphasis on objective and balanced reporting resulted in superficiality, similarity, and lack of vitality in political reporting. Adherence to these norms also results in a writing style devoid of liveliness. It dulls the reporter's capacity for sensitive discrimination, leading reporters astray from the reporting of the truth.[24]

Some critics contend that these norms are conducive to the presentation of news articles favorable to the ruling party and that they tend to constrain the development of news stories favorable to the opposition parties. In their view, the norms tend to function as a rationalization for the production of newspapers amenable to the ruling authorities.[25]

Honda Yasuhara, a former *Yomiuri* reporter, was blunter when he stated that the principle of objective reporting is nothing but "an illusionary attempt to stand on the objective fact that does not exist." The "objective fact" is the result and, in the final analysis, refers to a filtering process of a reporter's subjectivity. In this process, a reporter's choices are continually made as to what to pursue and what to ignore.[26]

The norm of objectivity has led to two contrasting attitudes. The first is a tendency to avoid and discourage controversial opinions. The lack of reporting during the initial period of the Tanaka corruption charges is a case in point. Rumors had long been heard, but the newspapers did not have in their possession "objective facts" and hence felt unable to write about the pos-

22. *Gendai Janarizumu* 2: 68.
23. Ibid.
24. *Shimbun ga Abunai*, p. 66.
25. Ibid., p. 68.
26. Honda, *Taikenteki Shimbunshi Gaku*, pp. 23-24.

sible corruption charges. At the same time, the norm may lead to the entirely opposite tendency; it is permissible to write anything as long as there is "an objective fact," regardless of its consequences. Extensive newspaper reporting on the intra-Liberal Democratic party plot by certain factions to unseat Prime Minister Miki in May 1976 provides an example. Individual reports on anti-Miki moves within the party were indeed based on objective facts observable to the reporters. However, these reports were insensitive to and ran counter to the apparent popular sentiment calling for a vigorous investigation of the Lockheed affair under Miki. While editorials, letters to the editors, and social affairs pages showed positive enthusiasm toward this popular stance, the political affairs pages tended to discourage the trend by portraying the demise of Miki as an inevitability or a fait accompli.[27]

Norms of Nonpartiality-Nonpartisanship and Neutrality

According to Ishimaki, the prevalence of the norms of neutrality, impartiality, and nonpartisanship make the newspapers susceptible to manipulation by the existing government. He believes that upholding these norms is intrinsically impossible in the arena of opinion. The norms themselves represent a certain political standpoint; yet they are often used to justify the basic ideological tendency of the newspaper management.[28]

The application of these norms to reporting tends to exclude stories that appear contrary to the interest of the establishment. As a matter of fact, the newspapers usually refrain from openly supporting a particular political party on a certain issue. At times, special care is given not to voice any opinion that conforms with the position of a particular party. The first paragraph of the *Asahi* newspaper's charter declares "its intention to safeguard the freedom of press by standing on the ground of nonpartiality and nonpartisanship and to contribute to the completion of a democratic state and the establishment of world peace." The logical end of a commercial newspaper would be

27. Ibid., pp. 24-29, 39-42.
28. *Gendai Janarizumu* 2: 66-67.

met by printing everything, maintaining the stance of non-partiality and nonpartisanship. With the exception of illegal reporting and the expose of primary obscene material, the newspaper could implement the policy of reporting on all political activities including both extremes, right or left. Equal weight could be allocated for opposition activities as well as those of the governing party. In actuality, however, the newspapers may be said to practice a nonpartiality or nonpartisanship in the sense that they avoid reporting on both the extreme right or left, which are outside the framework of the existing political order. Furthermore, within this framework, the practices of the newspapers tend to be advantageous to the ruling party. For example, when the newspapers introduce to the readers the policies of various political parties after the dissolution of the parliament, the then ruling party is likely to be given preference in the order in which the party position is presented and in the amount of time allowed. Another example is that the norm of nonpartiality and nonpartisanship is not applied to new emerging political forces.[29]

The norm of *fuhen-futo* (nonpartiality and nonpartisanship) may be interpreted to require the selection and reporting of news on behalf of or for the people of all political persuasions or standpoints. This interpretation, however, runs into practical difficulty. The limited space requires allocation of priorities. A critic goes so far as to argue that the norm functions to select and report news that does not make much difference to all sides of the political spectrum.[30]

The progressive forces sometimes complain that the critics apply the norm of impartiality strictly to the leftist tendency, while the partiality to the right is ignored.[31] News of American atrocities published by Hanoi was either ignored or given little play, while the pronouncements of the American military in Saigon were given detailed treatment. They contend that unless special effort is exerted, the reporters tend to naturally be favorable toward the powerful force.

It is important to note that the invocation of the norms of neutrality, fairness, and *fuhen-futo* is criticized by the writers of

29. Honda, *Janarizumu Ron*, pp. 36-37.
30. Ibid., pp. 126-27.
31. Ibid.

right-wing persuasion as well. Their point is that the newspapers are in fact biased, while proclaiming that they are neutral or impartial. In their view, the norms are nothing but a facade.[32]

One reason why the Japanese newspapers profess the posture of neutrality is that these papers enjoy nationwide circulation. Unlike American newspapers which have a specific, limited territory, the major newspapers in Japan are national newspapers and must sell to a larger proportion of readers.

The widespread acceptance of the norm of *fuhen-futo* can also be ascribed to the commercial character of papers. The newspapers are a commercial undertaking designed to sell a commodity called news, entertainment, and advertisement. The papers are concerned with the production of a page that will be of interest to the customers. The norms of *fuhen-futo* or neutrality in a sense constitutes a veneer to make the commodity more attractive.[33]

A decision to report a particular piece of information as news and the desk's decision to print that particular news story involves more than one value judgment. However, the norms require an effort to seek and report any contrary views and facts as well. When these norms are thought to be desirable and socially sanctioned, and when the need to report any contrary views is recognized, the tendency for biased reporting might be corrected.[34]

Despite some cases of policy advocacy contained in editorials on such issues as Vietnam and China, one usually finds the editorials reflecting an artful practice of the norm of *fuhen-futo*. Editorials are often devoid of a clear-cut stance on the issues. Thus, within the space of a single editorial, both the Liberal Democratic party and the opposition parties might be criticized. Contrary arguments might be presented in tandem without indicating where a newspaper stands.[35]

While editorials practice *fuhen-foto*, news reports are less constrained by the norm and more often characterized by

32. Den, pp. 196-97; Fukuda, p. 49.

33. Fukuda, pp. 51-53.

34. Tsujimura Akira, *Shimbun yo ogoru nakare* (Tokyo: Takagi Shobo, 1976), pp. 58-61.

35. Fukuda, p. 62; Ikuta Masaki, *Shimbun o kiru* (Tokyo, Sankei Shuppan, 1968), pp. 140-42.

subjectivity and emotionalism. A few words are in order on the related question of consistency between a basic perspective underlying a particular news story on the one hand and the position taken in editorial pages on the same story.

Most reporters feel that the position taken in the editorials and the stand taken by news reports and analysis on other pages should be consistent. Thus, a former editorial writer of a major paper recalled that when he wrote a certain editorial in relation to the question of Chinese United Nations representation, a department head lodged a complaint that it made things difficult for him to compose news sections. His response was that whatever direction the editorial leans, that should not affect news reports and commentaries.[36]

Professor Ikuta Masaki's judgment in this respect is different. The Japanese newspapers, he has argued, lack an overall unity or harmony. Very seldom are the newspapers consistently biased. Rather, they are opportunistic and do not have a consistent stand. Even if the managing editor attempt to give the newspaper a consistency or unity, the mammoth size of the organization makes it impossible to do so. Occasionally, there is inconsistency in the stands taken by editorials and news articles. Bias shown by a newspaper may not necessarily last long. Even though some individual stories are biased, in most cases the newspapers as a whole may not be necessarily biased. Sometimes the tone of a newspaper changes, depending on who the desk is at a given time, making it difficult to discern a consistency over a two-day period.[37] Policy advocacy appearing in Japanese newspapers is often ambiguous. Under the name of neutrality, biases are not consistently unidirectional, at times leaning either toward the left or the right, but are sensitive to the trends of the time. Most Japanese newspapermen appear to feel that a uniform and consistent position must underlie the treatment of similar stories found throughout the pages of a newspaper. Hence, they are reluctant to introduce views differing from their own.[38]

After joining a newspaper, a reporter learns over the years the limits on expressing a particular point of view. An *Asahi*

36. Fukuda, p. 198.
37. Ikuta, pp. 26-28.
38. Yano, pp. 110, 140.

reporter, for example, reads the editorials of his paper and learns what they say, how they say it, what their logic is, and to what extent they express themselves. He comes to realize the limits his own articles must observe. He learns even how to express the views which are contrary to the editorial line or the dominant mood pervading his organization. By virtue of the "editorial right," a newspaper may declare that it supports the United States-Japan Security Treaty. However, regardless of the paper's editorial line toward the treaty, the reporters could write articles critical of or opposing the treaty, depending on the style of writing. Unless one examines all the specific articles on the subject in advance, one cannot selectively regulate the direction of the entire newspaper writing on the subject.[39] However, the tendency of the reporters to conform to the editorial position in their newspaper is unmistaken.

Most dailies in Japan, as members of the Japan Newspaper Association, are pledged to observe the Editorial Principles of Newspapers. These are a set of self-imposed rules agreed upon by the member firms concerning news gathering, reporting, sales, and advertisement. The statement of ethical principles, identified as the guiding spirit of the association, consists of seven items: freedom of the press, the limitation on reporting and commentaries, attitude on commentaries, fairness, tolerance, leadership responsibility, and pride.[40] The four norms embodied in the statement of ethics—freedom, responsibility, fairness, and dignity—are specified as the criteria governing the conduct of the reporters. They are thought to be applicable, and so recommended, to all other employees of the newspapers.[41]

Article 2, on the limits of reporting and commentaries, specifies five rules:

1. The basic principle of reporting is to convey the true picture of an event accurately and faithfully.

2. In reporting news, the injection of a reporter's personal opinion is absolutely forbidden.

39. Honda, *Janarizumu Ron*, pp. 316-17.
40. Inaba and Arai, p. 106.
41. Nihon Shimbun Kyokai, *Shimbun Henshu no Kijun* (Tokyo: Nihon Shimbun Kyokai, 1976), pp. 141-43.

3. In handling news, one must take great precautions so as not to be used as a means of propaganda for someone.

4. Critical comments on an individual should be confined only to the extent that they can be spoken directly in the presence of the individual concerned.

5. One must realize that a biased commentary which tends to deviate from the truth is deliberately contrary to journalism.

Article 5 on tolerance states that to assert one's own freedom and at the same time to recognize the other's freedom to make assertions constitutes the principle of democracy and that this principle must be clearly reflected in the editing of newspapers. Tolerance as shown by the allocation of space for introducing and reporting those policies that are contrary to one's own principles and assertions is identified as the proper function of a democratic newspaper.

In addition to the Editorial Principles of Newspapers, there is a series of guidelines which are authoritative interpretations on relevant legal provisions that member newspapers are expected to observe. They cover such topics as obscenity, privacy, defamation, the reporters' club, and reporting on crime by minors and kidnapping cases. Some of these were discussed in an earlier chapter.[42]

Many reporters in Japan maintain within their organizations a group which is devoted to the close scrutiny of their own newspaper with respect to accuracy, appropriateness of value judgments, protection of human rights, and dignity. The result of their review is passed on to those who are responsible for news gathering and processing. The association itself monitors all newspapers including those of nonmembers, checking to see if the general principles of ethics and pertinent legal provisions are observed. The Office of Examination of the Secretariat reports any violations of legal and ethical norms to the Editorial Committees and the governing Council of the association. After review, the association may take the necessary actions such as warning and recommending withdrawal from the association. At times, the result of this monitoring is published in the organ of the association so as to enhance the ethical standards of the newspapers.[43]

42. Ibid., pp. 13-140.
43. Inaba and Arai, pp. 107-8.

CHAPTER XII

Reflections on

Selected Findings

This final chapter is not intended to be a comprehensive reca-
pitulation of the findings presented earlier. Rather, it provides
my reflections on one selected aspect of the reporters' activities,
namely, their interactions with government officials. The
interactions with government officials constitute the dominant
and most important part of the political reporter's activity.
Moreover, they constitute a most crucial decisive factor shaping
the substantive contents of political reporting.

In the pages to follow, the reporter-official interaction are
viewed from three distinct perspectives: the analyst's, the
reporter's, and the official's. Two topics will receive special
attention: (1) the nature of the reporter-official interaction and
the degree of impact such interactions have on the official and
(2) the nature of the official-reporter interaction and the degree
of impact such interactions have on the reporter.

The Nature of the Reporter-Official Interactions and
Their Impact on Official Behavior

Analyst's Perspective
From the analyst's perspective, the reporter may be said to perform the following four functions, though in varying degrees:

1. Neutral Transmitter. Reporters perform the function of a
neutral transmission belt, providing information to and for
officials. After all, what appears in print and what they tell the
officials in private comprise part of the information on which
the officials base their perceptions of reality. News is consumed
by both the public and the officials. News may become relevant
to policy making directly, in the sense that officials become
sensitized to certain developments, or by affecting the demands

and expectations of the population vis-à-vis government, thus indirectly shaping the behavior of officials.

2. Agenda-Setter. The reporter performs the function of agenda-setter by focusing attention on certain events. He is instrumental—wittingly or unwittingly—in politicizing certain issues and in establishing priorities, thus turning the official's attention to these issues and giving rise to a need to respond to them. This would in turn shape the process of policy formulation and implementation.

3. Policy Participant. The reporter may play the role of active participant in policy formulation by consciously advocating a particular course of action either in print or in private conversations with the official.

4. Watchdog. The reporter may be said to perform the function of watchdog by way of probing and criticizing any wrongdoings on the part of the official. What analytically distinguishes this from such a function as agenda-setting is that the focus here is on the exposé of wrongdoings in the personal and official conduct of an official.

From the analyst's perspective, the impact of the reporter's activity may be said to occur in two analytically distinct ways. One is through his collective output, i.e., what has been printed in the newspapers, whether in the form of articles or editorials. The other is the impact the reporter exerts on the official through and during his news-gathering activities before the appearance of written reportage.

Reporter's Perspective

How do reporters themselves assess the manner in which they influence government policy and the degree of such influence?

As indicated in chapter 5, in their response to open-ended questions, Japanese reporters spontaneously refer to one or more of the four functions identified above—information transmitter, watchdog, agenda-setter, and policy participant—roughly in that order of frequency and importance. They tend to focus primarily on how the government uses the press for gauging public opinion and effectively disseminating information the government wants publicized in order to mobilize public support for government policies. They seem more impressed with the government's ability to use the press than with their own ability to influence government policy.

Japanese reporters say without hesitation that the press exerts "considerable" or "very much" influence on government policy making. Such responses relate primarily to the first three functions, not so much to advocating or other active forms of participation in policy making.

We have seen that the role of the press was decisive in such political events as the Kurashiki and Masuhara affairs. The course of various power struggles within the Liberal Democratic party, such as that involving the emergence and demise of Prime Minister Miki, was also significantly affected by the press. However, the impact of the press is limited when measured in terms of successful policy advocacy, especially from a short-range perspective. In the foreign policy arena, the press seldom advocates—and rarely successfully—a specific course of action. However, the impact of the press through agenda-setting and information transmission is considerable, as was evident with the case of the development of Japanese policy toward the People's Republic of China. Although not treated in this volume, the issue of the Okinawa reversion is another case in point.

Official's Perspective

How do officials see the ways in which the press influences government policies? How do they assess the magnitude of such influence?

Judging from their spontaneous responses, officials evidently think of the press primarily in terms of its utility in information transmission. They find the press helpful in gauging the "public mood" and essential in transmitting government views to the public. To them, commentaries and interpretations contained in newspapers are not particularly useful.

When asked specifically to identify the ways in which the press influences government policy, administrative officials are, on the whole, reluctant to acknowledge the existence of influence, either direct or indirect. The officials of the Ministry of Trade and Industry are relatively willing to concede such influence; most say that they take press views into account, while some even go so far as to ascribe considerable direct influence on policy formulation to them. Foreign Ministry officials generally deny press influence, particularly direct influence, asserting that the influence of the press is at most indirect. A single dominant view among them—approximately a majority of those interviewed—is that they do not take press views into account but merely take note of them.

Legislators tend to ascribe greater influence to the press than administrative officials do, rating the role of the press higher with regard to all four functions.

The interviews I conducted previously with Foreign Ministry officials in connection with other research projects on Japanese foreign policy indicated a similar assessment. The only press influence they said they could recall was that the timing of the announcement of some foreign policy decisions was affected by speculation in the newspapers. They could not readily recall any cases in which the press had affected the substantive contents of foreign policy decisions.

What facts might best explain the variations in willingness to ascribe influence to the press? The features of one's position, i.e., the nature of the office and the degree of responsibility one holds, are clearly associated with the variations observed. The intervening variables that provide linkage between positional differences and variations in ascribing influences are: (1) the intensity of felt need for and perceived essentiality of press cooperation in pursuit of one's goals, whether personal or collective and (2) the availability of alternative means of information collection and dissemination. As mentioned earlier, legislators tend to ascribe greater influence to the press than do administrators. This holds true of the legislators who serve as ministers. Of the bureaucrats, MITI officials tend to ascribe greater influence than Foreign Ministry officials.

The variations in ascribing influence are also associated with differences in the normative conception of the role of the press. Thus, those officials who are negative toward the reporter's consciously attempting to influence government policy tend to dismiss the possibility of press influence on their activity. Such a difference in normative conception may, at least in part, be explained by an in-service socialization associated with the requirements of a given ministry.

Factors Shaping the Reporter's Activities, including Interactions with Officials
In this volume three groups of factors were examined: recruitment, orientation, and organizational requirements.

1. Factors Related to Recruitment. Several features of recruitment seem relevant to an understanding of the reporter's activities. There exists a formal channel for the recruitment of reporters. The system of competitive examination, designed for college graduates, provides a pool of highly educated professional reporters. Despite frequent rotation in assignments, their broad training in liberal arts and intellectual background enable them to cope with assignments in different fields.

No clear pattern emerged in this study, but the prevalence of reporters with humanities backgrounds may be related to a different set of political values, beliefs, and attitudes—different from those which reporters of social science backgrounds have. Reporters with social science training appear to experience fewer tensions with government officials, perhaps because of their tendency to judge officials' performance in more realistic terms.

Reporters with more prestigious educational backgrounds enjoy more advantages in obtaining access because of the respect accorded them by officials. The sense of affinity based on school ties is a factor, since the overwhelming majority of ranking officials are from prestigious public universities such as the University of Tokyo.

Systematic early recruitment provides the opportunity for a long period of common socialization. In addition, the following factors also contribute to intense loyalty to one's own news organization, exerting pressure for conformity with the norms prevailing within news organizations: the virtual absence of lateral entry into or mobility between news organizations; the practice of permanent employment with a single employer; and the traditional norms concerning "group orientation" and "conformity."

The existing system of assignments and promotion brings about a situation in which relatively young reporters in their twenties and thirties assume the primary responsibility for news gathering by interacting with senior officials of higher age brackets. The disparity in age and the reporters' relative lack of expertise and experience have an impact on the effectiveness of their interactions. However, regardless of what officials may think of inexperienced young reporters, what is salient to the officials is the prestige and power of the newspapers that the reporters represent, for which due deference is shown.

About the time the reporters reach the age of forty, they are usually assigned to managerial posts with limited roles in newspaper making. This, together with early retirement in their mid-fifties, is a factor conditioning the effectiveness of news gathering. And this in turn attenuates the stifling atmosphere generated by the sense of hierarchical relationships and buttressed by the traditional values associated with a "vertical society."

2. Role Conception and Other Orientations. The following kinds of orientations were examined in chapters 5 and 6:

a. The normative conception of a reporter's job
   (1) the general conception
   (2) whether a reporter should shape public opinion in addition to informing
   (3) whether a reporter should attempt to influence government policy
   (4) whether a reporter should participate in government policy making
   (5) whether a reporter should act in the role of opponent or watchdog

b. The normative conception and the perception a reporter has of press-government relations, i.e., whether the relationship should be or is conflictual

c. Criteria for selecting stories to write and publish; conception of what constitutes good news

d. Conception the reporter has of what criteria the official should use in releasing information

e. Perception of whether and to what extent the official cares about what the reporter writes

The normative conception of the job of a reporter is perhaps the reporter's most fundamental orientation. The Japanese reporter generally holds an activist orientation, that he should shape public opinion, should attempt to influence government policy, and should act in the role of opponent and watchdog. This is mediated through the working criteria for selecting stories and determining good news and the criteria that the officials should use in releasing and withholding information.

It is reasonable to assume that the orientations specified above at least partially condition and explain the reporter's actual news-gathering activities. They constitute the norms to which their actual behavior is directed in the absence of impediments.

The point here is that if the reporters operate with an essentially passive role conception, their behavior might be different from that which obtains. For example, if the reporters did not believe in or perceive the basically conflictual nature of press-government relations, their actual interactions might be different.

We have seen a remarkable degree of consensus among interaction partners on most of the orientations examined. This adds further strength to the assumption that Japanese reporters have internalized these orientations and that their behavior conforms to a significant degree with these orientations.

As is shown in the chapters examining the behavior of reporters, actual behavior, including the substantive contents of newspapers, seems generally consistent with the orientations specified above. The most dominant general role conception is that the reporter should report accurately, fairly, and objectively. Apparent deviation from this norm embodied in the most general role conception is due to an important degree to organizational constraints and dominant subcultures (i.e., political tendencies) within the respective new organizations.

3. Organizational Factors. The reporter's news-gathering and processing activities are shaped to an important degree by what may be called organizational constraints.

a. Internal distribution of power and standard operational procedures. The role of desks (deputy chief of Political Affairs Department) is the most crucial in the entire process of newspaper making: their leadership and relationship with front-line gatekeepers (those reporters covering various beats). Other organizational factors shaping newspaper making include the allocating of responsibilities regarding gathering and transmitting news stories to the home office and all the established procedures for editing that are observed by the Political Affairs Department and the Makeup Department.

b. The requirements of the job. It will be recalled that Japanese newspapers under study publish both morning and evening editions. They rely heavily on their own reporters even for the collection of factual information. Thus, the reporters operate under immense time pressure and are expected to produce stories in time for their deadlines. The requirements of the job under the organizational setup make it difficult to meet the norms of accuracy and objectivity.

Besides, the reporters are acutely conscious of intense competition among the major newspapers for a larger share of the readership. This awareness, together with high sensitivity to the substantive contents of rival papers, gives rise to a drive to be first with a news item, leading to sensationalism and mutual emulation.

c. Established procedures for news gathering. The process of newspaper making is in a most direct way affected by the established mechanism and procedures associated with the reporters' club. While this mechanism provides a useful, convenient channel for both the reporters and the government, it also constrains news gathering. This sytem of the reporters' club, together with the virtual absence of by-line articles, is conducive to the reporters' evasion of responsibility, facilitating government manipulation of the press and sometimes resulting in self-censorship.

The Nature and Degree of
Officials' Influence on Reporters

Analyst's Perspective

Government officials could influence the press by regulating the operations of news organizations.

1. Legal/Formal Constraints. Japanese reporters work in a society where the freedoms of speech, press, and other forms of expression are regarded as inviolate and fundamental human rights and their guarantee is accepted as a basic principle of government. According to a prevailing constitutional interpretation, the freedom of reporting is included under the protection of the freedom of expression stipulated in the Constitution. As for the "freedom of news gathering," it is considered as "worthy of respect" in view of the spirit of Article 21 of the Constitution. As explained in chapter 7, reporters might be prosecuted for disclosing classified information, and the "right" to withhold the sources of information is not firmly established. However, there are virtually no legal impediments to news gathering and reporting in Japan.

2. Indirect/Informal Constraints. Government leaders may bestow special favors on news organizations, for example, by expediting the sale of state-owned land to a newspaper for the construction of a new office building. They could formulate and administer laws (e.g., concerning taxes and postal services) in such a way as to affect the operations of news organizations.

Officials can and occasionally do regulate the flow and contents of new stories indirectly and informally through their information policies. A variety of techniques is available. De facto regulation is attained by helping to structure and maintain the channels of news gathering and by controlling the degree of access to the sources of news. This can be done by:

a. Helping to operate the reporters' club
b. Cooperating in and regulating the frequency and quality of press conferences and briefings of all kinds
c. Aiding selected reporters in obtaining scoops through deliberate leaks or by impeding access
d. Cooperating with reporters in the practice of the "morning run" and "night attack" methods of news gathering.

De facto regulation may be achieved by the deliberate use of media by officials. Other than to obtain useful information from the reporters and newspaper pages, officials may and do attempt to actively use the press to their advantage to:

a. Enhance their visibility and to project favorable images (personal or collective)
b. Gauge public moods by floating trial balloons
c. Mobilize public support for a proper course of action
d. Enhance Japan's bargaining position vis-a-vis a foreign government
e. Strengthen their positions relative to rival political groups and individuals

3. The Analyst's Assessment of the Degree of Officials' Impact. Government officials' capacity to affect press activities through the use of legal or formal constraints is more potential than actual. The capacity to have an impact on press activities through the employment of indirect or informal constraints is substantially greater. However, basic norms governing press-government relations that are widely accepted in Japan provide the broad limits beyond which the officials could not impose constraints. Other factors further inhibit the government's restrictive influence on press activities. The multiplicity of

major newspapers and their intense competition as well as the perceived need for and utility of newspapers as seen by officials reduce the incentive for and effectiveness of any constraining measures adopted. The perceived utility is associated with the institutional requirements and with the sense of job security.

The Reporters' Perspective: How Reporters Assess the
Nature and Degree of Government Influence on the Press
Reporters maintain that there are no legal constraints on their newsgathering and processing activities. They talk about difficulty in penetrating the veil of official secrecy on matters related to national security, but they add that they understand that such is the rule of the game.

They also talk about government-imposed restraints, such as a nonattribution rule regarding a background briefing, an attempt to suppress a particular piece of information, and the restrictions on reporters' visits to government offices during specified hours at certain agencies. However, they are not particularly upset about these restraints. Few challenge the legitimacy of the system of the reporters' clubs or offer major criticisms regarding the operations of the clubs. (Free-lance reporters constitute an exception.)

On the whole, Japanese reporters operate with a firm belief that they are under no government-imposed constraints. They are, of course, aware that government officials attempt to use newspapers to promote certain interests and sense from time to time that they are being managed. And yet, they offer no critical remarks about the practice and in fact accept it as being inevitable. Their attitude toward the question is tempered by the awareness that officials' need of an dependence on the cooperation of the press is what aids their own access to the officials. Reporters maintain that they occasionally feel they are being used, but for a reporter with the responsibility to cover a particular agency, whatever the officials of the agency say or do constitutes a news item!

On the whole, then, Japanese reporters do not feel or perceive any undue restraint or limitations imposed on their activities. Whatever de facto constraints exist are accepted as given, and they feel that it is their job to overcome these hurdles or inconveniences.

The Officials' Perspective: How Officials Assess the
Nature and Degree of their Own Influence on the Press

Of different ways of exerting influence, government officials see the informal and indirect method of regulating the flow of information to be most realistic and effective. The legal or formal method is discounted as politically unfeasible; they are resigned to the democratic rules of the game. Officials do voice their dissatisfaction over the inadequate legal protection accorded official secrets and are ambiguous toward the issue of protecting news sources. They realize that they could, to a certain extent, regulate on a de facto basis the degree of access that reporters have to official sources of information. However, they are also conscious that their capacity is limited in view of their own dependence and prevailing democratic norms, which are supported by the presence of opposition political forces and the reality of the power of the media organizations. Their own assessment is that their influence on the press is limited and modest.

As examined in Chapter 9, on matters deemed important to the interest of the ruling party and the government, the party and the government leaders feel that they ought to and at times do make strenuous efforts to shape media views. Normally, however, on most issues the officials' attitude is one of gauging the moods of the "general and elite publics" and of passively reacting to, rather than actively shaping or manipulating, media views.

The present study has shown that officials are generally dissatisfied, to varying degrees, with the substantive contents of newspapers. The dominant viewpoint of government officials is that, generally speaking, news reports and commentaries are overly critical and antagonistic toward the government. This sentiment is shared by the legislators of the ruling party. Opposition legislators are no less dissatisfied with newspapers, but for different reasons. They are unhappy because they perceive the lack of militant, sharply crticial attitudes toward the ruling party and government. They contend that the newspapers are in effect facilitating Liberal Democratic party rule in the name of "neutrality" and "nonpartisanship."

Opposition political leaders tend to ascribe greater influence to the government in shaping the contents of the media than the government itself perceives to be the case. It is also opposition leaders who ascribe a greater role and greater utility to newspapers than government party leaders and officials.

Cross-national Notes

In his pioneering study, Dan Nimmo specifies three role types for reporters: the recorder, the expositor, and the prescriber.[1] The recorder is concerned with objectivity in his reporting and is aware that his function is to select what is newsworthy and what facts are essential for his readers. As compared with the recorder, the expositor perceives himself as more of a specialist who should go beyond fact recording to the level of interpretation. The prescriber perceives it as his duty to referee or call fair/foul plays, articulate public opinion, and prescribe future courses of action. He sees himself as a generalist, concerned with a wide range of issues, and his mode of reporting is highly interpretative.

In Nimmo's terms, the role orientations of Japanese reporters partake of the characteristics of all three role types. Most Japanese reporters verbalize the expositor orientation, with some of them subscribing to the prescriber orientation as well. For them, the recorder orientation is simply subsumed and taken for granted.

The role orientations of Nimmo's "information officers" are typed into informer, educator, and promoter. Informers are concerned with getting out the facts. Educators feel that their duty is more than transmission of facts; facts require a frame of interpretation. Promoters are concerned with timely and adroit promotion of information that will create a favorable image for their agencies.

As for Japanese government officials' role types, on the whole they subscribe to what Nimmo calls educator and pro-

1. For comparative purposes, see the following works: Bernard Cohen *The Press and Foreign Policy* (Princeton, N.J.: Princeton University Press, 1963); Dan Nimmo, *Newsgathering in Washington* (New York: Prentice-Hall, 1964); Delmer Dunn, *Public Officials and the Press* (Reading, Mass.: Addison-Wesley, 1969); Leon Sigal, *Reporters and Officials* (Lexington, Mass.: D. C. Heath, 1973); Steven Chaffee, ed., *Political Communication* (Beverly Hills, Calif.: Sage Publications, 1975).

moter, particularly the latter. Concerning the role orientaion held by officials about the normative conception of the reporters' job, it is predominantly that of recorder, and of expositor to a lesser extent.

Following Nimmo, one may say that the roles of informer and recorder are compatible and their relations tend to be cooperative. The interactions between the educator and the expositor show some points of convergence conducive to a compatible relationship. The interactions between the promoter and prescriber types are more likely to be characterized by antagonism.

William Chittick conducted an empirical study of the opinion and policy process in foreign affairs in the United States. He examined four groups of actors: State Department policy officers, information officers, foreign affairs reporters, and nongovernmental organization leaders. The focus of his study was the extent of perceived antagonisms among the groups. His major thesis is that antagonistic interactions result from the incompatibility of the requirements of democracy and foreign policy making regarding information dissemination. The behavior of the occupants of each position is a function of role expectations that they themselves hold and of those held by the counter-position occupants. For Chittick, role expectations appear to constitute the crucial link between the incompatibility and perceived antagonism. Yet he goes on to state that role expectations are merely one of several variables explaining perceived antagonism. He identifies such independent variables as position of each actor within his group, demographic variables, such as age, education, and length of professional service, and career patterns.

How might one explain the degree of perceived antagonism? Theoretical insights obtained through the present study of Japanese reporters are as follows. The conflict arising from the requirements of the job (demand for publicity and secrecy) are mediated through the two factors: (1) the degree of perceived utility in interacting with the counter-position in successfully discharging one's own job and securing self-enhancement and (2) the degree of acceptance by interaction partners of the legitimacy of the role of reporters.

The degree of perceived utility and the degree of congruity in the role conception of the reporter in turn are shaped by such independent variables as demographic characteristics, the particular subculture within a news organization, the intensity of partisanship, and the sense of political competence. If one can assume stability in the degree of perceived antagonism that individual reporters have vis-à-vis government officials, it may be useful to measure the degree of perceived antagonism and employ it as a major explanatory variable for overt behavior. However, to the extent that antagonism is intermittent and is subject of fluctuation in specific situations. It must be viewed as one of many variables explaining the patterns of reporter-official interactions. The degree of antagonism may also vary with different issue-domains. One may alternatively conceptualize reporters' behavior (in interactions with officials) as basically a function of a generalized feeling of antagonism mediated through such factors as situational exigencies, particular role concept, behavior of counter-role incumbent, and perceived utility of interaction. This way one does not have to invoke proper nouns such as Foreign Ministry or Ministry of International Trade and Industry (MITI), saying situation X obtains in the Foreign Ministry while situation Y prevails in MITI.

Appendix: Interview Schedule for Reporters

1. Name

2. Position

3. Place of birth and age

4. Sex

5. Marital status

6. Education

7. What was your first job after graduation?

8. How long have you been in the journalism field?

9. Have you done any other work?

10. How did you become interested in the job of a reporter?

11. Generally speaking, what kind of people go into the field of journalism?

12. What do you think of the current method of selection?

13. What are the major criteria the selectors apply?

14. What do you think of these criteria?

15. Would it be preferable to have people with different backgrounds and training come in?

16. How would you describe the job of being a reporter (director of editorial bureau, department head, deputy department head, etc.)?

17. What are the most important things you should do?

18. Are there any important differences between what you think this job is and the way your department head (deputy department head, editor, etc.) sees it? What do they expect you to do?

19. How about your readers? What do they expect you to do?

20. I understand that there are some informal rules of the game—certain things reporters (director, etc.) must do and things they must not do as they go about doing the work. Will you tell me what they are?

Interviews were conducted in Japanese. This schedule is merely a translation of the Japanese language version used. Additional questions were used depending on the nature of the respondent's work (e.g., editorial writers, makeup department personnel). Comparable questions were used for government officials.

21. Who defines your duties? To whom do you report within your organization?

22. Who determines what stories to print?

23. What criteria are used?

24. Are most of your stories used?

25. How do you determine what stories to write on a given day?

26. Generally speaking, what sources of information do you rely on most heavily for news stories?

27. What do you think are the characteristics of a good news story?

28. What do you think your reader likes to read about?

29. What does your deputy department head (department head, editor, etc.) consider a good news story?

30. What are the most important attributes or qualities a reporter needs to be effective in his job?

31. Now let us talk about the government agency you cover. How did you get the assignment to cover this particular agency?

32. Would you describe the kind of things you do generally to report about what is happening in this agency?

33. Which officials do you generally see in connection with your work? How often do you see them? Where?

34. How would you describe your relationship with these officials? What are the reasons for the relationship being as it is?

35. What do you suppose these officials think of the reporters?

36. To what extent do they care about what you write?

37. In what ways do you think the press shapes or influences government policy? And to what extent? Could you give some examples?

38. Do you see a role for yourself as a participant in government policy making?

39. In reporting on this ministry (Diet) have there been any occasions when you were helpful to particular officials (members of the Diet)?

40. Would you give some examples?

41. If an official of the ministry takes exception to your story, would he be most likely to contact you, the editor, department head, deputy department head, or someone else?

42. Have the officials (Diet members) ever communicated their reactions to your superiors?

43. How would you advise new reporters to go about developing news sources? How about maintaining them?

44. During the past week, what sources have you used for developing your stories? Would you say they are fairly typical sources?

45. Have you ever felt that there are limitations on freedom of the press?

46. How would you describe the role of the journalists' unions in gathering and processing news? What role should they play?

47. Have you ever had any difficulty in obtaining information from the government agency for your story?

48. To what extent do you believe government officials are obligated to inform the public of their activities?

49. Do you believe that public opinion should influence government policy? To what extent?

50. Do you think government officials do in fact base their decisions on public opinion?

51. Do you see a role for yourself in expressing and shaping public opinion as well as informing the public?

52. Do you feel the government-press relations are basically conflicting or basically harmonious? How would you describe this relationship?

53. Do you think they should be conflicting or harmonious?

54. Would you describe the relationship between the reporters and the officials as being
    a. always cooperative
    b. usually cooperative
    c. sometimes cooperative
    d. seldom cooperative
    e. never cooperative

55. How would you rate the officials with whom you deal on the following qualities:
    a. intelligent
    b. well informed
    c. trustful
    d. helpful
    e. personal integrity

56. To what extent do you feel that reporters should or should not try to do the following? To what extent are they doing this?
    a. Report the facts without any interpretation.
    b. Write without regard for the editorial views of their news organization.

    c. Attempt to influence government policies.
    d. Act in the role of opposition or watchdog.

57. To what extent do you feel that government officials should or should not do the following? To what extent are they doing this?
    a. Release information selectively because it may strengthen the government's negotiating position.
    b. Release information because it may promote domestic political support for official policies.
    c. Release information because the public has a right to know.
    d. Withhold information because it may endanger national security.

58. Now I would like to ask you a few questions about the various jobs in your organization.
    a. What role should the director of the editorial bureau play?
    b. What does he do actually?
    c. Are you satisfied with the way he does his job?
    d. How about the deputy director? What role do you think he should play?
    e. What does he actually do?
    f. Are you satisfied with the way he does his job?
    g. How about the department head? What role should he play?
    h. What does he actually do?
    i. Are you satisfied with the way he does his job?
    j. How about the deputy department head? What role should he play?
    k. What does he actually do?
    l. Are you satisfied with the way he does his job?
    m. How would you describe the relations between director, deputy director, department head, and deputy department head?
    n. How would you describe your relations with the deputy department head, etc. deputy director, director)?

59. What do you think of the way your newspaper has been reporting about developments in China?

60. How about the reporting on the Soviet Union?

61. How about the reporting on the United States?

62. What political party comes closest to your own political views and attitudes?

63. Do you consider yourself as belonging to a social class? Which one?

64. Are there any magazines you read more or less regularly?

65. Are there any newspapers other than yours that you read more or less regularly?

66. How would you characterize these newspapers? Are they very different from your own? In what ways?

67. In terms of social prestige, where are the journalists placed in your country?
     How about in relation to government officials?

68. If you were ever to begin again, would you choose the same career? Why? Why not?

Index